KT-539-838

PELICAN BOOKS

EXPLORATION IN MANAGEMENT

Wilfred Brown was born in 1908 and educated at Rossall School. He joined the Glacier Metal Company in 1931 and was its Chairman and Managing Director from 1939 until 1965. He was determined to use scientific method and knowledge in the running of the company and spent sixteen years with his company and the social scientist, Dr Elliott Jaques, on the Glacier Project. This consisted of research into every aspect of organization, manning, and management of industrial enterprise.

The Glacier Metal Company merged with Associated Engineering Ltd in 1964 and Brown joined the Board of the latter company while remaining chairman of Glacier.

Wilfred Brown is the Pro-Chancellor of Brunel University. He received a life peerage in 1964 and is a minister of state at the Board of Trade. He has been chairman of the Docks Modernization Committee since 1965. On taking up this latter appointment he severed his ties with Glacier.

His other books are: *Managers, Men and Morale* (with Winifred Raphael, 1948), *Piecework Abandoned* (1962), *Product Analysis Pricing* (with Elliott Jaques, 1964), and *Glacier Project Papers* (with Elliott Jaques, 1965). He is married and has three sons.

WILFRED BROWN

EXPLORATION IN MANAGEMENT

WITH A FOREWORD BY
MICHAEL SHANKS

PENGUIN BOOKS

Penguin Books Ltd, Harmondsworth, Middlesex, England
Penguin Books Australia Ltd, Ringwood, Victoria, Australia

—

First published by William Heinemann Ltd 1960
Published in Pelican Books 1965
Reprinted 1968, 1969

—

Copyright © Wilfred Brown 1960

—

Made and printed in Great Britain
by Hazell Watson & Viney Ltd
Aylesbury, Bucks
Set in Monotype Imprint

This book is sold subject to the condition
that it shall not, by way of trade or otherwise,
be lent, re-sold, hired out, or otherwise circulated
without the publisher's prior consent in any form of
binding or cover other than that in which it is
published and without a similar condition
including this condition being imposed
on the subsequent purchaser

*A Description of the Glacier Metal Company's
Concepts and Methods of Organization
and Management*

THE GLACIER PROJECT SERIES

CONTENTS

Contents

Contents

Contents

FOREWORD TO THE PELICAN EDITION

by

MICHAEL SHANKS

THE English scene contains two traditional folk-heroes who, between them, have done untold harm to the image and performance of British industry in recent years. One is the Inspired Amateur – the scholar-gentleman who, on the basis of native genius and a good classical education, can solve any problem and surmount any obstacle with effortless superiority. The other is the Wise Craftsman, possessor of a mysterious skill which nobody else can master and which he himself cannot explain and can barely communicate. These two archetypal figures have presided benignly over our comparative industrial decline for more years than it is pleasant to remember. They represent a survival from the Dark Ages of technology, and it is surely time to let the daylight into their twilight world.

The fact is that many of the craftsman's traditional skills have been superseded by modern technology, and human judgement increasingly replaced by scientific measurement. Today the craftsman, particularly if organized in a tightly exclusive union, is one of the main obstacles to progress. And the role of the industrial manager is no less radically affected by the scientific revolution. The content of business is becoming increasingly technical, and the manager who does not understand technology is at a serious disadvantage. It is not enough to have one's experts hidden away in the boffins' back room, 'on tap and not on top', available to answer questions from non-technical executives; it is not enough because too often these executives do not know the right questions to ask and cannot understand the answers they get. (Nor does this apply only to industry. The whole business of government has been transformed by the scientific revolution, and by the increasing involvement of the State in the economic process – through planning, through the complexities of the defence programme, through the growth of the public sector, through the Government's responsibility for promoting research and development. These changes call for a new type of expertise among our predominantly humanist civil servants, and among our political leaders.)

The content of management is changing with the business environment. As industry becomes more capital-intensive and the consumer market becomes more affluent, and therefore more capricious, the rewards of success and the penalties of failure become greater. In bad times workers can be paid off, but capital has to be serviced whether or not the goods it is producing can be sold. In these conditions the job of the manager becomes harder. On the other hand, he has more knowledge available to help him, if he is equipped to use it. The computer provides him with a tool of incomparably greater accuracy and sophistication than any hitherto available. And in the sphere of business techniques and understanding of the environment in which business operates, the amount of knowledge accumulated over the last half century, and particularly in the last few years, is impressive and extensive. Management, in short, is itself ceasing to be an incommunicable craft and becoming more of a precise technique, the elements of which can be taught. The imponderables of luck, flair, and judgement will always remain important in determining the success or failure of a business enterprise, but they are no longer – if they ever were – all-important. The argument that there is no point in teaching business studies because Rockefeller got on all right without them is equivalent to saying that there is no need to teach anybody English literature because there is no evidence that Shakespeare studied it. The besetting failure of the English educational philosophy is that it is geared to the needs of the near-genius and not to the average man or woman who – no doubt unfortunately – happens to make up the great bulk of our population.

Acceptance of the professional manager, therefore, has been slow in Britain. But the tide is turning, and certain prophets are now at last beginning to find honour in their own country. Among these is Wilfred Brown, one of the self-taught pioneers of professional management in this country, who has made his company, Glacier Metal, into a virtual laboratory of business management which is of enormous value to social psychologists (without in any way adversely affecting its competitive efficiency in the process).

The essence of the professional is that he operates by rational calculation rather than by intuition, and this has been the guiding principle of Wilfred Brown's career. At each stage he has tried to analyse the nature of the work he is doing, and the criteria for its success. What is the essence of the manager's job? Whence comes his authority? What are the social relationships within a factory, and what are the mutual obligations of its various members? On what principles should authority be delegated and financial rewards determined? These are the kind of questions, within the great society of the State, with which political philosophers have concerned themselves since Plato. But, despite Plato's pleading, philosophers have rarely been accorded executive authority by society. This has usually been left to the no-nonsense 'practical' men, who, to quote Keynes, 'are usually the slaves of some defunct economist'. Wilfred Brown insists that his methods of management at Glacier Metal are not revolutionary – and this is strictly true. What *is* revolutionary at Glacier is the extent to which practice has been analysed and codified, and the degree of involvement on the part of managers and men which this process has involved. Glacier Metal has become a self-conscious political society (in the broadest sense of these words) in a way which applies to few other business enterprises. The record of this development over two decades is given in this book. It is not an easy book to read. It represents the intellectual odyssey of a remarkable man – a man who has had to combine in himself the role of theoretician and executive, exponent both of the theory and the practice of management. Other managers and potential managers will find it valuable and stimulating, but they will not find in it solutions to all their problems – for many of the methods and measures propounded here are solutions to problems which were peculiar to Glacier or arose out of Wilfred Brown's particular objectives and sense of values. And as Brown himself stresses, by no means all the problems at Glacier have yet been solved. The chief value to the outside world of Brown's work is probably as an exercise in methodology. *This* is how the business process strikes this highly conscientious, highly articulate man who has been a practitioner for twenty years. *These* are the problems, the relationships, the obligations; *these* are, at any rate, one man's solutions. Light has been shed into dark corners – not in an isolated laboratory experiment, but in the hurly-burly processes of real life.

LITTLE KINGSHILL   MICHAEL SHANKS
December 1964

FOREWORD TO THE ORIGINAL EDITION

by

ERIC L. TRIST

Chairman, Research and Training Committee, Tavistock Institute of Human Relations

THERE are not many men who combine in themselves the theory and practice of management. Wilfred Brown is one. This book has resulted from twenty years of doing and thinking, developing and analysing. It attains a precision of formulation about problems central to the tasks of management which breaks new ground.

On the eve of the late war, Wilfred Brown, then a very young man, assumed full control over the Glacier Metal Company as its chairman and managing director. During the twenty years which have followed, he has maintained the faith that he would be a better manager of the affairs of his company if he could become clearer about the bases of his own conduct as an executive.

In seeking to understand the nature and conditions of executive action, he has sought the help of social scientists. Indeed, his first book, which appeared in 1948, was in co-authorship with Winifred Raphael of the National Institute of Industrial Psychology. Since then his company has become a centre of pioneer studies in the social sciences as applied to industry. In 1951 *The Changing Culture of a Factory* appeared, which reported the results obtained by a research team from the Tavistock Institute led by Elliott Jaques. This study modelled a new role through which the social scientist could gain access to the material which lies under the surface in organizational as much as in personal life. It showed how an organization might increase its ability to undergo change in a direction desired by its constituent groups. Dr Jaques has remained working with the company as an independent research consultant, and in 1957 his *Measurement of Responsibility* showed a novel approach to the rewarding of work – in terms of the amount of discretion used in carrying out the tasks appertaining to a given role.

The impression may well have become current that it is the social scientists at Glacier who do all the thinking. *Exploration in Management* will correct that impression; for it is Wilfred Brown's own account of the system of thought which has gradually evolved in his company through his own efforts and those of his subordinates, aided by the social investigations which they themselves have requested. The account shows how deeply he has been involved in these developments, and how much he has had them constantly under the test of his own continuous experience as a manager. Throughout one hears his voice speaking as managing director to his immediate subordinates and company members generally. He has written this book – in such time as he could redeem from the daily executive round – because it had become necessary for someone to make an overall description of the concepts and methods which have come into common usage in the company. In Glacier this someone could only be himself.

A number of us who have been associated with the developments going on in Glacier were eager that this study should be made available not only to the internal company audience, but to industry generally, and to all those in the social sciences concerned with the study of organizations. As one of these, I was particularly anxious that the book as externally presented should retain the living form of the original. I am glad, therefore, that Wilfred Brown has consented to allow it to appear as a practical communication to his own people. His achievement is that the ideas expressed are not merely aspirations, but theory already being converted into practice – even if the practice is as yet imperfect and even if there are many areas left where the thinking itself is still unfinished.

In his recent book, *Leadership in Administration*, Philip Selznick suggests that organizations transform themselves into true social institutions, as they come to embody in their structural form and canons of behaviour a set of values appropriate to their institutional ends. The Glacier Metal Company has become a social institution in this sense, and the tradition which it has developed is embodied in the present book. The development of an organizational tradition of this kind, containing as it does so much that is new, is not something which happens automatically. It requires leadership. In Glacier the organizational leadership has been supplied by the man occupying the central position, who all the time has also had to carry the overall strategic and economic responsibility. It is this which gives to the sociological thinking of this book an authenticity and reality uncommon in management studies.

Broadly, three approaches are detectable in the history of management studies. The first is what Daniel Katz has called the machine theory of organization. This regards the human agent exclusively as an instrument. It is characteristic of Taylorism. The excesses of this approach were corrected by the 'human relations' movement. As Peter Drucker has recently said, 'It has been fashionable of late particularly in the human relations school to assume that the actual job, its technology and its mechanical and physical requirements are relatively unimportant compared to the social and psychological situation of men at work.' The human relations school was set going by Elton Mayo and the Hawthorne experiments. While much of value remains in what it has brought to light, 'good human relations' as a management philosophy is giving place to what may be called the 'task' approach. In this, both instruments and people are considered, but in relation to the work that has to be done.

This is the approach adopted by Wilfred Brown. In a very early chapter we find him setting out his credo as follows:

Effective organization is a function of the work to be done and the resources and techniques available to do it. Thus changes in methods of production bring about changes in the number of work roles, in the distribution of work between roles and in their relationship to one another. Failure to make explicit acknowledgement of this relationship between work and organization gives rise to non-valid assumptions, e.g. that optimum organization is a function of the personalities involved, that it is a matter connected with the personal style and arbitrary decision of the chief executive, that there are choices between centralized and decentralized types of organization etc. Our observations lead us to accept that optimum organization must be derived from an analysis of the work to be done and the techniques and resources available.

I believe this approach to be consistent with that adopted by my colleague A. K. Rice, who is concerned to show that all aspects of the enterprise must be subordinated to what he calls its *primary task*. It is not only industrial enterprises, however, which must remain loyal to their primary tasks. This is so of all human groups, for these are all compelled, in order to maintain themselves in existence, to undertake some form of appropriate action in relation to their environment. This line of thinking derives from basic social psychological studies of the nature of human groups at the psycho-analytic level, such as those of W. R. Bion. An organism, whether individual or social, must do work in order to keep itself related to its external environment, that is, to meet reality.

Many years ago Freud showed that the ego had this function in the growth and maintenance of the personality, and psycho-analysts have come to talk of the work of the ego. It is Bion's achievement to have transposed this concept of work from the individual to the group and so deepened our understanding of what we all think of as work in the everyday sense. More recently these ideas have obtained general reference through the development of open system theory, based on the work of the biologist von Bertalanffy. Social scientists are now coming to realize that prime importance attaches to the fact that living systems, as distinct from physical systems, maintain themselves in existence only by carrying on active transactions with their environment. They import material into themselves, transform it, and export some of this transformed material back into their environment. In the most general sense, this active maintenance of the steady state by use of the environment constitutes the work process. Enterprises must be understood in these terms as much as other living systems. By contrast physical systems are closed systems, to be understood largely in terms of their internal activities and characteristics; they are inert towards their environments. Closed systems follow, in consequence, the second law of thermodynamics, growing towards maximum homogeneity, instead of increasing differentiation, of their parts. They attain the steady state only by the cessation of activity, instead of by its maintenance. It would not be appropriate in this context further to elaborate these ideas. I mention them to show that there is a growing and convergent body of thought in the social sciences which supports the fundamental ideas about organization, and its relationship to work, which Wilfred Brown has arrived at from his own experience as a manager.

This viewpoint has only gradually evolved in Wilfred Brown's thinking; which is scarcely surprising, as no one was looking at things in quite this way during the period of the war when he first began to fashion an operating company as a cohesive society. He was at that time severely bothered about the nature of executive authority and the source of its sanction. Until he could be clear on these matters, he did not feel free to command people as he felt they should be commanded and to mobilize them fully for the tasks that had to be done. He saw the extent to which managerial authority was perceived by the workers as both absolute and arbitrary. So long as this was so, marginal participation only could be expected of the operatives in the work of the enterprise. This led him quite early to develop an unusually advanced form of works council in his company. The way in which the wartime version of this was transformed from a two-sided to a many-sided institution in the post-war years is described in *The Changing Culture of a Factory*, and the written policy which this council has gradually produced is described in the present volume. A social scientist would say that, in order to understand the nature of executive authority, one must examine its 'boundary conditions'. This is precisely what Wilfred Brown, in collaboration with Elliott Jaques, has done.

There have, however, been misunderstandings on the part of a number of people regarding the achievement of the company. These misunderstandings arise from the mistaken belief that the Glacier Metal Company has deviated from the orthodox form of a public company in the private enterprise sector of our economy. This is not so. The Glacier Metal Company remains an entirely orthodox firm as regards the responsibilities of its board to the shareholders and of the board to the employees. Within the basic form of the orthodox company, however, there is immense scope for variation – what in Glacier is called 'conditional' policy as distinct from 'definitive' policy, which proceeds from the board's obligatory relation to the system of legal and financial rules governing the transactions of industrial enterprises. What Wilfred Brown has shown is the unexpected scope for participation by groups at all levels that lies within the orthodox framework. In his belief, however, these inherent possibilities can only be realized if there is a radical separation of the representative and legislative systems from the executive. One of the research discoveries at Glacier, during the original project carried out by Dr Jaques, was that it was just through making this separation that it became possible to develop the strong executive organization which the company so badly needed. A greater freedom to take managerial action was won by doing a lot of hard work on the sources of managerial authority. This paradoxical relationship between executive action and its boundary conditions is not at all well understood in most of industry.

Having won this freedom, Wilfred Brown and his managers have in more recent years been able to concentrate on the search for an optimum model of an executive system. As March and Simon remark in their recent book on organizations, a fundamental distinction has to be made between the adequate and the optimum; adequate solutions enable one to get by; optimum solutions enable one to attain the highest results. In the industrial field, as in most others, adequate solutions only are attempted for most problems, and problem-solving at the level of the adequate is the conventional standard. As our knowledge advances, however, it is becoming possible not only to aspire to the optimum as an ideal, but – with increasing precision – to formulate the conditions of its attainment. The more of these conditions that can be described and the more precise the descriptions, the more does it become possible to approach the optimum state in workaday reality. Wilfred Brown's contribution, in collaboration with Dr Jaques, to extending the area of the precise formulation of such conditions is one which, in my belief, changes our level of working knowledge in this field. And one need not agree with all their formulations to hold this view. But the kind of rigorous definition of concepts and operating procedures attempted in this book is one which substantially increases the resources through which managers in an organization can take effective action. This does not mean that these resources will necessarily or always be used – even in the Glacier Metal Company they are only beginning to be used and rather imperfectly. But a tool-making job has been done which has not been done before, and the tools must be made before people can avail themselves of them.

It is not until one comes to the chapters on specialist work that Wilfred Brown's views on organization will become entirely clear to the reader. Here the traditional notions of line and functional managers are rigorously redefined in terms of the task approach. The primary task of any enterprise inherently involves the development, manufacture and sale of certain products. The activities directly concerned with developing the company's products, and with making and selling them, constitute phases of the primary task of the enterprise. These activities are referred to as operational work, and those who control them as operational managers. All other activities undertaken are carried out to support operational activities. These are referred to as specialist work, and those responsible as specialists – some of whom carry staff authority. Specialist work itself is analysed into three dimensions: technical, programming and personnel. What is to be included in each of these is worked out with great rigour and with some surprising results. Accounting, for example, is separated from programming. A number of economists now adopt this view. Responsibility for organization is placed in personnel. Several studies recently carried out by the Tavistock Institute support this contention, for example that by Dr A. T. M. Wilson of the personnel function in a Unilever company; but this view is only slowly gaining ground.

Another surprising conclusion is to regard research and development as a phase of operational work, rather than as a resource within a specialist division. This, again, will arouse controversy, but the case Wilfred Brown has made is a strong one and may do much beneficially to alter the way research and development departments are perceived in industry.

In field theory terms, what Wilfred Brown and his colleagues, working with Elliott Jaques, have done is first of all to work out the requirements of the primary task in activity space, and then, in social space, to set about designing a system of roles and role-relationships likely to be optimum for the activities. This leads to the emergence of what I have referred to in my own work on the mining industry as a socio-technical system, the object of which is to make work organization optimum for the task in hand, considering the resources available. My colleague Dr F. E. Emery has recently shown that open system theory involves considering the enterprise as a socio-technical and not simply as a social system.

In building role systems Wilfred Brown is concerned to get the relation of specialist to operational work right at every level of management. He has therefore surrounded himself at managing director's level with technical, programming and personnel staff officers. It is through the interaction of these divisional managers with himself that he hopes to get balanced policy appreciations and a coordinated plan for action. The same treatment is repeated at the level of general manager and even of unit manager. Full specialist resources are made available but there is no blurring of the line of command. The specialists are built into the domains of each operational manager, and the rules which regulate their communication with each other in the technical channel are explicitly formulated. This pattern coincides with a strong preference for product as opposed to process organization, and for keeping the number of essential steps in the hierarchy as few as possible. The result is a self-consistent executive system made up of a succession of unambiguously accountable and internally serviced managerial domains. Everyone knows his place in such a system. The advantage of this, according to Wilfred Brown, is that it provides the security required by the individual before he can become free fully to develop the discretionary component in his own role. In other words, rigidity and flexibility are not regarded as mutually exclusive. Rather is the one seen as the condition of the other. It is the relation between the two which is felt to be important.

This tendency to think in relational terms is fundamental to Wilfred Brown's outlook, as in his formulations concerning organizational 'states' or 'modes'. The terms he uses – 'manifest', 'assumed', 'extant' and 'requisite' organization – are not likely to appeal to many people but there is no doubt that we must somehow think of organization in more than one modality. Many sociologists will translate 'manifest' and 'assumed' into 'formal', and 'extant' into 'informal'; some will regard 'requisite' as equivalent to 'ideal' in the Weberian sense. But the conventional terms do not carry quite the same implications as regards the relations between the various modes as do Wilfred Brown's. It is the nature of these relations that future research must work out, rather than spend too much time demurring about words.

The book is presented as a work in progress, and as one in which many of the problems uncovered are left without satisfactory solutions having been found. It has been a disappointment to many people at Glacier that so much of 'the split at the bottom of the executive chain' still remains, despite so much having been done towards creating a participant organizational structure and climate. From my own observation, I would say that the level of worker participation, both as regards task and enterprise commitment, is higher at Glacier than in the average firm. It still, however, falls far below that expected by Wilfred Brown and his colleagues. The 'alienation' of the worker in contemporary industrial society is a problem which has not yielded, to more than a limited extent, to any remedy that has been tried, whether political, economic or sociological. It remains for the future to find a general solution. But in the search for such a solution those sets of conditions under which a partial reduction has been effected merit serious study. The ideas and practices which have emerged at Glacier provide one such set.

Wilfred Brown remarks that concepts and methods such as he and his colleagues have worked out cannot be fully applied, even in a company such as Glacier, until a fully equipped personnel division has been developed, based on a recognized expertise of its own. The development of such divisions is a long-range project, requiring the collaboration of industry and the social sciences over many years. As a contribution to the basic knowledge on which such an expertise must rest, this book by Wilfred Brown will have a lasting place.

LONDON   E. L. T.
January 1960

ACKNOWLEDGEMENTS

The content of this book is based upon work done by very many employee members of the Glacier Metal Co. Ltd, of all ranks. Special thanks are due to the following:

The general and divisional managers who, over the past ten years, have played such a large part in the development of policy.

Mr D. J. Clarkson for making many constructive suggestions and for his work on the Company Policy Document.

Mr J. M. M. Hill for writing the glossary, reviewing the text and drafting many amendments.

The Tavistock Institute of Human Relations for the constructive base which they helped the company to lay for the development of organized policy during their three-year research project with the company from 1949 to 1952, and for valuable advice on the structure of the book which led to extensive amendments.

Dr Elliott Jaques who led the project and has since been associated in a consultant capacity with the company for a period of eight years. Many of the concepts which I have discussed had first been stated explicitly by him. His technical comments have had a major effect upon the content of this book.

Mr Colin Legum for editorial advice on construction and continuity, and for detailed work on expression and writing.

Miss M. Lucas for preparation of diagrams.

Miss M. Davis for a great volume of work concerned with typing, correcting, checking and sub-editing.

And last, but not least, to my wife for actively encouraging me to write this book, and providing the setting in which I was able to tackle the job over nearly two years of week-ends.

W. B.

CHAPTER I

ANALYSIS OF ORGANIZATION

SOME years ago I was a member of the Education Committee of the British Institute of Management. We received a communication from the American Management Association, asking: 'In Britain, is the foreman a member of the management team?' The committee argued the question at great length, but the discussion became not in fact an attempt to answer the question, but an examination of the meaning of the words 'foreman' and 'management team'. Clearly, no answer could possibly be found until there was agreement about the content of these words.

The absence of a language, concepts and a general theory of administration is a serious impediment to the efficiency of industry. Its competence to grapple with the problems which are emerging from the rapid growth of technology and the steady increase in size of the individual industrial unit is dependent on there being a constant flow of trained managers. In the absence of a body of knowledge which can be taught, training has to rely on the uncertain process of 'learning by doing'.

This is a 'hit or miss' approach, which is just as capable of leaving minds fogged by fantasy notions and *unreal* ideas as of instilling sound knowledge. It can perpetuate unfortunate practices which reduce morale, damp down initiative, drive potential managers into other professions, lay the basis of strikes and resistances to necessary change, and generally fail to focus objective thinking on to problems which cannot be solved by other means. One has only to imagine what would happen if engineering, physics, chemistry or medicine had to be learned almost solely 'on the job', without the assistance of a general body of confirmed knowledge, to realize what would be gained if the problems of management could receive the same systematic study that has been applied in these other fields.

Professor Homans, the American sociologist, has written:

Exploration in Management

The practical value of any science is that by making experience subject to explicit intellectual control it speeds up the learning process and so sets intuition and judgment free to work on new ground rather than old. In something as important as management, anything that even begins to get us free of empiricism or to set empiricism free for new advances, makes a contribution.[1]

Writing about a different phase of the same subject, under the title 'We Need to Understand Better', the Earl of Halsbury has made this important observation:

The twin battles to compete in world markets and to reduce inflation are in reality but one battle, the battle of productivity in which engineers are constantly engaged. There are two ways of contributing to any such affray; one is to dash into the fight and hack away with the rest of the army; the other is to climb a hill so as to obtain a comprehensive view of what is going on with the object of directing it. For the majority who must willy-nilly be thrown into the battle, the spectator's role is an unheroic one but it is important none the less. I shall adopt the unheroic role on this occasion by considering how much the nation loses through a certain lack of perspective on the part of those engaged in industry. I refer to the simple fact that there are some 56,000 industrial establishments in Great Britain and that most of us in the course of a working career acquire familiarity with but half a dozen or less.

It is often said that production engineering is not an academic subject. So be it! Nor was electrical engineering at one time. It has become one because electrical engineers made it so. It is likewise up to production engineers to make their subject into an academic one. This means reducing each of its component aspects to intellectual good order and discipline seriatim. The Institution of Production Engineers is currently making a drive at clearing up the domain of materials handling. The time to do the same for production patterns is probably not yet. Beginnings have to be made by individuals and the type of classificatory and anatomical study advocated here awaits a few individual enthusiasts who will endow it with a beginning.[2]

Though I have never been able to state it so succinctly as Professor Homans or so interestingly as Lord Halsbury, I have for

1. 'Scientific Management', *Nature*, December 1955.
2. *Metalworking Production*, March 1958.

a long time shared the view differently expressed by both of these men. Accordingly I have increasingly supported a policy of studying how we do our jobs as managers, analysing the processes which we use and endeavouring to extract from a mass of experience any principles or concepts which appear to have general validity in our circumstances. The purpose of this book is to record the current state of the company's knowledge in this field.

What is the present state of explicit conceptual knowledge about administration in general? There is no general theory, and a great paucity of concepts and hypotheses about managerial processes. The meaning of many of the words which we use in discussing our problems has no established or widely accepted content. No words exist at all for many ideas and situations which occur daily in the lives of managers. Such ideas can only be discussed in terms of lengthy and often inconsistent description. Many of the words which are used with great frequency, such as 'manager', 'supervisor', 'specialist', 'policy', 'subordinate', 'authority', have no generally accepted and precise meaning. How then can we use them in discussing industrial problems? In fact, we spend most of our time arguing about the meaning of the words we are using, instead of discussing the problems themselves. In the absence of a language, such as, for instance, the physicist has had to evolve, it is extremely difficult to start substituting intuition by explicit knowledge.

The universities realize the need to equip graduates with as much knowledge as possible about management. They have been under pressure from various quarters in industry, and from the British Institute of Management, to set up chairs of administration. There is, however, *no body of knowledge* available of the appropriate level of abstraction on which a degree course could be founded. There are as yet no 'laws of management'. The first concern of a university department of management would be with research in order that the required body of knowledge could then be established.

Here again, however, difficulty arises. University departments can function only in so far as they produce concepts having an integral connexion with the real industrial situation.

This would seem to involve much deeper relations with industry than at present exist where administration is concerned. Is there as yet any real acceptance in the universities of the need for deep and prolonged study of this subject by the best brains available? Moreover, when concepts emerge they will have to be tested in industrial situations. If the engineering department of a university produces new ideas on, say, some aspect of production technology and wishes to have these ideas tested by a particular company, they then would need to make contact with that company's production engineers who are responsible for advising its management on production techniques and for implementing changes. But in the field which I am discussing, no such specialist branch yet exists. Great difficulty would arise, therefore, in getting new notions tested.

A theory of industrial administration cannot be developed in isolation within the laboratories of a university. Unlike the physical sciences, it is not possible to import samples of the 'materials' which interact in social processes or to build models of the processes which require analysis. These things exist only in the work setting; their transplantation to a laboratory disrupts their reality. Picture what would happen if universities and other bodies were to turn seriously to research in this field and industrial companies were to set up groups of specialists responsible for implementing the results. Interchange of ideas about principles and concepts between research workers and industrial specialists would lead to the emergence of ideas that were of general validity for industry as a whole. It would gradually become possible to teach administration. A manager's task would be greatly helped by the existence of accepted laws of administration, for his field of choice in making almost daily decisions would be narrowed by his knowledge of principles. The engineer who knows his fundamentals can, by reference to them, reject many choices which an untrained man, dependent on his intuition alone, might accept – to his own and his company's later discomfiture.

I do not wish it to be inferred that managers can be made in the university or college of technology; for some, by personality and intellect, are fitted for the task and others are not. But a man who is psychologically suited to the tasks of management by the accidents of heredity and environment can be helped to do a better management job by education in an appropriate set of ideas. Given a series of principles of administration, a company can decide explicitly how it wishes to operate, and can instruct its own managers in the appropriate policies to be pursued. But in the absence of definition, language, principles and concepts, everybody within that company has to imbibe a knowledge of what is wanted slowly, painfully and intuitively. When change in these policies is required nobody can state explicitly what it is that requires change.

The study of administrative methods is the study of people at work, their behaviour, their relationships, the way work is split up between different roles, and the often unrecognized social institutions which companies have established and are using. Barriers exist in the carrying out of such studies. There is too little evidence that the work pays off. Such studies cause anxiety and individuals rationalize their fears by denying the value of the studies. Few trained people exist to carry out this work and it is extremely difficult for managers themselves to do it because their own involvement in what is being studied makes it very hard to maintain objectivity. The institutions capable of training such people are themselves short of financial support, because our community has not yet fully accepted the need for such schools of thinking.

Our company was fortunate. In 1948, Mr Herbert Morrison, then Lord President of the Council, set up a Committee on Productivity. The Human Factors Panel of this Committee sponsored a joint research project into industrial social issues by the Tavistock Institute of Human Relations and our company. The project became a study of how the company carried out its operations. The result of the work done has been fully reported in *The Changing Culture of a Factory*,[1] a book which was the official report of the three-year research programme. When this programme came to an end in 1950 the management, in collaboration with its representative works council, decided to invite Dr Elliott Jaques, who had led the original research team, to carry on the work. This he agreed to do on the basis of a contract to be renewed each year by agreement with

1. Published by Tavistock Publications, 1951.

representatives from the company's London factories and their management.

Thus it is that we have at our disposal the results of twelve years' continuous research. In the course of doing this work it has become clear that at least two distinct approaches towards work of this kind are possible. It is appropriate at this stage to define them.

(1) *Executive analysis of work and organization*

This occurs when an employee member of the company attempts the analysis of work and the manner in which it is distributed between various roles. It is the type of analysis which will, I hope, be carried out on a wide scale when we as a company are able to set up a fully established organization and personnel division. The personnel technician has available to him facilities similar to those employed in the analysis of, say, production methods. He can use the resources of time, money and people put at his disposal. He can ask for those data which are on record to be produced. He is, however, faced with certain difficulties. He can make observations but, because he has a work relationship with those whom he is observing, he will have to make allowances for the effect of his presence. He can ask for the views or feelings of those concerned in the field which he is studying; but all the communications which he receives are conditioned by the fact that both parties are members of the same organization. Completely free communication is not, therefore, available to managers or technical people carrying out such analysis. To command people to speak freely is a contradiction in terms.

(2) *Independent analysis*

This takes place when the person carrying out the analysis is not an employee member and has no executive relationship with anyone in the company. The Tavistock Research Team took up such a role at the beginning of the project and Dr Jaques has continued in it since then. It involves:

(*a*) The completely confidential nature of all communications to the independent analyst, unless specific permission is given to make public.

(*b*) The undertaking of analysis of work only at the request of those individuals, managers or groups responsible for that work.

Given such circumstances, 'unconditioned' views and feelings may become available. It has been our experience that this approach to the understanding of the way in which the company operates has permitted the emergence of data and ideas which would not otherwise have been obtained.

This book sets out, in a manager's language, the concepts, principles and ideas that have emerged during this period of research. This research will, I hope, continue vigorously, for the work which has been done has already served to point to many fields where knowledge is required: for example, selection of people to fill vacant roles remains almost entirely intuitive; in managerial jobs we are unable to quantify work; we are still unable to make conceptual statements which seem to fit about supervisory jobs; we have insufficient conceptual clarity about the sort of organization required for research and development work on our products; the role of accountancy and costing requires much more penetrating analysis than it has received, and so on.

On the other hand, a great deal has been discovered. For example, we know now that there are a number of different systems of interconnected roles in operation in the company: the *executive* system, the *representative* system and the *legislative* system. People move in the course of their daily work from a role in one system to a different role in another system; and it is essential that this be recognized and that behaviour appropriate to the role be adopted if trouble is to be avoided.

(*a*) We are beginning to learn about the principles within which we operate these social systems. On the basis of this knowledge we have constructed a statement of the policies within which the company operates. This is a most important document constantly referred to for guidance by people at all levels in the company. It is the basis of our managerial training programme.

(*b*) We know some of the basic criteria upon which work is split up between different positions and we can, by setting principles to govern the decisions which affect the way we build our executive organization, free intuition to do work in other fields.

(*c*) We know that change of the work we are given to do by our customers implies change in the structure of work roles, and we can increasingly derive from change in work-load the appropriate change in executive structure that is implied.

(*d*) We have learned how to define and differentiate between managers and specialists, and we are able to make some precise statements about the authority and responsibility of the latter and their relationship to managers.

(*e*) We have learned about the sources of managerial authority and we also know something about the measurement of the level of responsibility of a given job of work.

These are samples of the gain in knowledge which have flowed from this study, and which will be set down in detail in this book.

We realize now that our company requires not only all the recognized essential functions of a successful business – sound organization to develop good products, manufacture and sell them – but also a highly formulated knowledge of what makes up good organization, how it is brought into being and manned by the people who can operate it successfully.

We have gained a great deal of this formulated knowledge about organization from the research done. In the course of getting it, many managers have learned a great deal and much reorganization has been brought about; but we have not, as yet, got a technical team of specialists on organization. Without such continued technical help for managers there is no guarantee that we shall continue to use the knowledge we have gained and implement the principles arising out of it. This is our next task.

The idea of setting up a technical team of specialists to implement fresh knowledge is certainly not new, for this is the way that all successful companies maintain advance in technical work based on the physical sciences. It is new only in relation to work in the field of organization and social matters. Conventional personnel management only touches the fringes of it. If a sufficient number of companies were able to set up the kind of organizational and personnel teams that I envisage,[1] which could be given the authority to teach and implement the type of organizational concepts which are set out in this book, then I think advances could be achieved in the efficiency of business and in the satisfactions gained by those who work in industry.

Such work, coupled with the granting of full opportunity to external research workers to carry out independent analysis when it became clear that new concepts were required, would lead to the emergence of a general theory of administration. This book is a contribution to the building of such a theory. There is a real need to generalize and systematize knowledge about management. Bonner and Phillips in the introduction to their book, *Principles of Physical Sciences*, have stated the point well in regard to the sciences.[2]

Without abstract concepts, which help scientists to generalize and systematize knowledge, and which reflect the relations of different sets of occurrences to one another, science would be little more than a vast catalog of events. As our study of physical science progresses, we shall see that often its most stunning successes have been triumphs of generalization – discoveries of interrelations among phenomena which had previously appeared unrelated. Yet the importance of the phenomena themselves cannot be overlooked. Indeed the great generalizations have value only so long as they aid exact description and interpretation of particular observations, and help scientists to bring new phenomena to light.

Some years ago the vice-chancellor of a university communicated what I thought were some very wise thoughts to the graduates of a technical college. I must paraphrase his remarks because I cannot recollect his exact words. He reminded these young technologists that when they took up positions in industry, they were to remember that it was not always the role of the technical specialist to tell managers and craftsmen what they ought to do, but more frequently to tell them in

1. I have defined the new kind of personnel function to which I refer in Chapter 13.

2. Addison-Wesley Publishing Co. Inc., Reading, Massachusetts, U.S.A.

conceptual terms 'what they were doing'. He reminded these students that the companies they would enter were 'going concerns', producing a variety of excellent goods of high quality with great efficiency; although improvement was, of course, often possible, before a specialist could possibly suggest improvements he had to gain a very clear and objective appreciation of the methods in use. If these methods could be stated with clarity and in terms of general descriptions or concepts, then such descriptions could by themselves be as useful as suggestions for innovation. People who had, for some time, been practising particular methods were often unable to describe such methods in objective terms, and the availability of accurate statements about their practice would very often enable the practitioners themselves to introduce the most valuable improvements.

His comments are supported by the experience of one of my colleagues who, before joining our company, had fifteen years' experience as a senior industrial consultant. His finding was that very few managers of factories could give an accurate description of how the various processes in their factories operated, and that as soon as he started the investigation for which his services had been retained, discrepancies between the managers' appreciation of current practice and the actuality as observed by him began to emerge.

I suggest that if a number of experienced senior managers were to describe in detail a particular process in operation in their factory, and were then asked to vouch for its reasonable accuracy, they would be chary of doing so. Furthermore, I suggest that if their descriptions were checked by careful observation by an experienced person, considerable and important inaccuracies would be exposed. I think we are all aware that if we have what we think is a clear picture in our minds of a particular situation *for which we are ultimately responsible*, then when we get close to it and attempt to observe it objectively, we tend to 'see' what we expect to see rather than what is actually taking place. We project on to the scene of our observations that mental picture of the situation which we already possess.

The social research into organization which has been going

on in our company for the last ten years has been carried out by independent observers who had no preconceived notions. Their terms of reference have been to help solve social and organizational problems which individuals or groups of individuals felt to exist, and about which such people were prepared to talk in confidence. The method of helping has been to extract, from a mass of unorganized description offered, the simplest statement that sums up all that has been said, pointing also to the inconsistencies in various descriptions or statements of 'fact'. By a series of successive approximations made in the form of such statements, a more accurate picture of the problem and the situation comes into view. In the course of such a process concepts like those described in the following chapters emerge. This is the process which has enabled us to describe organization as it exists in the company in conceptual or generalized terms.

There are strong grounds for the belief that this description of organization is valid for industry in general. Some of these grounds can be stated:

(*a*) Our company is subject to all the normal cultural pressures of British society and British industry.

(*b*) We employ 3,600 people. With a sample of this size it would be unrealistic to maintain that we were not an average cross-section of the British population.

(*c*) We have a constant influx from other industrial companies of newcomers of all ranks – general managers, technologists, accountants, technicians, engineers, craftsmen and operators. Such newcomers, when introduced to these descriptions of organization, do not find they run counter to their own notions and experience. To them the only unusual feature of the situation is the fact that their own previous experience can be stated in these general terms.

Thus it is that this book has a twofold objective: (*a*) To record for our company a description of our own organizational ideas, and (*b*) to set before other industrial readers a general description, in conceptual terms, of organization as it is believed to exist in industry.

In no sense is this book to be regarded as a record of a number of new organizational ideas which readers are recommended

to adopt or to try out in their own companies. When, however, I have lectured on this subject, audiences have very
often assumed that what I have said is to be taken as a series
of recommendations. In the discussion which has followed
such lectures, one participant after another has opened his
remarks by saying: 'Your scheme of organization, Mr Brown
. . .', or 'The ideas which you are recommending', or 'These
new ideas which you advocate', and so on. I have always
replied:

'No – I am recommending nothing except that you absorb
these ideas, and then see if in your actual experience they are
not a description of your own practice – I am not recommending new organizational practices or ideas to you, but I am
giving you, in general terms, a description of what I believe
goes on in your own company.'

You, the reader of this book, will, I expect, compare your
ideas about your own organizational practices with the concepts I am about to advance, and you may feel the two to
be inconsistent. I would, however, ask you to consider the
following: Are you quite sure that your notions about your
own practices are consistent with the reality of what really
takes place in your company? If you are not sure then I ask you
to consider whether the apparent inconsistency between your
own practice and the general notions I have put forward
might not be dispelled once you have obtained a more objective
picture of your own organization. In other words, until you
possess an objective picture of your own extant organization
you will not know whether the concepts described in this book
fit your own experience or not.

I am aware, of course, that the foregoing paragraphs contain
very challenging statements, but I have good grounds for making them. It has been my own constant experience over the
last ten years that, on many occasions when faced for the first
time with some of these general statements about organization,
I have dismissed them on the grounds that they did not fit my
experience of industry or the way in which our own organization was arranged. Very often, however, I have subsequently
discovered that what to me manifestly existed in our company
did not, in fact, exist. The exploration of some of these appar-

ently new generalizations about how we did our work forced me to accept the fact that for years my own notions of how the company of which I am chief executive was organized were strangely at variance with the facts. Such discoveries used to make me feel foolish. They do so no longer, for I have come to realize that the price of realistic perception of this dynamic thing called organization is constant exploration and adjustment of attitude in the face of the facts as they emerge.

PART ONE

STRUCTURE

CHAPTER 2

SOME ORGANIZATIONAL CONCEPTS

THIS book sets out in detail the policies and organizational ideas that have been in daily use in a light engineering company for the last five years. They are essentially very simple ideas and I hope that they will appear obvious to the reader; at the same time they may have a 'newness' about them because they are stated as far as possible in conceptual rather than descriptive terms.

I have been faced with the continual difficulty during writing of a tendency to wander from the subject in order to refer the reader to certain fundamental notions from which many of the conceptual statements were derived. I decided, therefore, to start with an orientation chapter which would, so to speak, get rid of these more basic notions by stating them at the beginning, and thus avoid the necessity of making constant reference to them in later chapters. With this background I think the rest of the contents will be readily understood.

Role and structure

The social structure of a company is the more or less recognizable organization pattern variously referred to as 'the authority chart', 'the hierarchy of positions' or 'the managerial tree'. It includes also the consultative or representative system, various grading systems and other types of stratification.

Structure in this sense is made up of a network of job positions which can be occupied by individuals. These positions are defined as work 'roles'. Thus, for example, the social structure of our executive system is made up of the network of roles of managing director, divisional manager, general manager, unit manager, section manager, supervisor, operator, etc. It is by the process of taking up a role in the executive system that an individual becomes a working member of the company.

Language

One of my aims is to set down for our company a description of the policy currently in operation. Because of this it is written in 'Glacier language'. In default of a generally accepted and defined terminology, it seemed better to take one which, though in some ways particular to our company, has, at least, grown out of a serious attempt at definition. There is, in Appendix 1 (p. 299), a glossary of terms used.

Company Policy Document

I have made constant reference to the 'Company Policy Document'. It is the fourth edition which is accepted by the board of directors, the management of the company and representatives of all who work in it as the basis upon which the company should be operated. This document, reproduced in Appendix 2 (p. 309), is available to all who work in the company.

The work on analysis of organization which we have done in recent years is based on a number of fundamental ideas. These are each listed and discussed in turn.

The relation of organization to work

Effective organization is a function of the work to be done and the resources and techniques available to do it. Thus changes in methods of production bring about changes in the number of work roles, in the distribution of work between roles and in their relationship one to another. Failure to make explicit acknowledgement of this relationship between work and organization gives rise to non-valid assumptions, e.g. that optimum organization is a function of the personalities involved, that it is a matter connected with the personal style and arbitrary decision of the chief executive, that there are choices between centralized or decentralized types of organization, etc. Our observations lead us to accept that optimum organization must be derived from an analysis of the work to be done and the techniques and resources available.

Some of the most familiar examples of change of organization arising out of change of work are in connexion with the changes from small quantity to large quantity production. The nature of the work alters in terms of the length of run.

Some Organizational Concepts

The techniques change, tooling and fixtures are provided, the speed of operations rises, some of the discretionary element in operating the actual machines is removed by mechanization; the skilled craftsmen, turners, millers, grinders, etc., are needed by growing tool-making departments; people of lesser capacity and training can operate the machines. Their manager, instead of being in charge of a team of skilled men who were able to continue their work for considerable periods of time without his attention, is now in charge of a much larger number of less skilled people, and he will require supervisors and machine-tool setters to help him keep the complex mechanized set-up going. These changes on the shop floor will have repercussions on the organization right up to the top.

Consider the changing job done by our own selling organization since 1930. First, four salesmen in touch with engine builders. Then the level of understanding of the metallurgy and hydrodynamics of bearing operation begins to rise and a technical service to back this sales effort is forced into existence. The need arises to sell overseas, and contracts officers to handle agency agreements are appointed. Technical salesmen, who can travel overseas, are needed. The internal organization of the sales department has to go through progressive adaptation as the range of products and the markets to which they are sold changes, and so on.

A company that manufactures household appliances may have a sales organization with two or three managerial levels coordinating the efforts of perhaps 150 salesmen, and another, say, shipbuilding company with the same turnover may have one very high level salesman who does the whole selling task personally.

Research and product development departments are notoriously difficult to organize because if any one result of a given activity cannot be predicted, then resources required for a specific result cannot be estimated with any certainty. In addition, constant change in the work implies a capacity of the organization to adapt itself constantly to the different forms made necessary by these changes in task.

Uncontrolled organizational adaptation and its effects

Not recognizing the relation of organization to the nature of the work to be done has several results:

(*a*) The organization may partially adapt itself to these changes, albeit with considerable difficulty. New work has to find, so to speak, a role into which it can fit. Pressure of work causes some person willy-nilly to accept it. Some work disappears and leaves other roles with a diminished quality or quantity to be done. These changes are felt by people in these roles in terms of overwork or underwork, loss of status or gain in status.

(*b*) The level of work available to a single role either drops or rises. If it drops, the occupant of the role will get uneasy and may start complaining about his future prospects. Unless he has recognized the alteration to the work in the role, the manager will have difficulty in understanding what is happening. He will feel that the complaint is unreasonable and he may act unsympathetically. If the level of work rises the occupant of the role may be able to cope with the work; but he will begin to feel underpaid. Or if he cannot manage the higher level work, his manager will begin to feel that he is deteriorating, and may become critical.

(*c*) Because these changes of organization of work are thrust upon the structure in a manner that is not explicitly recognized, a feeling is generated that the situation is slipping out of control. Such uncontrolled adaptation at the dictate of forces which are not understood does not produce optimum organizational forms.

(*d*) Where there is lack of technical insight into change of work and method, the necessary change in the structure of roles comes into being as a series of *ad hoc* decisions made in response to pressures that are felt rather than understood. Only by *understanding* can managers have a mastery of the situation. If they do not understand, the situation masters them instead.

(*e*) People can accept changes when their sources of rationale are understood, but when change arises in the manner described then the scene is set for anxiety and resistance to new methods.

Some Organizational Concepts

If situations like these are to be avoided, and if organization is constantly to be adapted to the changing quantity and quality of work and to changing methods of doing it, there is a need for objective analysis to be carried out periodically. But it needs to be carried out in such a way that the implications of the change in executive structure can be seen.

Definition of work

One of the striking things emerging from exploration into the meaning of organization is how difficult it is for people in industry to think about work. We had no definition of work, and we consistently described it in terms of the people who did it. We talked of skilled work, boring work, satisfying work, highly paid work, managerial work, technical work. But these are in fact psychological descriptions of people's reactions to the work, or descriptions of the type of person who does the work. They are not descriptions of the work itself. If we glance through the columns headed 'Situations Vacant' in our technical press, we note that there is seldom any description of the work which the applicant will have to do. What appears is a description of the person who is wanted to do it, whatever 'it' may be.

We have now defined what seem to be two of the major components of work: the prescribed components – those things that the person in the role must do; and the discretionary component of work – those decisions or choices that the person in the role must make.

This definition is not complete, for we have as yet no means of describing quantity of work; although it now seems possible to measure the level of work by reference to the discretionary component of work and to mechanisms for reviewing discretion.[1] Analysis is greatly helped by this definition. It has never been difficult to specify, in principle, what the prescribed component of any role is, although a complete statement of it can be very arduous. We have in our Company Policy Document,

1. I shall not attempt here to describe this approach to measurement of level of work because it has been fully discussed in *Measurement of Responsibility* by Dr Jaques (London, Tavistock Publications, and Cambridge, Mass., Harvard University Press, 1956).

for example, standing orders, directives and various written routines – extensive written examples of some of the prescribed content of various levels of the job. We have been able to add to this by describing the discretionary content in terms of the types of decisions which the occupant of a role must make. The following extracts from the job specification of the general manager[1] of the service group give an example of the written specification of a part of the discretionary content of a role.

Within the limits of his budget, the General Manager has to arrange for such modifications and extensions as may be required to the buildings and property within his command. He must continually *decide* whether or not these are sufficient now or will be sufficient in the future to enable his work to get done....

Within the command of the General Manager there are some 150 machine tools, metalling equipment and handling equipment. . . . He must *decide* whether the requirements of his planned work load for the next few years require either the replacement of existing equipment or the addition of new equipment. On the basis of *his decisions* he must make recommendations to the Managing Director for the necessary capital expenditure, and will be held accountable for failure to make such recommendations where it can be shown that they should have been made....

The General Manager must ensure that estimating procedures are adequate in his judgement and must *decide* policies with regard to profit loading....

The General Manager must himself *decide* upon the kind of developments in methods and techniques that are required to meet the changing and competitive demands of the business and pursue such developments. He must *decide* what new developments in production methods occurring elsewhere in the Company are the concern of Service Group . . .

The General Manager is responsible for *deciding* when to take

1. We use the term 'general manager' perhaps differently from most companies. There are at present six general managers, all immediately responsible to the managing director, as follows: Two of them command manufacturing organizations, each employing over 1,000 people. One is in charge of a group of three service stations, employing in total about 230 people. One is in complete command of a subsidiary company. There is a general manager in charge of the sales organization and another in charge of the company's research and development organization.

the initiative in making contact with potential customers. He will himself *decide* when to visit customers. . . .

The General Manager has to *decide*, within Company Policy, on methods of recruitment, selection, training and advancement of existing personnel . . .

The organizational structure of Service Stations is under the *discretion* of the General Manager and, within the limits of Company policy, he must *decide* on the size of managerial section he uses, the use he allows to be made of supervisory staff, the employment of specialists, etc.

Understanding organization in action

The planning of organization implies understanding of a range of ideas, and I shall therefore first give some definitions to make clear the meaning which we now give to certain words and phrases.

Decision – is a commitment to action. Examples of action are the giving of an order to a subordinate, the signing of a letter to a customer to inform him of the terms on which the company will accept a contract, etc.

Role – is a position into which decision-making work is allocated.

Executive system – is the term used to imply that structure of interrelated roles from which the people who man these roles may do the work of the company. This system of roles, variously referred to in industry as the 'hierarchy of positions', the 'organizational tree', etc., we refer to as the 'executive system'.

Planning of organization – implies, in the first place, analysis of the situation, because it is often not accurately known. It also implies the job of deciding what the role structure of the executive system shall be and into which roles responsibility for taking specific types of decisions shall be placed.

Analysis of organization – should be taken to imply the job of discovering the type of decision which individual people are making and the roles which they occupy when they are making them. In the analysis of organization we now have four helpful concepts. These are as follows:

Manifest – the situation as formally described and displayed.
Assumed – the situation as it is assumed to be by the

individual concerned. There may or may not be consistency between the 'assumed' and the 'manifest' situation.

Extant – the situation as revealed by systematic exploration and analysis. (It can never be completely known.)

Requisite – the situation as it would have to be to accord with the real properties of the field in which it exists.

The ideal situation is that in which the manifest, the assumed, the extant and the requisite are as closely as possible in line with each other. The circumstances, of course, are always dynamic, so that the tendency is for these four to be moving out of adjustment with each other. How often systematic analysis requires to be done in order to bring them back into line with each other will depend on the dynamics of the situation. The more dynamic and unstable the situation, the more frequently will analysis have to be made. I will explain the use that can be made of these ideas by taking the simplest possible situation.

Manager A has in his office an organizational chart. This shows that he has three subordinates B_1, B_2 and B_3. B_3 is on loan temporarily to another manager in another part of the factory; and it has virtually been decided that he will in the future stay permanently in what up till now has been his temporary job. Outwardly, however, and to the rest of the organization, B_3 is still responsible to A. The position of A with three subordinates, B_1, B_2 and B_3, is the *manifest* organization.

A, on discussion, will agree that the actual situation is that he has two subordinates B_1 and B_2, and that all instructions given by him go to B_1 and B_2 who receive instructions from no other role. That is the *assumed* organization.

Analysis of the situation discloses, to the surprise of A, that some of the instructions given to B_1, who is in fact a good deal older than B_2, seem to go to B_2 and are carried out by him. In short the occupant of role B_1 sometimes gives what are, in effect, instructions to B_2. A's assumption, however, is that B_2 is in no way a subordinate of B_1; thus the *extant* situation differs from the assumed one.

A, having discovered that for some work B_2 is receiving

orders from B_1, investigates further and comes to the conclusion that some of the problems he has experienced in the past are due to the fact that B_1 is giving such instructions and, further, that optimum organization insists that he himself should give these instructions and not B_1. A, therefore, reorganizes the situation so that, in fact, all instructions received by B_2 come from him alone and he has, in this respect, achieved *requisite* organization. In this context, *requisite* organization implies change so designed that people may keep within role when making decisions, giving orders, etc. A recognizes, for instance, that as long as B_1 is giving instructions to B_2, B_1 is in fact sharing a part of his own role. The sharing of roles in this manner is complex and gives rise to serious psychological difficulties, e.g., the occupant of the role B_1 will become both the colleague of B_2 and his part-manager. In carrying out analyses of organization we have frequently come across the type of situation described. Usually it is caused by non-recognition of the existence of a specialist staff role, which is actually part of A's role. The subject of specialist roles is discussed at length in later chapters.

Here is a live example to illustrate further the meaning which we in the company now give to these four words, *manifest, assumed, extant* and *requisite*.

Decisions about what types of bearings our company should manufacture and sell have been arrived at in complex ways after much discussion. Various individuals have, in fact, from time to time taken the actual decisions. In day-to-day working, questions like the following have frequently arisen. 'We make and sell white-metal-lined steel-backed bearings, but do we make them of this particular size or design, or do we make them in this particular specification of material?'

These questions gave us much trouble. General managers of factories frequently complained that orders were taken for designs or sizes which could only be manufactured by them at the cost of high scrap or increased expense.

The *manifest organization* at one stage was that the managing director had set a range of policies, and by reference to these, everybody knew what we officially did or did not make. Most people also knew that, in fact, these policies were quite insufficient to guide people to correct answers to all the many questions that arose.

The *assumed organization* was that in cases of doubt, where the overriding factor was the performance of bearings, the general manager in charge of research and development of our products specified what should be manufactured and sold. These decisions had grown into his ambit on the grounds that he knew best what products it was safe for us to offer to engine builders from the point of view of their performance.

Investigation showed that the general manager sales was making these decisions by accepting orders from customers, thus committing his colleague general manager in charge of a factory to manufacture them. Hence the *extant organization* was that the sales manager was, in fact, giving instructions to the general managers of factories. Clearly, however, the issue of an instruction to the general manager of a factory could only come from the managing director who is his immediate manager. Decision as to what should be made and sold is binding on the general manager sales and the factory general managers, and is *requisitely* in the managing director's role. When, therefore, the general manager sales made such decisions he was *requisitely* in the managing director's role. Arising from that investigation, I decided to do what I should always have done: accept responsibility myself. In facing up to the detailed work involved in making such decisions it became clear that I must set an adequate range of policies about the type of products that we made. These policies would have to be in terms of material specification, size, dimensional limits of accuracy, degree of finish, manufacturability, design from the point of view of function, and so on. Such specifications would have to take into account the views of the general manager sales, of customers' wishes, of general managers in charge of manufacturing on manufacturability, and of general manager research and development on function. By the time this book is printed a product manual will be in existence setting out these policies, and reference to it will answer the questions which have caused us much trouble in the past. It will require continuous work to adapt the policies set out in this manual to changing circumstances.

As soon as the manual was started two more useful facts emerged:

(*a*) That there were some bearings which, because of their characteristics, we could not produce without risk. It therefore became very necessary that we should equip ourselves rapidly in order to be in a position to produce these bearings without trouble, thus preventing loss of business.

(*b*) That, as soon as these manuals are available to our technical representatives, it will be possible for many problems and questions, which are now passed back to headquarters and dealt with by correspondence, to be settled by them on the spot with customers – in a way that benefits everybody.

This notion of requisite placing of work enables us to discover an answer to the question 'Who ought to be making this type of decision?' by simply ascertaining what the decision is intended to achieve. If such a decision sets terms of reference within which a person must perform his work, then that decision must be made by the manager in charge of that person.

We shall in the future gradually be able to make greater use of this notion, and we shall be able to create an increasingly more effective organization as our ability to analyse jobs in terms of discretionary content increases.

There is another useful way of talking about this notion in current use in some parts of the company. The key phrase of this other approach to the idea of *requisite* placing of decisions is 'the cross-over point'. The idea is stated diagrammatically in Figure 1.

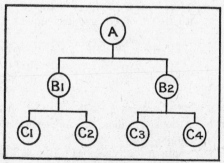

FIGURE 1. The cross-over point

In our terms, B_1 is the cross-over point between C_1 and C_2, his subordinates. But A is at the cross-over point between C_1 and C_3. Thus any decision that is binding on B_1 and B_2 must be made at the cross-over point A. Equally, any decision that is binding on C_1 and C_3 can only be made at the cross-over point, i.e., in A's role. This is merely a different way of stating that the decisions binding on B_1 and B_2, or on C_1 and C_3, are *requisitely* in A's role.

It is clear to me that if we can discover decisions that are assumed to be made at, say, the B's level, which *requisitely* belong to A's role, then equally it must be possible to discover decisions being made extantly by A which requisitely belong to the roles of B or even of C.

This use of the concept has great potentialities, for it could be applied to tell us when decision-taking was being placed at too high a level in the organization, as well as when it was being placed too low. There must be many examples of this failure to achieve *requisite* organization in our company. This is a field in which further work will have to be done.

I began this chapter by describing the set of ideas which, as a result of our attempts to understand what really happens in our organization, have come to form the framework of our company's thinking. In concluding this chapter, and by way of summing-up, I will now try to state in a slightly different manner the assumptions on which we base our organizational and social approach:

(*a*) That the company's organization and social institutions exist primarily to facilitate the optimal discharge of the company's work with the resources and techniques at its disposal;

(*b*) That changes in the work itself – the methods of doing it or of the resources available – set up pressures for change in the pattern of roles in the executive system and of the distribution of work between roles;

(*c*) That a company which is unable to adapt itself, consciously or unconsciously, to those pressures will cease to be a viable economic proposition;

(*d*) That our continued existence as a competitive unit is evidence of the fact that we have introduced at least some of the changes implied by changes of work, resources and methods available;

(*e*) That the degree of our adaptation to these pressures is one determinant of our state of competence to discharge our work as compared to the optimum attainable.

(*f*) That, with our present lack of insight into these matters, much of our adaptation is done not as a piece of conscious planning, but is forced upon us by feelings of pressure whose source is not always recognized;

(*g*) That our approach to the problem of establishing better organization and more appropriate social organization is by analysing the way in which work, resources and methods have changed and are likely to change; the adjustments implied by these changes; and the extent to which these adjustments have already taken place.

Thus we conclude that a study of how we are actually organized (the extant picture), as compared to the manifest or the assumed picture of the situation which we possess, will lead to knowledge of organization and a capacity to tease out and build the requisite organization which is necessary if we are to approach optimum levels of performance.

It is because of the approach described that many of our plans for 'reorganization' in various parts and phases of the company are felt by those affected to be 'not new', and to be little more than an explicit recognition of what has existed in unrecognized form for some time past.

This kind of reorganization work can only be carried through if it is done on a continuous basis and at the necessary level of sophistication – in fact by allotting it to a specialist branch of the company. It constitutes part of the large area of work which at present is being left aside, or intermittently done by managers, which requisitely belongs to an enlarged and more highly skilled personnel division.

Some of the gains arising from the approach to organization described in this chapter are:

(*a*) The fact that members of the company can in this way be taught how the organization is operated;

(*b*) Greater consistency of action arising out of this shared common perception;

(*c*) The fact that the changes which emerge as a result of this approach are often felt to be obvious and, therefore, necessary. Thus resistance to change is reduced;

(*d*) The increased adaptability which insight into t he source of change and the function of organization give us;

(*e*) Some reduction in feelings of confusion and frustration stemming from the increased sense of control over the situation and a decreased dependence on the whims of personality.

CHAPTER 3

THE EXECUTIVE SYSTEM

THE company at present employs about 3,600 people. This means that although the board of directors delegates to a single person (the managing director) the task of developing, manufacturing and selling certain products, this man must depend upon 3,600 others to ensure that this task is, in fact, accomplished by apportioning the work among immediate subordinates chosen by himself.

The managing director's work changes with the changes imposed on the company by the needs of the market. This, in turn, affects the work delegated to subordinates; and it may cause a rise or fall in the volume of their work. It is for the managing director then to decide: whether to re-allocate the work among his subordinates; whether to increase or decrease the number of his subordinates; and whether to allow his subordinates to expand or restrict the number of people on whom they rely to carry out that portion of the work allocated to them.

The company can be said to get its work done by a process of setting policies and delegating work; that is, if the managing director can successfully share out the work among his subordinates and their establishments according to their capacity to fulfil the tasks allocated to them. This statement needs thorough explanation.

The managing director cannot say to a factory manager, 'Make this product', and leave it at that. He must specify the quantity, quality, target costs and delivery times required. Nor can he leave the factory manager in a position to employ anybody he may decide upon at a rate of pay he deems suitable. He cannot give him complete freedom of choice as to the techniques he will use in producing nor can he permit him the use of unlimited resources.

The managing director must limit the discretion of the factory manager in a number of dimensions, and in such a manner as will ensure that the work of the factory is coordinated with the work of the product development organization and the selling organization. The factory manager may employ only such resources as are commensurate with the total resources available in the company. He must use the best-known techniques of production available within the company. He must select, pay and train people in a way that conforms with the total pattern of approach towards such matters in the company. Delegation without policy-setting and routinization is not, in fact, a viable proposition, because the uncoordinated acts of a manager's subordinates would not get the work of the company done.

This process of splitting-up work, policy-setting, routinization and delegation results in the setting up of a large number of different roles. Nobody can operate one of these roles except through certain minimal relations with persons in other roles. For example, a section manager in charge of thirty shop operators producing on the floor of one of our factories has manager-subordinate relationships with those thirty operators, as well as a relationship with his own unit manager, certain defined relationships with his unit manager's specialists, and relationships with his colleague section managers. He cannot get his work done without operating all these relationships. This series of interconnected positions we call the executive system, because it exists to execute the work of the company.

It will be necessary, throughout the remaining chapters of the book, to use a number of diagrams to illustrate the various parts of the executive system; and Figure 2 shows the standard symbols which we in the company use to represent these parts.

The *executive system* is defined in our Company Policy Document as follows:

The network of positions to which the Company's work is assigned. It is made up of positions which shall be called Executive Roles. The Executive System includes all members of the Operating Organizations, a member being in his Executive Role while he is carrying out his job responsibility.[1]

1. The phrase 'Executive System' as defined includes operators, craftsmen, clerks, etc.

The Executive System

The executive system is a social structure. The nature and function of each role can be studied and made the subject of

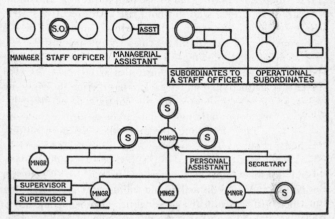

FIGURE 2. The standard symbols used to represent the executive system

explicit statements. The relationship of one role to another can be understood and regulated.

This system exists irrespective of people. An individual position can be vacant because the person who occupied it has left the company and has not yet been replaced; but the position does not disappear. Change in the company's work brings about change in the work content of particular roles within it. The work in a role decreases or increases in importance, without the people in those roles necessarily changing their personal capacity to do that work. New roles can be added to the system – to cater for change in the amount and kind of work to be done – before ever any thought is given to the person who should fill those roles. The work allocated to a given role can disappear; hence the role is no longer needed and a person is redundant, which results in the search for other vacant roles to which that person can be moved.

This social structure exists as an entity in itself. It can be made the subject of explicit thinking, analysis and alteration. (This is not in any way to suggest that an executive system can be designed without reference to people. Any such approach would be highly unrealistic, and would result in a system of roles which would either fail to use people's full potentialities, or call for supermen who did not exist.) An executive system can be designed in its own right, bearing in mind that people subsequently will have to fill the roles set up within it.

It is necessary to distinguish between social systems and the people who comprise them. Difficulties arise from failure to make this distinction. Though each of us entering the company takes up an executive role by the contract of employment which he accepts, and though as our career within the company grows we change from one role to another, we do not think explicitly about the social system within which we are working. We are not asked to think about it, because we find a pattern of relationships already established around us. When the individual runs into difficulties, he will usually blame it on his own personality, or on the personalities of other members of the company. The idea that the difficulty could be a function of the design of the social system, of which his role is a part, seldom occurs to him.

The word 'relationship' is perhaps something of a stumbling block in itself. It connotes to most people the interplay of their personality with the personality of another, and therefore tends to have a purely psychological meaning. A *role relationship* – the terms of which are set by the interplay of the work content of two roles – is a relatively new idea. Thus there is often very little conscious perception at all of the existence of an executive system, and the place of a person's executive role within the system as a whole. My own experience suggests that there seems to be quite a considerable tendency to construe all problems in industry in terms of the personal behaviour of people, and to exclude the notion that we can design trouble into, or out of, an executive system.

Any competent engineer confronted by faults in a complex piece of machinery, incorporating gears, levers, cams, hydraulic and electrical systems, etc., would tackle the problem along two lines. He would look for faulty manipulation of the machine by the person responsible for controlling it, and he would look for trouble inherent in its design. If he assumed that all troubles in machines of this kind were due to the people operating them, he would not get very far. Furthermore, he would be quite unable to make helpful adjustments or modifications to the machine without a very clear notion of the function of each part of it, and the relation of each part to the rest. We all know the trouble we can get into if we try to adjust part of a complex mechanism on the basis of a faulty perception of its function. I well remember a very trying week-end some years ago when I essayed the task of repairing our grandfather clock. I thought I understood how it worked!

This experience can be generalized. If the assumed appreciation of how a system works is unsound, then change based upon this faulty appreciation will also prove ineffective. The extant situation has to be discovered before effective change can be introduced. The discovery of the extant situation in any system may lead to the exposure of requisite implications for change, which in turn will lead to modification and improvement.

The company must seek to promote a growing awareness that the work of developing, manufacturing and selling bearings is done through a social structure, and that this structure must be specifically designed to carry out that work. Because the work is constantly changing, this mechanism requires constant adaptation. The clearer the perception of what exactly the system is, of how it works, and of the relationship of its various roles to one another, the more readily will we be able to adapt it as the work of the company changes.

I will now try to draw up a definition of a *role* in the system by reference to its position in the system; its relationship with other roles; its work content.

(A) *The position of a role in the system*

Our work on the positioning of a role is not finished. Nevertheless, we have made some headway in our thinking. Six years ago there was no rational way of comparing the level of work, and therefore the implied status, of, say, a production engineer with an accountant or an operational manager, except on the basis of hunch. Managerial hunch was often different from the hunch of the person who thought that the status of his job was too low. There was thus a strong tendency for the status of a role to depend upon the number of positions through which instructions from the managing director's role had to flow to reach it.

Thus in Figure 3 role Y, being twice removed from the managing director's role, was felt to be of higher status than role C, which is three stages removed, whereas in some cases it was plain that the level of work in C was higher than that at Y.

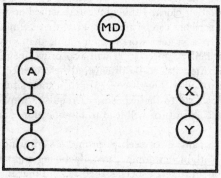

FIGURE 3

Since then, much analysis of work in various roles has been done, and this has produced the idea of measurement of level of work by reference to the concept of maximum time-span of decisions in roles.[1]

This approach to measurement of the level of work is in tentative use in the company. It is proving helpful in planning organization, but is not in general executive use at the time of writing. Despite the limited application, however, the thinking and discussion which has led to its evolution has given us an incomplete and tentative, but still very useful approach to this problem of fixing the position of a role in the executive system.

Figure 4 is an attempt to describe diagrammatically the way

1. The maximum time-span of decisions made by a person in a role is the maximum lapse of time that *does* take place between the taking of a decision and the review of that decision either by the person's manager or by some indirect mechanism. See Jaques, *Measurement of Responsibility*.

in which we now look at the question of differential levels of
work in the executive system. It shows the five ranks[1] into
which we assemble all roles; the time-span bracket which, on
the basis of sample measurements, we attach to these ranks;
and the salaries which, again on the basis of a sample, are
apparently felt to be fair pay for such levels of work.

ORGANIZATION	RANK	TIME-SPAN BRACKET OF WORK LEVEL according to Jaques	SALARY BRACKET felt to be fair by those whose work has been analysed by Jaques (about 1000 people) and who are occupying roles at these discrete levels (as at December 1961)
⑤	5	5 YEARS –?	£5500 + P.A.
④₁ ④₂ ④₃	4	2–5 YEARS	£2800–5500 P.A.
③₁ₐ ③₂ ③₃ ③₁ᵦ	3	1–2 YEARS	£1500–2800 P.A.
②₂ₐ ②₁ ②₃ ②₂ᵦ	2	1 MONTH –YEAR	£878–1500 P.A.
①₁ ①₂	1	UP TO 1 MONTH	UP TO £16–17–6 PER WEEK

FIGURE 4. Differential levels of work in the executive system

Five ranks seem appropriate, because this is the maximum
number of roles which, in any line of authority, span the

---

1. It is not intended to convey that all executive work can be
appropriately assembled in five ranks but merely that the level and
quantity of work being done in the Glacier Metal Co. Ltd at the time
of writing requires five ranks. Smaller companies may have only three
or four ranks; larger companies six or seven, or more.

system from managing director at the top to operative or clerical worker at the bottom. Whether such a categorization has essential validity we do not know; but it certainly enables us to discuss organization more meaningfully. The placing of roles within particular ranks is still largely based on managerial intuition, but we are aided in these decisions by analyses that have already been made of a number of roles. As the number of these analyses increases, the intuitive content of the decisions will decrease. When we are able to measure the work content of all roles regularly we shall, in so far as this method of measurement is valid, have a consistent basis on which to rank all roles relative to each other.

For the last two or three years we have been dealing with ranking problems within this tentative framework, and I think it has produced what feels to most people a more consistent and satisfying situation. The evidence for this statement is that, before this kind of thinking developed, there was almost unremitting pressure on the management of the company to upgrade large numbers of roles, and great anxiety was constantly expressed about differential pay and status; whereas for the past two years such anxiety and pressure has receded very noticeably indeed.

The level at which work is being done *within* the rank timespan bracket appears to be assessable at this stage only by the judgement of the immediate manager in charge of that role. Thus although we appear to have found a means of measuring work to determine rank, the element of managerial assessment still remains very much in the picture in determining pay, etc., *within* the time-span bracket.

It seems clear that Jaques' work will eventually enable us to clarify our knowledge about roles, pay and responsibility. Here are some examples of what we have already learnt and of the possibilities opened up to us by these particular ideas.

(1) Although theoretically there is as yet no support for the suggestion that organization must proceed in these particular discrete stages of time-span bracket, it nevertheless appears that these are the particular brackets which enable our work to get done with the smallest number of managerial levels. In other words, it would seem that the smallest chain of command

through which we can get work done – from the production of bearings on the floor of a factory to the managing director – is five ranks, with these time-span brackets and salaries attached to them.

(2) We are able to analyse the work content of a single role in terms of time-span, and thus to say within which bracket and, therefore, within which rank it falls. Here it should be noted that where time-span measurements of work in individual roles produce brackets which cross a rank boundary, we tend already to be regarding these, status-wise, as belonging to the higher rank.

(3) We now know that people engaged in a wide variety of occupations have extremely consistent ideas as to what are fair brackets of pay for their jobs, provided that the work in those jobs, when analysed, falls into the same time-span bracket of discretion. 'Felt fair' brackets of pay are also pretty consistent with managerial hunches as to what the pay-bracket for such work ought to be.

(4) We have limited but consistent experience of ranking jobs intuitively and paying accordingly. We find that decisions made within this matrix of thinking have produced less feeling of frustration about pay and status than we used to get in the past.

(5) We know that we cannot determine rank by counting the number of times the role is removed from Rank 5, because of the existence of 'half-rank' roles. For instance in Figure 4, we designate 3_{1A} and 3_{1B} as at Rank 3_A and 3_B respectively. If we counted 'removes', then 3_{1B} would have the same status as 2_{2A} or 2_3. This head-counting was probably one of the causes of underpayment, and led in the past to the awarding of inappropriate status.

(6) We know that most of the half-rank role positions are to be found in the specialist commands, embracing engineers, metallurgists, accountants, production control personnel, etc.; though there are a few examples in operational (line) management.

(7) We believe that some jobs which are paid on an hourly rating, and which we therefore used to regard, on an intuitive basis, as Rank 1, are doing work in Rank 2. This has explained to our satisfaction (though it is not yet supported by evidence

such as will, I hope, later be derived from selectively made measurements of the time-span bracket of work in these roles) why some of these hourly-rated jobs are paid more than many weekly-salaried jobs. This has removed a feeling that we were being inconsistent in paying any hourly-rated job more than any weekly-salaried job. We believe that when we can move forward – for example by taking time-span measurements of such jobs to determine the corresponding ranking – that the feeling of 'non-recognition' experienced by some skilled craftsmen and others in the company may be dissipated.

(8) From time to time specific roles come under particular observation – perhaps because the work is not getting done effectively; because of the apparent difficulty in filling the role with a suitable person; or because of confusion about who is responsible for what. This sometimes leads to strong pressure from the manager to change the salary available in such a way as to break the rank brackets of salary. We find that when situations like this arise, these difficulties, confusions and pressures are often the result of the work content of a role having undergone change that has not been recognized; and that, in fact, the role is wrongly placed, ranked and salaried.

This is a summary of the position we reached in December 1957 and the extent to which we are able at the moment to define executively the level of work and, therefore, the position of a role in the executive system.

(B) *The relationship of one role with another*

The emergence of the idea of an executive system produced a flow of ideas about the nature and relationship of the various roles composing it. We defined many of these ideas in precise terms. These precise definitions will be set down in succeeding chapters as the ideas are brought into play. For the purposes of this chapter I merely list some of them.

(1) We defined operational activities, and differentiated them from specialist and staff work;

(2) We defined the different phases of operational work by recognizing that work is done by *people* in an organization, according to a balanced *programme* using specific *techniques*, and we are thus able to talk about the different types of

specialist work, i.e., personnel, programming and technical;

(3) We defined the various levels of operational command, i.e., managing director, general manager, unit manager, section manager and operator; and so are able to talk about role relationships between these different levels in language which communicates reasonably precise ideas;

(4) We defined the various types of different role relationship which can arise in our executive system, e.g., superior-subordinate relationship; collateral relationship between colleagues when their work is interdependent; colleague relationship between people in roles which are all responsible to the same manager; conjoint relationship between specialists responsible to the same manager; relationship between a manager responsible for providing services and the manager receiving the services, and so on;

(5) We defined and set out various mechanisms for overcoming the difficulties which can arise when people in different roles are collaborating with each other in various ways to get work done. The Policy Document describes, for example, mechanisms for contracting executive lines for the purpose of communicating; seeking and providing prescriptions and services; dealing with disagreements; manning the organization; getting agreement on change of policy; dealing with grievances; and dealing with disagreements about the interpretation of policy.

(c) *The work content of a role*

Having introduced the idea that work has two components – prescribed content (the actions which have to be taken) and discretionary content (the decisions which have to be taken) – we can now talk about the work content of a single role. The following is a brief description of a single role in these terms.

Take the fairly typical job of designer draughtsman, the occupant of which is engaged in designing small items of equipment for use in production. The kind of matters which would be prescribed, and therefore about which he would be left no choice, might include the following.

He would have to conform to the requirements of overall company policy and to standing orders as regards starting times, stopping times, sickness, holidays, etc. His total working conditions – that is, where to work, at which drawing board, under what conditions of lighting, heating, etc. – would be prescribed. The kinds of paper and the type of draughting equipment he could use would be laid down. He would have to adhere to the practice of his drawing office with regard, for instance, to numbering, codes, dimensioning, tolerances. The range of materials, such as the various kinds of steel that could be incorporated in the designs, would be laid down. There would be a range of standard items, such as screws, dowels, bushes, which he would be required to use instead of employing special parts. When instructed to design a particular piece of equipment, it would be within a specification and would be for a particular purpose. He would not be allowed to design another piece of equipment. He would have to work within cost limits. Important also, but sometimes difficult to discern, would be the prescribed end-product of his work. Whether, for example, he was expected simply to produce a drawing which would be scrutinized and either accepted or rejected by his superior, or whether such a drawing would be expected to pass unreviewed into production use with the prescribed result of satisfactory operation.

All the above, then, would act as a limitation to his activities, but within this limitation he would be authorized and, indeed, expected to use his judgement and to make choices as regards the following:

The general design features of the equipment he was designing; what materials to use; how the materials would be arranged and how they would be assembled together; individual dimensions, tolerances, etc. And also such matters as, for example, the method of lubrication. He would be expected to select from among the prescribed range the kind of standard items, such as screws, bushes, dowels, to incorporate in the final design. He would be expected to balance economy of manufacture with efficiency of use, and to avoid extremes of very efficient and costly equipment as against cheap but, possibly, unworkable equipment. As to social behaviour, he would have to judge within the norms laid down how to behave towards tracers, production engineers, shop-floor personnel and others with whom he might have to make contact in order to get his work done. Physically, he would have to judge how actually to arrange his drawing implements and how to make his printing neat and legible. He would have to decide when to ask for advice or assistance. He would have to decide how quickly to work on each individual aspect of his total task in order to finish his design within the prescribed time. In setting about his job he would have to decide in what order to do it; for example, whether to make a general sketch first or whether to begin with the detailed design of certain parts. Again, within any prescribed limits, he would have to decide how many elevations would be necessary and the amount of explanatory wording which he should add to his drawings. Important, also, he would have to decide how much discretion to leave to those who use the drawings, i.e., how much himself to prescribe for others. It is interesting to note that in this way *his* discretion becomes the prescription limiting *another's* job.

I have now outlined: (*a*) means of describing and placing a role in an appropriate rank in the executive system; (*b*) means of defining a role by reference to its relationships with other roles; and (*c*) means of describing a role with reference to its work content.

I will now describe one role in our executive system by reference to these three 'dimensions' and take that of general manager service group as my example.

(*a*) This is a Rank 4 role, 2–5 years' time-span of discretion.

(*b*) It is a managerial role immediately subordinate to the managing director; having three Rank 3 operational subordinates, namely, service station managers in London, Manchester and Glasgow; and having two Rank 3 specialist subordinates, namely, group technical manager and group programming manager; relying for personnel, maintenance and buying services on the general manager No. 1 Factory, and for accounting services on the financial division manager.

(*c*) Work content of this role has already been used as an example in Chapter 2 (see p. 46).

These 'dimensions' of a single role (i.e., position in the system, relationship with other roles and work content), if fully used, can lead to a degree of definition which greatly facilitates not only organizational planning but also the solution of many types of day-to-day problems as they arise. The chapters that follow are in themselves examples of how the ideas which have been discussed so far can be used.

An example of the way in which organizations become confused

If we accept the idea of an executive system as a planned social mechanism, then we begin thinking about optimum forms of organization. This leads to the scrutiny of existing organization and the detection of faults. Here is an example of the way in which such situations arise.

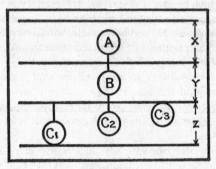

FIGURE 5

In Figure 5, Z is the range of work available to B's subordinates, Y the range available to A's subordinates. C_1, C_2 and C_3 are performing work at a different level but all their work is appropriately within the range.

At the stage shown in the diagram, C_3 is doing work for B and is his subordinate. C_3 is young and his capacity for work at a higher level is growing rapidly. In the near future he is either going to get a job in the organization which will involve work at Y level, or he will get restless and look for a post outside the company.

This situation is, at least partially, recognized by both B and A. The need arises for work to be done on an important new development. A gives the job to B in the light of his knowledge that B has as a subordinate C_3 whose ability and performance have become noticeable. C₃ tackles the whole job vigorously, and virtually takes it over from B. A, who is very concerned about the job, has many meetings about it with B and C₃. A begins increasingly to have direct contact with C₃ who has, requisitely, moved into a job at a higher level.

This is only one example of a very large number of different types of situation which can very easily arise where faults have crept into the executive system. If they are not detected, they can give rise to ill-feeling, inefficiency, mistakes and resignation of valuable people who are needed by the company.

Instruction. Before leaving this subject of the executive system itself and proceeding to the next chapter which discusses the role of the manager, I want to discuss rather fully the meaning of a word which must appear with great frequency in any book about management. That word is 'instruction'.

What is an instruction? The executive system is a command system for getting work done. Any discussion of how it operates will inevitably make constant use of the word 'instruction' or 'order'. I must, therefore, introduce a definition of what we in the company mean when we use this word. The definition given in the Company Policy Document reads as follows:

> *Instruction* is any communication from a superior to one or more of his subordinates when they are in their executive roles. This definition includes not only orders, but also requests for information, advice or assistance, the passing of information, etc., which always contain, either explicitly or implicitly, an instruction.

I will take just one implication of this definition and discuss it as a means of explaining the importance of the definition itself. Once the definition is accepted, it means that a manager who communicates to a subordinate his own preference for a particular line of action has, in fact, given that subordinate an instruction. At first sight this proposition may seem absurd, for the immediate implication is that a manager cannot give advice to his subordinates (since technically this is an instruction). I am now quite sure that the proposition and inference is completely realistic in the context of an executive system.

Consider the position of B who has received advice from his

manager A to follow a particular line of action. There are two possible courses he can take: either to ignore the 'advice', or to accept it. If he ignores it and still achieves a successful result, nothing will be said, although A may feel rather foolish. If, on the other hand, B ignores the advice and fails, then he will certainly be criticized by A for risking a course in defiance of the 'sound' advice he had been given. If B accepts the 'advice' and this leads to success, B will not feel responsible for that success, nor will A feel that he deserves commendation for it. If B accepts the advice and it leads to failure, he will not feel responsible, though A might try to pin the responsibility on to him. Clearly, if a manager gives 'advice' to a subordinate, he expects it to be accepted, and he cannot escape the responsibility for having done so. Advice is a confused way of giving an instruction. It might be termed 'instructional advice'.

I remember once being faced with the news of a rather large bad debt and the feeling with which I tackled one of my immediate subordinates for his failure to act with greater speed and thus save us from loss. He pointed out that months before he had expressed anxiety about the account and suggested action, but that I had 'advised' a tolerant approach because they were old customers. At the time, I resented his quoting back of 'advice' given; but I came to realize that by giving it I had taken over responsibility in the matter. By the same token, requests from manager to subordinate for information or assistance are merely 'polite' instruction.

If a manager describes to his subordinate, with obvious approval, the technique being employed for a particular job elsewhere, it is an instruction to his subordinate to learn about it. The more deeply one thinks about these managerial-subordinate communications, the clearer it becomes that they are always instructions.

Now consider the situation when B_1 says to his *colleague* and equal, B_2: 'I advise you to do this or that', or 'Please supply me with the following information or assistance'. Clearly, no instruction has passed. The position that arises, therefore, is *that the same words have quite different meanings according to the roles occupied by the people between whom communication takes place.*

All of us, I imagine, have always known that the tone of voice, emphasis given to different words, facial expression, physical movements made while talking, modulate the meaning of the words used. Here is just as important a finding: that if A says certain words to B_1, it is an instruction. If B_1 uses the same words to B_2, it is advice for which B_1 will not later be held responsible (i.e., irresponsible advice). If B_1 uses the same words to A, this again is advice, but in this case he will be held responsible by A for using poor judgement if the advice leads to failure (i.e., responsible advice). We thus have three quite distinct meanings for the same word, according to the role position: 'instructional advice', 'irresponsible advice' and 'responsible advice'.

This is intuitively known by all experienced people in industry. But it is not explicitly known and stated in the form above; for explicit recognition of the truth of the preceding proposition only follows out of recognition of the existence of a structured executive system, and definition of the various types of role within it, e.g., manager, subordinate, specialist, colleague.

The meaning of a sentence is a function not only of the words used, but of the field within which the words were uttered; and a part of this field is the role-relationships of those between whom communication is taking place. Once this is accepted, it follows that if role-relationships are not clear, then communication between roles can be deprived of clarity. For example, if B is not really sure whether A is his manager, then equally he is not sure if A's 'Please do this or that' is an order or not. Such unclarity leads to all the executive evils of delay, failure to develop, frustration, loss of good people, failure to get good work done, and so on. That, then, is just one example of the value of clear conceptual thinking about executive systems. The rest of the chapters of this book provide further examples.

CHAPTER 4

THE MANAGER AND HIS SUBORDINATES

HISTORICALLY, a manager was a person who was put in charge of a venture by a company of people who, in order to finance it, had joined together and subscribed the necessary money. If he could 'manage' the venture single-handed, then he was not a manager in the full sense in which we in the company now use the word. But if he required the assistance of others in his task and chose subordinates to whom he could delegate some part of his work, then his function corresponded to the managerial position we have in mind. His delegation of part of the work in no way affected his total responsibility. He alone remained responsible to the company of shareholders. He was, in fact, completely answerable for any failure on the part of his subordinates.

This total responsibility of the manager is one of the properties of executive systems, and from it arises the inevitability of the manager being in a position to choose his subordinates. If, for example, the shareholders instruct him to employ as a subordinate some person of *their* choice, then he is not totally in charge of the operation of the venture. His role is not a full managerial one. In the same way a manager must have the right of discharge of his subordinates if, by their performance, they cause him to feel that they have ceased to be persons to whom he can safely continue to entrust part of his work. The inevitability of this proposition is supported by the observation that if the manager is unable to discharge his subordinates, then, in effect, the subordinates are put in a position to bring first discredit and then dismissal to the 'manager' by their own inefficiency.

The use of these two criteria – the right to choose and the right to dismiss subordinates – enables us to distinguish managers from non-managers.

The Manager and His Subordinates

The manager defined

We define 'manager' in our Policy Document as: 'A member who has subordinate to him authorized roles into which he can appoint members and determine their work; he is accountable for his subordinates' work in those roles.'

We lay down policy about the work of a manager as follows:

Assignment and assessment of work:

A manager shall be accountable for the work assigned to him, including the work which he assigns to members under his command. In assigning work, a manager shall determine the extent to which he requires his subordinates to make reference to him before making their own decisions (E.3).

A manager shall appoint, train and maintain as his immediate command a team of subordinates who are competent to carry out the work he requires of them, and who conform to the generally accepted standards of conduct. He shall assign and display an order of seniority among a sufficient number of his subordinates to ensure that his work is done in his absence (E.4).

He shall set standards of executive performance and attainment for his immediate subordinates, and shall make these standards clear to them (E.4.1).

He shall assign work to each of his immediate subordinates at a level consistent with the standards he has set (E.4.2).

He shall judge the executive performance of each of his subordinates in relation to the standards he has set, and their conduct in relation to the standards accepted in the Company.

(a) He shall ensure that each subordinate is rewarded at a level appropriate to the work of his executive role.

(b) In the event of a subordinate performing below the standards he has set or contrary to the generally accepted standards of conduct, he shall acquaint him of this fact and, in the event of continued inadequacy, he shall decide whether to retain him in his command (E.4.3).[1]

A manager shall limit his immediate command to the number of people he can effectively control, and amongst whom he can maintain cooperation (E.4.4).

1. It should be made clear at this stage that there is an appeal mechanism which exists in explicit form in the company. This is described in detail in Chapter 18.

The above clauses shall not necessarily apply to a manager on probation or in training, the extent of whose responsibilities his immediate manager shall decide (E.4.5).

The managerial–subordinate relationship

Managerial decisions concerned with the choice, training, assessment, promotion or dismissal of subordinates are fundamental to the success of a company. They are also, I think, among the most difficult of all decisions to make.

I believe the work done by psychologists and psychiatrists in establishing better means of assessing personality to be of considerable value to industry. Until, however, it is possible to equate a particular personality to a specific task, then such personality assessment will be of more value in rejecting candidates for jobs than in helping to decide which candidate should be appointed to a job. I am not aware of any objective aids to the manager who, faced with three or four candidates for a job, has to decide which to choose. Such decisions have still to be made on an almost entirely intuitive basis. It seems inevitable, in these circumstances, that a very large number of marginally poor decisions are made. The importance, therefore, of putting a manager squarely into a situation where he has the necessary authority and responsibility for assessing his immediate subordinates and for coming to decisions to train, to promote, to point out shortcomings and, if necessary, to reject subordinates from his command, is paramount. If this is not done, the accretion of the results of bad decisions in selection will gradually clog up the whole executive system. It is to be noted that when capable people of the right calibre are appointed, they progress either to higher positions within the company or, if such positions are not available, leave the company altogether; whereas those who are marginally of too low a calibre tend to stick for ever. I notice a very strong tendency on the part of managers to abdicate this task of criticizing or rejecting an immediate subordinate.

It is not difficult for a manager to know, or to find out, whether or not one of his subordinates has carried out the *prescribed* component of his job. It is not too difficult to deal with a subordinate who has failed in this way; for such failure is usually a straightforward mistake or, very occasionally, insubordination. It is much more difficult when we come to the *discretional* component. Then, although there is not necessarily too much difficulty about detecting the use of sub-standard discretion, judgement has to be used in deciding when the quantity, or the effect, or the nature, of this failure has reached a point when confidence in the subordinate is beginning to be inadequate.

This seems to me to be the really difficult part of a manager's job. He is called upon to judge the executive work of one of his fellow human beings. I think everybody tends to shrink from such a task. The manager is faced with the fact that his decisions in these circumstances may have a considerable bearing on the future career of his subordinate and on the fortunes of his home and his family. In my experience, managers feel acutely that they have in their hands the happiness of a fellow human being. These considerations set up emotional barriers which tend to hinder the full taking up of the responsibilities inherent in the managerial role. There is no doubt that unfortunate judgements and bad decisions by a manager can temporarily halt a subordinate's career. Note, however, the contents of Clause E.18.4 of our Policy Document:

A manager shall have the right to dismiss a subordinate from his own immediate command. When taking such action he shall, in the following order:

(*a*) inform his own manager,

(*b*) inform the member so that he may seek alternative employment in the Operating Organizations,

(*c*) inform Personnel Department.

The dismissal is subject to appeal. If the appeal is not upheld, or if the subordinate is unable to find alternative employment in the Operating Organizations within the period of notice, the manager's notice of dismissal shall be taken as dismissal from the Company.

This policy means, in the first case, that the subordinate has a fair opportunity of having the soundness of his manager's appraisal tested in the light of company policy. If the manager's judgement is upheld, then the subordinate has the further opportunity of applying for, and being appointed to, other executive posts in the company. Obviously, in spite of these safeguards, a manager may do injustice to a subordinate; but it is necessary for him to realize that inaction may do even greater harm. If, because he is aware of the possibility of injustice being done, a manager takes no action, he may well be doing equal injustice to a much larger number of people whose degree of satisfaction at work is largely dependent upon the work-effectiveness of the company and the calibre of those to whom they are responsible. The retention of men in managerial positions who are not fit to do the job is an injustice to that manager's entire command.

The abdication by managers from these very difficult decisions rests, I think, on two main factors: the *under*-assessment of the ill-effect of retaining an incapable subordinate on the rest of his command; and the *over*-assessment of the effect on that subordinate of rejection from the job. It is a very bad moment in a man's career when he is dismissed, but he is not 'finished off'. There is many a man in our company today who started building a successful career on the day when his boss 'mercifully' brought to an end that trying period during which he tried to discharge a task to which he was essentially ill-fitted and forced him to change over to a job which he could do with reasonable competence.

Society, to quite a marked extent, has a picture of industry being authoritarian in character. People outside industry often seem to think that a manager's normal behaviour involves the frequent discharge of subordinates without a sufficient sense of the possible injustice and of the grave effects that these decisions have. My experience is that the contrary is true.

The basis of assessment

The assumption is often made that a subordinate can be assessed on quantitative figures alone which indicate his performance. This assumption is, I think, motivated by the desire to escape from the personal business of passing judgement on another. If a manager can say to a subordinate, 'I am sorry, but you can no longer remain in this job – *I have no choice in the matter*, for on the results you have produced, as set out in this profit and loss account [or in this record of output, etc.], you have failed to meet the minimum standard which the company would expect of you,' etc., then he can feel that the subordinate has decided his own fate and he has avoided the penetrating anxiety which inevitably surrounds a decision to discharge somebody from his job.

Unfortunately, the assumption is usually not valid; facts and figures are, of course, an aid to assessment, but they are seldom the whole story. A few examples will serve to demonstrate this:

(*a*) I cannot wholly assess the work of a general manager in charge of a factory on figures of output, expense, quality, delivery, scrap, etc. I used to assume that it could be done. Manifestly it appeared possible, but extantly I have never done so. He may have been instructed to operate a hazardous process which makes low expense, high quality and good delivery almost impossible and yet it is in the company's long-term interest to persevere with the process. The figures are a factual indication of what has happened, but they do not indicate whether reasonable performance has been achieved under the conditions imposed. I must come to difficult intuitive judgements on the relationship of actual to optimum performance.

(*b*) A managing director may largely be judged by a board of directors on the profit made; but his activities have, in fact, been carried out within a series of policies set by the board, which will have exercised a very substantial effect on profit. The board must assess the extent to which their policies have contributed to the results, as well as judge by the figures.

(*c*) An operator may produce low output and poor quality, but unless his machine, the material on which he works, the prescribed method of work, the tools, etc., are identical to those of others, then his manager cannot wholly assess him on figures of output or scrap and is driven to the use of judgement.

There are many facets of performance which cannot be quantified, e.g.:

(*a*) How much change in method ought a subordinate to have developed in the way he does his job, as a means of improving it, over a given period of time?

(*b*) Should he have been able to foresee trouble that did, in fact, arise; and should he have been ready with a solution?

(*c*) Is it his fault that some of his own subordinates are of poor calibre and have not performed well; or does this trouble arise because of the policy operated by the company with regard, say, to salaries, which has led to a situation where he has been unable to get together as good a team as necessary to do the job at the required standard?

In short, the results obtained in any manager's command are a function not only of his own decisions but also of those of his superior manager, and of the policy operated by the company as a whole.

A manager has the responsibility of making assessments of the work and of the behaviour of his subordinates. This is inescapable.

A special point on criticizing behaviour

The right of a manager to critize work is clear; but the right and duty to make personal criticism of behaviour because it is such as to interfere with work by setting a bad example, disturbing relationships with others, introducing discord into the company, is not so clear. For example, if a manager has a subordinate whose 'code' is low and who in a time of rationing gets his 'stuff' on the black market or behaves like a spiv, then so long as such activity does not manifest itself in the company, it is not his manager's business. If, however, he talks about it, then his manager has the right and duty to stop him talking and to point out that such conduct is not approved and not allowed in a manager of the company, because it lowers the status of his authority, and that any reference to or continued display of such conduct must cease forthwith. A manager has a duty to criticize and to limit vulgarity, the exhibition of extreme prejudice about non-work issues, scruffy appearance, etc., not because he happens to object personally, but because such things interfere with the executive work of the company. This right and duty, however, vanishes if the matter is clearly not affecting work. It is only the *executive effects* of such behaviour which come within the realm of comment and assessment by a manager.

In short, a manager must keep his assessment of a subordinate confined to the manager–subordinate relationship. Thus it is that a manager who meets a 'subordinate' in the role of a representative cannot criticize him about his performance in that role. It is essential that managers should be clear about this matter; for it is outside company policy for them to carry into their assessment of subordinates considerations that arise from performance in a representative role.

I have dealt with this subject of assessment at length with a single purpose in mind. Managers must review subordinates because, if they fail to do so, they fail to give those subordinates the opportunity to improve their performance, and so saddle the organization with people who may be unsuited to their roles. They perpetuate inefficiency because they are unable to make executive criticisms of subordinates. And this inefficiency, slowly but surely, inflicts its results on other members of the organization. In the long run, managers who fail to assess, to criticize, to train and to appraise their subordinates, lose their own jobs.

Assessment of appropriate levels of pay of subordinates

At the time of writing, measurement of the level of responsibility of various jobs is still a subject of research, development and some executive activity in the company. I believe, however, that we are making marked progress towards a situation where the level of work in a role can be objectively measured. If I am right, this will make a substantial contribution to our ability to plan organization, allot work appropriately between roles, pay fair rewards for work, and deal with what at present is the very difficult subject of differential pay levels. We are slowly moving towards a situation where, by watching the career history of an individual and noting the ages at which he proved himself capable of doing different levels of work, we shall be able to establish the potential career assessment curve of that individual. The intuitive judgement of a manager *vis-à-vis* his subordinates will then have to be used in assessing how nearly the individual is conforming to the potential career curve which his previous history has indicated. This represents a considerable narrowing of the field in which intuition has to be used. The aid given to intuition by the techniques which are emerging should help very considerably indeed.

We have these ideas about the measuring of responsibility and the pattern of career growth; but at present they are research findings. True, many managers in our company have done work with these ideas and have used them to obtain help in making difficult decisions; but we are not yet in a position to use them for the formulation of general policy. We cannot, for instance, describe the salary review policy which we propose to follow at a given review period by saying, 'For this review managers are to give such increases as will keep all subordinates on the curve indicated by their potential career assessment unless, in their judgement, this is not warranted in certain individual cases for specific and stated reasons.' We are not able to issue such an instruction to all managers because a great deal of groundwork remains to be done, not only to validate these ideas but also to get us into a position where we can use them. When the groundwork has been done, managers will still require considerable technical assistance to operate these techniques; for we cannot expect our managers also to be technical experts in the use of methods of measuring work and individual capacity.

All this adds up to the fact that, in order to move forward on this front and get into a position to make use of the research we have done, we must be able to set up a personnel division staffed with a larger number of technically oriented people. Such people do not exist at the moment; individuals with the necessary capacity will have to be found and trained. This is a slow process, and in the initial two or three years it would be nearly all expense and little net economic gain. Once established, however, such a personnel division would, I think, help the company economically in a major way.

Quantity of work done and amount of resources required by subordinates to discharge their responsibilities

This is an aspect of work which has not as yet been the subject of intensive study and analysis in the company at anything above the level of manual and clerical work. At these levels, time study and work study have, in many areas, set up standards in terms of the number of standard hours that various jobs should take to perform; the quantity of fuel to melt a given tonnage of metal; the type of machine required to perform given work, and so on.

When we move to higher levels of the executive system we come up against such questions as: How many section managers, engineers, production-control personnel, should a unit manager be allowed to achieve a given output? How many technical representatives should be deployed in a given market? How many draughtsmen and development engineers should be allocated to the machine-tool-design needs of the company?

Simply to ask these questions is to make us aware that, at present, we have only experience and intuition to guide us in our decisions. If we can produce accurate descriptions of all the work, without getting so entangled in laborious detail as to make the effort uneconomic in itself, we should be able to quantify the resources required. In the meantime, we have the problem of having to judge subordinates not only on the quality of their work but also on the quantity which they get through with a given amount of resources or a given number of subordinates.

Most managers have experienced difficulty at times in judging the relative merits of two subordinates. The one seems often to be in marginal trouble in adhering to programmes, or does not manage to move very fast on new developments. Nevertheless, his demands on the company's resources of money and personnel are very modest in relation to the work done by him and his command. The second, a colleague, may get through a great deal of work and have a firm grasp of new developments. But he is felt to be a bit of an 'empire builder'. Almost any change in his work is followed by a request for an increase in the number of people in his command. Decisions on such matters are a matter of managerial judgement. We have to rely on 'feel' and intuition. I can offer no help, but mention it as a task that requires more study and analysis.

I have described the current situation at length, because I wish to make clear the in-between situation in which we are placed at the moment. This poses particular difficulties for managers in their responsibilities for assessing salaries of subordinates. Many people in the company are acquainted with our research findings and appreciate the greater objectivity of the techniques which these findings imply. They are waiting for such techniques to be used. In the interim – and it may be a long one – we must, however, continue to observe the policies which have been the bases of our decisions in the past. For the sake of completeness, therefore, I shall state the policies upon which salary assessment has been carried out up to date.

Current policy on salary assessment

Paragraph E.4.3(a) of our Policy Document states that 'A manager shall ensure that each subordinate is rewarded at a level appropriate to the work of his executive role'. The use of the word 'ensure' is inappropriate; 'attempt to ensure' would have been more realistic. Our operative method of conducting a salary review can be stated as follows.

Figure 6 depicts a manager and his immediate command. The range of salary which is available to roles of the Rank C is shown as 10–20. C_1–C_5 are shown diagrammatically to be receiving different levels of salary within this range. The responsibility of B with regard to salaries can be stated thus:

(*a*) He is responsible for considering the range 10 to 20. If he feels it is inappropriate he can raise the question of revision with his own manager.

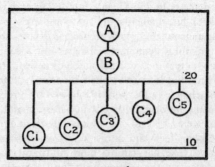

FIGURE 6

(*b*) He is responsible, at any time, for considering whether any of his subordinates are underpaid (or overpaid) and for seeking agreement from his superior for adjustments to be made.

(*c*) He is responsible, at a salary review time, for assessing the amount by which each of the salaries of C_1 to C_5 should be altered.

He may not, in fact, be permitted the full sum he has asked for; but he is responsible for deciding just how any total sum assigned to him for the reward of his immediate command should be allocated between C_1 and C_5. Thus manager B must judge the *relative* merits of C_1 to C_5, though he has not the authority to determine their *absolute* reward.

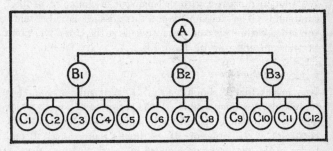

FIGURE 7

Let us now consider A's task with regard to rewards. At a salary review period, B_1, B_2 and B_3 (in Figure 7) assess their subordinates, and then seek a sum from A which will enable them to change the salaries of their subordinates in accordance with their assessments. In the absence of a means of making relative measurements of the level of work being done by, say, C_1 as against C_9, A will, to some extent, have to judge the level of work in these commands by the performance of B_1, B_2 and B_3. He will also have at his disposal all his previous experience of his immediate subordinates and of their work. B_1 may have consistently sought a generally higher average of pay for his subordinates than B_3, which A has not granted and for which he cannot see justification. On the other hand, A may have agreed a generally higher average because, for instance, he judges the work among B_1's subordinates to be of a higher level than that of B_3's. He may feel that the work delegated to B_3, and from B_3 to his subordinates, is not so well-executed as in B_1's command. He therefore concludes that B_3 is not such a good picker of subordinates as B_1, or that he fails to raise the standard of work of his subordinates, by training and criticism, in the same degree as B_1. These are examples of a few of the considerations that will cause A to differentiate between B_1 and B_3.

The concept contained in these considerations is that whereas the determination of differential rewards between *immediate subordinates* is the responsibility of their manager, the judgement about differential levels of salary between one *command* and another must rest with the manager in charge of all those commands. The decision about these issues is subsistently contained within A's role, because he is at the cross-over point of decisions affecting B_1, B_2 and B_3.

Choice of subordinates

If A insists that B should accept C as his subordinate, then requisitely A is responsible for the sector of B's work which he has to get done by C, although neither A nor B may be fully cognizant of the situation. If, in these circumstances, B fails badly in the discharge of some of his work and investigation shows that this is on account of C's failure, then it becomes clear that the failure belongs to A. A cannot therefore hold B responsible for that sector of work until he has agreed to B's right to fill C's role with a candidate who is acceptable to B.

The truth of what is said above is self-evident. But it often leaves a difficulty, for it is interpreted by many managers to mean that B must be allowed untrammelled choice of candidates. The difficulties that can arise out of this erroneous assumption are manifold. If B can choose anybody, then A has no certainty of being able to rely on finding candidates who will be acceptable to him for promotion to his own immediate subordinate roles; or B can affect the whole character of A's extended command adversely by consistently choosing undesirables, and so on. Here, then, are the properties of the selection mechanism which we use to avoid these problems.

In Figure 8, Role C is vacant, and E–K are candidates applying for the vacancy. A screens these first and finds E, F and G unsuitable for his extended command, but would agree H, J or K. B is left with the alternatives of deciding to appoint

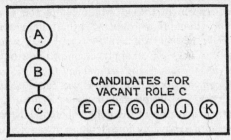

CANDIDATES FOR
VACANT ROLE C

FIGURE 8

H, J or K, or of turning them down and asking A to arrange
for further candidates (acceptable to A) to be offered to him.

The concept contained in these considerations may be stated
thus: the choice of a candidate to fill a vacant role is the job of
the manager to whom the candidate, if appointed, will be immediately responsible; the decisions about the general standards to which these candidates must conform, before they can
be offered to a manager for consideration, must, however, be
set by the manager once removed; he himself will have to conform to higher policies in making his decision about acceptance
standards.

Internal advertising of vacant roles

Paragraph E.18.3(b) of the Company Policy Document reads as
follows: 'Provided suitable candidates are available, vacancies
within the operating organization shall be filled by existing
members according to agreed procedure.'

This sentence is important. It implies that all vacancies
within the company shall be advertised internally before
external candidates are sought. Contrary to expectations, when
this policy was initiated, it was found that the level of internal
candidates applying measured up reasonably well to the requirements of the job. We did not, for instance, get large
numbers of people unqualified by experience or training applying for jobs when they had no real hope of appointment. There
have even been instances of jobs which carry a high level of
responsibility being advertised, for which there have been no
internal applications at all. It seems that the more realistic the

description given in the advertisement of the work of the vacant role, the more appropriate is the training and experience of the candidates who apply for it. If those who read the advertisement get a sound appreciation of the work that is to be done by the successful candidate, then the hopelessly optimistic type of application, which was expected at the time this policy was first introduced, does not eventuate.

The implementation of the policy quoted above involves a procedure for advertising, consideration of candidates and for their appointment that is complex. It is described in Standing Order No. 39/2 (of the London factories). It is worth noting that this is the second edition of this standing order and that no other standing order in the company has been the subject of so much discussion at our council meetings, or has had so much work done on it. At one time, there appeared to exist within the company a very strong feeling that it was, in fact, the duty of the company to provide opportunity for promotion for anybody whose performance warranted it. Desirable as such a situation would be, the fact remains that the operational task of the company is to develop, manufacture and sell bearings, and not to expand or contract itself in such a way as to suit the capacities of those who work within it. There have been, and there continues to be, strong feelings among large numbers of people that the company should be a place where there is always a role available to suit the growing capacity of any of its employee members. To the extent to which the essential real purpose of the operations of the company is faced, this feeling should diminish.

Long-term planning in filling vacant roles

If in the filling of vacant roles we were consistently, at one extreme, to appoint older people whose capacities (even with time) were not likely to develop – or, at least, not enough to enable them to carry out the work of roles at higher level than those to which they were appointed – we should soon reach a situation where expansion of the company would be rendered very difficult. Expansion means growth in the level of work of a large number of the roles in the executive system and of the creation of new roles, some of which would be at high level.

Unless candidates from existing roles can grow with the growth of the job, and unless candidates in other roles are available for promotion to new roles, the work of the company can only be efficiently carried out by seeking and training external candidates. This is expensive, time-consuming and hazardous. If, at the other extreme, roles are filled predominantly with younger people, their capacity for work at higher levels will inevitably grow and this will cause them either to seek and obtain promotion, or to leave the company. The presence of large numbers of young people thus stimulates expansion; but if expansion does not take place (perhaps owing to market conditions, or lack of resources, or old age at the top), waste will inevitably occur – since large numbers of young people will have been engaged and trained at considerable expense and to no purpose so far as the company is concerned. A balance must be struck.

Thus the appointment of a candidate to a vacancy is not only a matter of great importance to the immediate manager and to his superior manager; it is also one of a series of acts that will condition the future, and the possibility of growth and success, of the whole company. For this reason, the decisions of all managers appointing candidates to vacancies must be brought within the terms of a general company policy, devised with the long-term objective of providing for the future manning of the high-level jobs in the company. The work of detailing and making explicit such a policy in written form is in hand now.

We have reached a stage where we are beginning explicitly to fill vacant roles in such a way that we make provision not only for the work of that role, but for work which may arise in the future in other roles.

Drawing up job specifications

In Chapter 2, I have given some extracts from a job specification; this was to demonstrate the effects of detailing the discretionary content of a role as a means of conveying a more realistic appreciation of the work to be done. It is now company policy to establish, as soon as possible, a clear specification of the work content of all roles in the executive system. This is an exceedingly arduous task. We are not at the moment in a position to inaugurate those increases in the strength of the personnel division which makes this possible. In the meantime, the practice is to establish such a specification each time a role above Rank 1 becomes vacant, so that those applying for the vacancy can have a good look at the job 'on paper', and so that the manager concerned gains a more explicit idea of the nature of the work in that role. Here is the matrix upon which these job specifications are shaped.

Job specification

A. DESCRIPTION OF WORK CONTENT OF ROLE

(1) Main prescriptions limiting the role.
(2) Main areas of discretion, with illustrations.
(3) Effects of sub-standard discretion.
(4) Mechanisms in operation for reviewing work done by occupant of role.
(5) Any special working conditions.

B. POLICY ON FILLING THE ROLE

(1) Transit time range. (Probable time candidate is expected to remain in the role before being expected to be ready for promotion to a higher-level job.)
(2) Age range.
(3) Qualities likely to be relevant to doing the above work in terms of:
Formal qualifications; training; experience; skills; physical characteristics, etc.

CHAPTER 5

DISAGREEMENTS ON EXECUTIVE MATTERS

DISAGREEMENTS are part and parcel of an executive system. This statement is not a reluctant acceptance of the inevitable, for disagreement can be as constructive as it is sometimes destructive. New ideas frequently cause disagreement, and the greater the change which they represent, the greater the possibility of disagreement.

Procedure for dealing with disagreements

The problem that arises over disagreements is not how to prevent them arising, but what organizational mechanisms to set up in order that they may be dealt with constructively. The essence of such mechanisms is to ensure that a disagreement that has remained unsettled should be exposed to the manager at the cross-over point. He carries the responsibility for the inefficiency and trouble that stalemate or unsatisfactory compromises can cause, and he has the authority to work towards a solution by setting policies and giving orders that are binding on those concerned. Our company policy on this matter is somewhat wordy and might, I think, be stated more clearly; nevertheless, it contains the essence of the mechanism required.

General responsibilities of managers with respect to disagreements

A manager is accountable, where there is a conflict which affects the efficiency between one of his subordinates and another member, for ensuring that his subordinate takes the matter up with the other member with a view to resolving the conflict (E.13.1).

A manager shall discuss with the individuals concerned personal conflicts between members of his immediate command, which in his opinion they have failed to resolve and which reduce his command efficiency (E.13.2).

A manager is accountable for encouraging his own immediate

subordinates to state to him their opinions, whether or not they are in accord with his own. A subordinate should, whenever he feels strongly about the matter, state his differences of opinion with his manager to that manager (E.14). In the case of a difference of opinion between himself and a member or members of his immediate command, a manager shall manifest his readiness to submit such a difference to his own manager, should the subordinate so desire (E.14.1).

A manager shall draw the attention of members to their right to use the appeals procedure (E.14.2).

One very significant feature of our situation is that this particular part of our policy seems to be less consistently implemented than any other. I think the reason for this situation is failure to differentiate between personal and executive issues. Failure to agree is seen as personal failure. Disagreement is seen as something 'bad'. The idea that disagreement may be a function of lack of clarity about the structure of the executive system, about the work content of particular roles, or about the absence of clearly set policy on specific issues, does not occur; and thus the assumption is made that other people are being personally difficult. In the presence of such an assumption, the exposure of the dispute to a higher level feels like reporting on the shortcomings of a colleague, and therefore no action is taken. Personal incompatibility, prejudice, acts and decisions based on emotional feeling about others, and so on, do of course arise, and colleagues, rightly, will not expose such matters to their manager unless they are very serious indeed; for the assessment by one person of the personal behaviour of another is the task of a manager, not of a man's colleagues. The trouble is that many problems which are not a function of personal behaviour or of personality itself are nevertheless regarded as such, and their ventilation through the mechanisms set up is thus inhibited. The following examples illustrate this.

In recent years many countries have had to be regarded, from the company's point of view, as falling into one of two categories, either export markets, or territories where we could license the manufacture of our products. The two courses are sometimes mutually exclusive alternatives, for licensing agreements often preclude us from continuing the direct sale of our products in that market. Here, then, is a fruitful situation for disagreement; for decisions as to the best course to pursue are finely balanced judgements, which often cannot be made except after prolonged negotiation. During the period of negotiation, those concerned with selling, on the one hand, and licensing, on the other, can easily get at loggerheads in a personal sense, unless the very difficult nature of the executive judgements to be made is recognized, and unless there is realization that the different roles of selling and licensing contain responsibilities that are incompatible with each other.

A unit manager is responsible for processing material received from another unit into finished bearings. He calculates that despite his best efforts he will be unable to deliver these bearings on time. He therefore wants the other unit manager somehow, with the resources at his command, to make possible an earlier delivery of processed material to him. But the other unit manager, who cannot do what is asked of him without excessive expense and interruption to his own total programme of work, says that it cannot be done. Here is a case where rapid exposure of the disagreement at the cross-over point (i.e., the general manager) is essential.

The general manager of a factory operates a buying office which gives buying services to other managers on the same site but who are not in his extended command. The other managers feel that the buying service is not obtaining for them the goods they require; the buying-office manager feels that the manner in which these other managers utilize the facilities he provides prevents the efficient operation of the service. There is, in such a situation, great need to expose problems at the level of general manager, or even at a higher level if necessary, for otherwise it is very likely that money will be spent unwisely. This situation used to be a constant source of trouble and ill-feeling (it may still be). The provision of services by one manager to another is a difficult situation, and if unnecessary friction and inefficiency are to be avoided, it is essential to discuss the problems which arise.

Many years ago, I remember watching a colleague slowly but surely getting into real trouble with a problem which I believed could be solved by a proposal I had made. Because he regarded my action as interference I did nothing. We lost a customer. Given a policy which insisted that we both took issues of that kind to our manager, the situation could have been saved. Unfortunately, no such policy existed; and in the absence of such a policy, it was simply 'not done' at that time to raise contentious matters at the cross-over point. It would have been regarded as most inappropriate by our joint boss, no matter how important the issue.

The existence of clearly stated policy is the means by which executive disagreement is most constructively avoided. In my first example about selling and licensing, the decision that a particular country is one in which we will appoint a licensee settles the disagreement. In the second example (about unit managers meeting delivery dates), if it were possible to issue a policy to the effect that in circumstances where delivery of products on the date due was in danger, any level of expense which would correct the situation was permissible, then such disputes would not need to arise. Such a policy, however, is not usually possible, and problems of this sort have therefore to be taken to the cross-over point.

It is not possible to cover every eventuality which may arise by a prior statement of policy. The need for a policy frequently makes itself felt because of an unexpected new situation developing from the coincidence of a number of factors which have not previously all operated at the same time. Thus it is that executive disagreement is often the signal that new policy is required. If two colleagues in this situation fail to recognize what is happening and make a personal dispute of the matter, then nothing constructive will result. But, equally, if they get together and create a truce or a compromise they may, in effect, be making a policy which is not in the best interests of the company and which may be inconsistent with their own manager's responsibilities. If, however, they can see their own disagreement as a function of the absence of a needed policy, then the difficulty of exposing the matter to their manager is lessened, and the latter is given the opportunity of setting a policy and giving instructions which will help to avoid difficulty in all similar situations in the future.

Disagreements on Executive Matters

I have, over the years, experienced waves of difficulty between members of my immediate command. These difficulties frequently have the initial appearance of being cases of personal incompatibility. Under the stress of trying to deal with an increasingly difficult situation, one or other party begins to raise details of the difficulty with me. The other party criticizes this exposure of the problem as improper conduct. I often have difficulty at this stage in establishing the following points:

(*a*) That disagreements among my command are my business, for I carry the responsibility of the calamities which they can lead to;

(*b*) That, unless the disagreements are exposed, there is no way of establishing whether or not the two parties are in conflict over proper divergencies of viewpoint – that is, divergencies arising out of the differing needs of their separate responsibilities – and there is the danger that they will settle the matter by some compromise which they have not in fact the authority to make;

(*c*) That the dispute is, in any case, very likely to be a function of my own failure to set clear policy, or – worse still – a clash between two sets of policies which I have set.

Once these factors are established, we can wrestle with the problem. This, in the long run, always leads to the setting by me of new policy, which usually overcomes what initially was seen by my two subordinates as a purely personal matter.

I must end this section by pointing out that this chapter's title is 'Disagreements on *Executive* Matters'. Personal dispute matters do also exist, and it would be unrealistic for me to suggest that personal incompatibility can always be dealt with and overcome by executive mechanisms. In the long run, such unfortunate situations are solved by one or other of the parties changing his role to an area of the executive system where the amount of personal contact with the other is reduced or eliminated.

My main aim is to establish the fact that many disagreements which are felt by the parties involved to be personal can be shown requisitely to be executive matters; and that these are not only capable of solution by appropriate mechanisms, but also present positive opportunities for the setting of policies which will increase the effectiveness of the way the company gets its work done.

Collateral relationship between colleagues

This relationship arises when two operational managers, both of whom are responsible to the same manager, are partially dependent upon the effectiveness with which the other does his job for the extent to which they can discharge their own jobs efficiently. The relationship demands a capacity, on the part of each manager, to avoid making value or quantity judgements about the other, and yet, at the same time, to be able to take into account the other manager's statements of his problems and difficulties in planning his own work. The clearer the policy

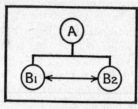

FIGURE 9

set by the manager to whom they are both responsible, the less onerous will be the collateral relationship. But it must be understood that each of the two managers is separately responsible for his own tasks set him by his manager, and that they are not in any sense jointly responsible to their manager. Thus, although there is a collateral relationship, this does not imply a joint responsibility.

A simple illustration is a salesman, B_1, in the field, and a contracts manager, B_2, in the sales office, both being responsible to the sales manager. The salesman carries out his responsibility in contacting customers, meeting them, arranging for quotations to be sent, samples to be made, tests to be carried out, and he relies on B_2, the contracts manager, to get these things done. A collateral relationship is thereby established. Both are carrying out tasks (set by the sales manager) *within prescribed limits* – yet each can interfere with the other's performance by failing to do his task efficiently. This is a difficult type of relationship to work effectively. It could perhaps be said that more friction is caused in the company by ineffective working of collateral relationships than by any other form of relationship. Part of the trouble is that the full nature of this relationship is not yet generally understood.

There is no such thing as collateral *responsibility*; B_1 and B_2, for instance, are not 'collaterally responsible' to each other, because their responsibility is to A alone. Nevertheless, a collateral *relationship* exists between them. For example, B_1 and B_2 are both section managers; B_1 manages a strip mill which lines coils of steel with bearing metal; B_2 manages a section which is responsible for converting the coils of bi-metal into bearing pressings. Both work within policies set by their manager A, which lay down limits of accuracy, finish, timing of output, quantity etc. Within these limits they each exercise their own discretion. If B_1 produces strip towards the top of the thickness limits set, it assists B_2 on certain jobs to avoid scrap; but it is difficult for B_2 to do this without taking special care, which tends to slow down output. In other words, if B_1 follows the course that is easiest for him, the efficiency of B_2's operation is marginally lowered. Alternatively, B_1 can give himself the marginal problem, and thus help B_2 to avoid it.

This is the type of situation which sets up a collateral relationship. B_1 cannot assess the effect of his decision on B_2's command, for this is the responsibility of B_2. B_1 will have to decide what to do in the light of B_2's assessment of the effect on B_2's command. Managers in collateral relationship have to listen to each other and decide on that basis.

I have, however, noticed that often B_1 does not listen to B_2 and assesses the situation in B_2's command as though he knew all about it. I will try and make this important point clear by describing two types of conversation that can take place in this situation.

(*a*) Here is one type of conversation:

B1 TO B2: You want me to produce strip to top limit on these specific jobs. That involves special setting of finishing tools and may produce reject material which is over top limit – merely because you have trouble with four or five particular press tools.

It is more economical for you to modify your press tools and accept strip within normal limits.

B2 TO B1: It isn't. Modifying press tools is tricky and expensive; *it is more economical for you to give me the strip I need.*

Note that both B_1 and B_2 are making judgements about the responsibility of the other. This is not uncommon and yet it is obviously unrealistic. Such behaviour is the cause of much friction and of marginally poor decisions. They can, of course, take the matter to their manager for decision; but, if this is done on every such issue, then their manager is being forced to reduce the discretionary responsibilities of both B_1 and B_2. He would have to state new policies prescribing when the general limits he has already set on strip material are to be modified, and in what circumstances.

(*b*) The appropriate conversation runs like this:

B1 TO B2: I reckon there is about £5 extra direct-labour cost arising in my command every time you want a batch of strip to special limits, and the added risk of rejected material. What does it cost you to do without the special limits?

B2 TO B1: I can get modifications made to the press tools at a cost which would certainly, over a year's output, be less than special strip each time; but I have no certainty on these few jobs that such modifications will clear the trouble. I have already made several attempts without success. Each attempt is likely to hold up a finishing line, and I feel that the only way of being certain is to ask for special limit strip.

B1 TO B2: O.K., you shall have it, but you must limit your demand – and do try and get over your problem some other way.

If both B_1 and B_2 started to quantify the effect of following different courses on their *own* operations and *accepted* their colleague's valuation of *his* position, then sound decisions would be more likely to be made and conflict might be avoided.

Some managers exaggerate the difficulty of their own position; but, in the long run, such characteristics become generally known, and pressures arise that cause them to modify their behaviour. Such managers earn the description 'uncooperative', and if this behaviour pervades their activities and persists, then their own manager becomes aware of it and can take action.

There have been cases where managers in a collateral relationship have gone into collusion to breach policy in order to get round difficulties. Their feeling seems to have been that if some set policy puts them both in difficulty, then because they are both in trouble, it gives them some sort of sanction to alter their manager's policy without referring to him; so they change it. This, of course, is out of order. The proper action is to raise the matter with their manager and get a change agreed.

The example I quoted above is not entirely real and may not be technically correct in detail; but I cannot easily quote a real situation because – by the very nature of the collateral relationship – it is very difficult for a manager to get a grip of the story of what happened; and the description of a real situation involves the disclosure, by inference, of the personalities concerned.

Distinguishing between matters which should be dealt with through a collateral relationship and those which should be referred to a higher managerial level. Two people (both responsible to the same manager), whose prescribed terms of reference are such that they can take decisions which may interact on each other's work, are in collateral relationship. They are not, however, in a collateral relationship when the only decisions which would interact on the other's work would infringe the policy set by their manager. Thus, when there is disagreement between two colleagues, it would probably be of great help to them in seeking a solution to discover the answer to the simple question: Has our manager set any policy which will tell us whether the interacting decisions about which we are in disagreement are in fact decisions which we ought to be making?

If such decisions lie outside the bounds of their discretionary responsibility, then clearly the matter must be taken to their manager for decision. If, on the other hand, the disagreement is concerned with matters within their discretionary authority, then they are in a collateral relationship. If it is not clear whether they have authority to make decisions in relation to this matter, then they must raise the issue with their manager. Note, however, that people in collateral relationship who persistently fail to resolve differences of opinion, and have therefore to take such matters to their manager, will inevitably find the area of their discretion curtailed in such a way as to inhibit the collateral relationship which they were unable to operate.

This can be illustrated by further reference to the example of the two managers already quoted in this chapter. If these two, each time that they have any troubles, go to their manager, he will always have to make the decisions as to what should be done. Eventually he will say to manager B_1 in charge of the strip mill: 'As you appear to be unable to resolve the problems involved when demands are made for strip to more accurate dimensions than your accustomed norm, you must, in future, refer such matters to me.' And to B_2 he will say: 'If need arises for specially accurate strip because of difficulty with press tools, then refer such matters to me.' Both have thus lost the authority to deal with these situations. I do not wish to suggest that this is some sort of punishment – the withdrawal of authority may well be entirely appropriate, because the interaction of the decisions of B_1 and B_2 may have been of too high an order to be satisfactorily handled at their level of authority.

PART TWO

POLICY

CHAPTER 6

POLICY-MAKING AND ITS EFFECTS

WHEN we talk about 'policy' in our company – which we often do – we think of it in terms of the definition described in our Policy Document:

Policy – Any statement adopted by a Council or laid down by a manager, or any established practice or custom, which specifies the behaviour required of members in given situations. It will be noted that policy so defined does not include the Definitive Policy which circumscribes the activities of the Board of Directors, i.e., the Memorandum and Articles of Association of the Company, Company Law or other legislation, and Stock Exchange regulations.

When a manager decides to set a new policy for his subordinates or to change an old one, he is exercising discretion. He is making a decision. The policy so arrived at becomes part of the prescribed work of that manager's immediate subordinates. Policy defines what people must or must not do, and thus delineates the area over which they must exercise their own discretion.

A managing director A who takes decisions, and thereupon issues instructions to his subordinates, is setting policy for them. This is the first level of executive policy. A second level is established when manager B – working within the prescribed limits of policy laid down by A – uses his discretion to make decisions that give rise to further policy which affects his own subordinates C_1, C_2. . . . These subordinates, in turn, will make decisions and set policy within which their subordinates must work; and so a series of policies is established at different levels.

If, however, manager A gives instructions, in precise terms, to B_1, B_2 . . . to instruct their subordinates, C_1, C_2 . . . , it can readily be seen that manager A has set a prescribed limit within which C_1, C_2 . . . can operate. Here then are two different sorts of policy setting. The first prescribes the work of a manager's immediate subordinates, leaving them to use their discretion in setting suitable policies for lower levels. The second type sets policy, not only for a manager's immediate subordinates, but for lower levels of the executive system as well (contraction).

Let us take a live example of these two types of policy-making. The board of directors decides that certain resources shall be devoted to the development and manufacture of a new type of bearing. As managing director, I must set a policy within which my subordinates may get to work. I make decisions concerning the range of size of bearing which will be made; the amount of resources which will eventually be deployed in the departments concerned with development, manufacture and sale; the time-table to which the various stages are to be kept; the limits on the resources to be used by each of my subordinates, and so on. This becomes the general policy within which work will proceed on the new bearing.

It involves, for the general manager in charge of research and development, for example, a number of requirements – target times for completion of design of plant; maximum amount of space that is available into which it can be assembled; output and size range of material to be achieved. Working within the framework thus set up, he proceeds to make more detailed plans: the allocation of design work to his subordinates; setting targets for the various stages of design work to be accomplished, and for certain pieces of research investigation to be carried out; setting general lines of design, including the type of technical process upon which design is to be based. This process will proceed, level by level, down to the bottom of his extended command.

Now for an example of the second type of policy. The new bearing contains aluminium. If even small quantities of the turnings (arising in the course of manufacture of this bearing) become mixed with turnings from the tin base alloys (which we use in large quantities), the value of the latter is greatly reduced. I can draft extremely detailed instructions laying down exactly how machines, working on bearings made from one material, are to be cleaned out in order to prevent contamination before being used again for work on the other material. In this way I will be setting policy at a very low level in the executive system.

Alternatively, I can use the first type of policy, by calling attention to the danger of the mixture of these two materials and instructing my subordinates to take appropriate action, thus setting a policy for my immediate subordinates only. This would require them to take every possible care in preventing contamination by setting appropriate policies for their own subordinates.

Centralization and decentralization

Much use is made in industry of the two words 'centralization' and 'decentralization' of authority. Although these two phrases are not used in our Policy Document, I should like to clarify what I believe to be intended when they are used. In the situation described above, when the managing director is confronted with two alternatives, *decentralization* might be said to occur if he pursues the first course (setting a policy for his immediate subordinates and leaving it to them to work out further policies for their subordinates); *centralization* would occur if he followed the second course (setting a policy which applies to levels lower than his immediate subordinates, i.e., depriving them of discretion in the matter). Complete centralization is clearly a practical impossibility. There is an optimum distribution of discretion between roles in an executive system. The phrase 'over-centralization' means a departure from the optimum in the direction of lowering the level of discretion. The phrase 'too much decentralization' means a departure in the direction of increasing the level of discretion in the lower ranks of the system. The process of distributing discretionary authority is depicted diagrammatically in Figures 10 and 11.

I do not wish it to be assumed from what I have said that it is possible to make general value judgements about the 'good' or 'bad' effects of greater or lesser degrees of centralization or decentralization. The extent to which a manager prescribes the work of one of his subordinates, or even of his whole extended command, must be determined by the facts of each situation. However, the following considerations seem to apply when decisions about the *degree* of delegation have to be made.

(1) If manager A can make a decision which prescribes the conduct in a given situation not only of $B_1 \ldots B_{10}$, but also of

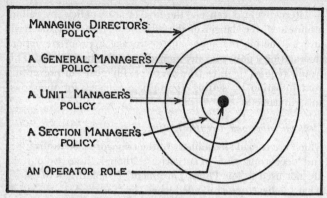

FIGURE 10. The different levels of policy

This shows the different levels of policy within which the discretionary content of one operator is bounded. Section manager policies and unit manager policies tend not to be expressed in written form, but communicated verbally; general manager and managing director policy requires to be written. The reasons for this are discussed in Chapter 9.

$C_1 \ldots C_{10}$ and $D_1 \ldots D_{10}$ in a manner that is beneficial to the organization, there is clearly no virtue in leaving discretion to $B_1 \ldots B_{10}$ to set the policies in this matter themselves. Such a course would merely give these other managerial levels additional work in the form of decision-taking. In other words, an A/BCDE policy should be set if there is the assurance that it will not reduce efficiency.

(2) If manager A has to give an A/BCDE type of decision rather than an A/B one (which bounds B's discretion and leaves it to B to decide the way he will bound the discretion of his own subordinates), it is necessary for A to explore the potential results of his policy at levels C, D and E in great detail. In such a situation A is necessarily involving himself in a great deal of work, which might be more easily done by B or C because they are more familiar with day-to-day events at the lower levels.

(3) If by setting an A/BCDE type of policy (with the uniformity it imposes), lower levels are prevented from taking the sort of decisions that may be in the best interests of the company, then in this case uniformity of operation has been gained at the expense of efficiency.

Managing Director's Policy	General Managers' Policy	Unit Managers' Policy	Section Managers' Policy	Operators' Policy
OVERALL	Sales Policy	Export Sales Policy	Export Market A	—
			Export Market B	—
		Home Sales Policy	Home Market A	—
			Home Market B	—
COMPANY	Manu-facturing Policy	Product A Policy	Process A	—
			Process B	—
		Product B Policy	Process C	—
			Process D	—
POLICY	Product Development Policy	Project A Policy	—	—
			—	—
		Project B Policy	—	—
			—	—
RANK 5	RANK 4	RANK 3	RANK 2	RANK 1

FIGURE 11. The different types of policy

This shows not only the different levels of policy which exist but also indicates the different types of policy which have to come into being if we are to get our work of developing, manufacturing and selling bearings done.

Here is an example of an appropriate A/BCDE policy or instruction. (At this point of the discussion, I shall change over from the use of letter symbols to rank numbers, and refer to a 5/4321 policy.) It is convenient, for the purpose of book-keeping, taxation, analysis and payment, that claims for reimbursement of personal expenses should be made on a single company form. Accordingly, I have given instructions that this form should be used by everybody in the company. This example is quite characteristic of 5/4321 instructions in that such instructions often deal with rather detailed subject-matter.

On the other hand, a general manager informs me that he proposes to obtain precise quantitative data about defective work in his organization. This is to be done through a system of defect reports which would involve having a form for each job done. He shows me a draft of the form. It has on it spaces for comments by the supervisor, the section manager and the unit manager; and it lays down that each of these levels should sign the report. Now, I point out:

(*a*) That the less writing and filling-in of forms in a machine-shop, where there is oil about and hands are dirty, the better;

(*b*) That at Rank 1 and 2 level, the customary method of communication is by word of mouth;

(*c*) That supervisors and section managers are often poor hands at any kind of report-writing because they get so little experience of it;

(*d*) Is the general manager sure, I ask, that his unit manager is not already in a position, by means other than the use of the projected form, to render just this analysis of defective jobs which he himself proposes to have made from these reports?

This, in my opinion, is a clear case of an inappropriate occasion for a general manager to set a 4/321 policy.[1]

Defective work is a very important subject, and control of quality is one of the major responsibilities of a section manager (Rank 2). But if he is asked, on every occasion, to fill in a form to be sent to a general manager (Rank 4), it may cause the section manager to feel that, having reported the matter, it is now out of his hands until he receives an instruction. If he is asked to give reasons for the defective work, he will often be in grave difficulty in stating them. There is frequently difficulty in deciding what constitutes 'defective work'. It will not, therefore,

1. In discussing policy in this chapter, I am, for the sake of clarity, over-simplifying the discussion by leaving out any reference to the problems of the reaction of the members of a manager's extended command to changes which the policy may imply. A particular policy may be objected to by all, or by a particular stratum of an extended command; such a policy cannot be implemented until the difficulties have been worked through. It is a manager's job either to know intuitively what changes will be tolerated, or, when in doubt, to obtain sanction through the legislative system before proceeding. I discuss these problems in Chapter 17, 'The Legislative System'.

always be clear when a report should or should not be written. This situation will lead to a tendency to under-report. Many other criticisms of this example of 'centralization' could be made.

Level of penetration of policy decisions

One of the important practical ideas that emerges from the foregoing is that there is need for managers, when setting policy and issuing instructions, to be conscious of the levels to which their action applies. My experience is that, when setting a policy, there is great value in being able to consider precisely which roles it conditions.

For example, some years ago it became obvious that control of credit given to the company's customers was not organized effectively. A situation had grown up that allowed a number of people at different levels to make decisions about extending or curtailing credit. As these different people, because of their different roles, did not always agree, disputes frequently came up to my level to be dealt with either by the company chief accountant or myself. A number of bad debts were involved which were clearly avoidable. There were instances of credit being given on a generous scale, where no clear benefit resulted to the company; and there were instances of failure to grant credit of a comparatively limited nature, which had resulted in the unnecessary loss of customers.

It turned out to be extremely difficult to rectify this position. A considerable amount of analysis was necessary to discover where responsibility for the different facets of policy should be placed. Various drafts of a directive on the matter were prepared. These grew longer and longer as more defects were discovered, necessitating additions to cover up loop-holes. The directive specified what action should be taken in given circumstances, not only by the general sales manager and the financial division manager, but also by people in roles at Rank 3 and 2 level. It described methods of putting the names of customers who were in difficulty with payment on stop lists; of notifying factory dispatch departments not to dispatch goods, and so forth. I realized that the whole problem was caused by the patchwork of instructions that had been given in the past to various roles at different levels in response to *ad hoc* problems of credit control.

The emergence of ideas about the level at which policy was to penetrate enabled us to get the whole matter more into focus. A policy on the control of credit is now in operation which sets terms of reference for my immediate subordinates, and leaves them to work out the details of implementation of that policy. Since the company provides credit running into nearly seven figures, laxity in control could make a great difference in the amount required to finance this credit – quite apart from the risks of loss. It can, therefore, readily be appreciated how important it was to the company to straighten out these control mechanisms, and to determine the manner in which responsibility was to be allocated. Since our experience with this particular problem, a number of complex situations have been much simplified by looking at the prevailing statement of policy in terms of the level of organization to which it was addressed. My own task has been greatly simplified by *first* deciding the level to which I wished my stated policy to apply, and then deciding what policy I wished to be followed.

Here is a different example to illustrate another facet of policy-setting. The company's expenditure on 'consumable supplies' runs into six-figure sums. The decisions initiating this expenditure are made at many levels in the organization, starting at Rank 2 section managers. It is therefore difficult to set and maintain a grip over decisions to use consumable supplies so as to ensure that the expenditure will not exceed its budget allocation; this difficulty is made greater by the fact that 'consumable supplies' include an exceedingly wide range of different materials and articles. Over the years, the total has shown a tendency to 'ride away'. Whenever this happens, the figures are reviewed; managers at all levels are seen; analysis of consumption is made; and, after a lot of work, the volume of consumption and expense is checked. Some years ago, as a result of a discussion about the need to check this expenditure, general managers gave instructions for the level of authorization for this expense to be raised, for a period, from Rank 2 to Rank 3. This single step seemed to produce a better result than the more detailed measures that had been taken in the past. One of the results was to provide managers at Rank 3 level with more knowledge on which to base the way they guided their own subordinates, once Rank 2 had reassumed authorization for the issue of the stores.

My experience shows that a great deal of what goes wrong when implementing instructions and policies originates in initial failure to decide the level to which they should be addressed. This failure to determine the right level in advance makes drafting difficult, and the instruction is accordingly confused. If, on the other hand, one can say: 'Yes, I know enough about this matter; what is needed is to prescribe the conduct of people down to and including Rank 3, but no further', then drafting can be simplified, and the instruction can be made clearer.

In Chapter 8 I quote from Section E.6 of our Policy Document dealing with the notion of contraction of executive lines: the situation that arises, for example, when a general manager communicates directly with levels below that of his immediate subordinates. This would constitute 4/32 policy-setting. I can now, therefore, define contraction more precisely in the terms used in this chapter. A 5/4 instruction, or a 4/3 policy, is not a contraction instruction because, in these instances, communication is from the manager to his subordinate and no further. But a 5/432 or a 4/32 policy is an example of a contraction instruction.

Thinking at different levels of abstraction

Awareness of the fact that people working at different levels of responsibility think at different levels of abstraction is important. I do not think it is possible to define a particular level of abstraction. But it is possible to know when one is moving in one's thinking from one level to another. This idea has a considerable bearing on the subject of setting terms of reference for subordinates.

A man goes to his manager and says to him, in effect: 'I have this problem on my hands – what shall I do about it?' The manager has the following alternative: either he can simply give his subordinate an instruction about what to do in that single situation. In this case he has not provided a policy, except for *precisely similar* situations – which probably will never arise. Or, the manager can explain the *general* policy to which he requires his subordinate to conform in the future. In so doing, he has raised the issue to a higher level of abstraction, and has set his subordinate a policy which will enable him in future to arrive at decisions unaided. I will now quote a real example.

A section manager is conducting a review of the pay rates of his subordinates. When he comes to consider X, he finds him rather slow, with low craft ability. He is, however, intelligent and very willing; because of this, his manager has, at times, used his services in the tool stores and other ancillary jobs, when the regular people have been off work. He has done such jobs very competently. The section manager is puzzled about what to do with him and goes to his unit manager. The unit manager might simply have said: 'Do not increase his rate.' Instead, raising his comment to a higher level of abstraction, he says: 'You cannot increase the rate of a man who does his own job poorly simply because he occasionally takes over some other person's job and does it well. You must assess your subordinates on their performance in their own jobs. If X gives you the feeling that he is more suited to a different kind of job, then you must discuss his career with him, point out his shortcomings, try and discover whether he wishes to change his occupation; let him know of the other types of jobs which are available in the company and more suited to his capabilities, and help him to apply for one of them if he wishes to do so.'

The unit manager has thus set his subordinate a clear policy in relation to such matters and has instructed him how to deal with all such issues in the future.

Here is another example at a higher level in the company. A general manager wishes to purchase two expensive new machine tools, one to reduce machining times on product A and the other on product B. His capital budget allowance will not permit the purchase of both. He comes to see me. What shall he do? I can simply say: 'Purchase the machine for product A, and delay the other machine.' Or I can raise the level of abstraction of my reply by saying:

'Product B is going to fade over the next two years. Purchase of new plant for its manufacture is not justified. You have done a great deal of work by way of exploring the market for the right type of machine, getting tests run and so on, but this work is now wasted. In future, before going into the matter as deeply as this, please consult with the programming division manager and discover the long-term situation with regard to products before starting on such work. . . .'

Every problem and question raised by a subordinate with his manager is an opportunity for the latter to set a new policy or to clarify an existing one. This is a dynamic method of setting policy, because it is done in response to real need and real situations. The policy set is immediately put to the test.

Setting policy for newly appointed subordinates

When a subordinate is newly appointed to a job, he should, if he has been adequately trained, know a good deal about the general policies on which we base the operation of the company; he should have available within himself a knowledge of the concepts which we now have at our disposal, but he will not know the detailed policies of his new manager. He needs, at this stage, a rapid and decisive introduction to and familiarity with those detailed terms of reference which, in fact, constitute much of the prescribed content of his new job.

It is necessary at this stage to say to him:

'If, on the basis of general knowledge of the company's policy, you really know what decision to take when faced with a problem, then take it without delay. If, however, at this probationary period you have any real doubt, delay the decision and see me. I will, during this period, make myself much more freely accessible to you both by telephone and interview than will later be the case. I wish you to learn those prescribed terms of reference of your job which I have not been able to write down, not by taking risks and making mistakes, but by bringing problems, and instances where you are in any doubt, to me. We will discuss them in such a way that you will quickly get acquainted with your terms of reference.'

Clearly, this is how a job should be learnt; but it is essential to give an explicit statement of the situation at the beginning, and to make the matter perfectly plain, if unnecessary problems are to be avoided. Newly appointed managers often tend to refrain, if possible, from asking many questions or bringing a large number of problems to their manager, because they feel that, if they do, they will give the impression that they are not able to fill the position or because they want to make an immediate demonstration of their competence by doing the job without guidance. It is a pity if the initial stages of a newly appointed man's career are marked by a series of mistakes and decisions which then have to be reversed by his manager. Much of this can be avoided by making the terms of reference for the learning period quite clear. By making this situation explicit it is, I think, possible to get through the probationary period much more quickly than would otherwise be the case.

Familiarity with policy enables a manager to work quickly

When a man knows what decision to make about any problem that arises almost without thinking about it, then he knows the prescribed limits of his job intimately. A manager with so much knowledge 'inside him' that many of his decisions are like reflex actions has, in one sense, much less work to do in keeping his job on the move. The normal day-to-day situations are easily handled, and he will be able to devote energy to improvements, innovations and thoughts in preparation for problems that may arise in the future. This is the real value of experience. It is not so much that one knows what to do – for mere practice can get a man into a deep groove of conventional behaviour – but that complete familiarity with his terms of reference enables a man to do a much larger quantity of work in a wider and developing field.

Managerial behaviour sets up policies

A manager's behaviour is an implicit means of setting policies for his subordinates; but this sometimes results in a manager unintentionally setting policies with which he himself is not in agreement. It is not so much a matter of his subordinates copying him, but of the public sanction that, by his own behaviour, he gives to various types of practice. If a manager walks round one of the departments in his extended command, and it appears that he has observed the practices that are in operation, failure to take any action will be accepted by his extended command as an indication that he has sanctioned those practices. This is why it is so essential for a manager to use his eyes when out of his office and among his own people. If he walks round his factory, office or production unit with his mind elsewhere, he will overlook many things which he is not prepared to accept. By so doing, he will make it very difficult for his subordinates to correct such matters; for when they start taking corrective action, they will be regarded as following a more meticulous course than is necessary. They are likely to be looked on as fussy or as super-disciplinarians.

Take as an example the problem of discipline at the commencement and finish of shifts. There are always some easygoing people who tend to start work late and finish working too early. If the unit manager or section managers are in the department and overlook such practices, it is very hard for a supervisor to do much about it. Once or twice in the past, when the question of such malpractice has arisen in discussion at council meetings, I have heard representatives say: 'If the managers are prepared to condone such practices it is no good blaming operators.' How right they are! When some operators or office workers get slack about this sort of thing, it becomes increasingly difficult for others who deplore such behaviour not to follow suit, because pressures arise which force them to. This example affects not only discipline about expenditure of time, but of most other things too – care of machinery, materials and fittings, consumption of materials, cleanliness of workshops and offices, care in attending to work, and so on.

Cash spent by people in carrying out their duties is a delicate subject. Nobody likes to be challenged on money matters, because it can feel like a criticism of their integrity. It is an auditor's requirement that I sign the expense accounts of my immediate subordinates. When I have a new subordinate, I scrutinize his expenses during the time he is working his way into the job. I can usually find some grounds for comment, and I take this as an opportunity for explaining more clearly the standards which we adopt in the company, and for giving a demonstration of the behaviour I require from him towards his subordinates. I have found by past experience that I must specifically sanction and highlight the necessity of managers taking up such issues with their subordinates. If this is not done by me, then although at times they may feel critical of subordinates on this score, there is a strong tendency to say nothing, rather than give a subordinate the impression that he is not trusted. Through the years many managers with whom I have raised this subject initially showed signs of being quite upset, but by the time I have made it clear that it was my duty to set standards and, furthermore, to set them an example to be followed by them with their own subordinates, the heat goes out of the matter.

I have referred in an earlier chapter to the great importance of a manager boldly assessing his subordinates individually. It is not much good telling a subordinate to do this, and then failing to do it oneself. If I do not see each of my subordinates individually and tell them as frankly as possible what I think about the way they are performing their jobs, I can scarcely expect them to follow such a practice themselves. Every act of a manager, no matter how trivial, contains its contents of instruction for his subordinates. The greater the perception of this, the better the example set.

To summarize, I have now discussed the subject of setting policy for subordinates in terms of:

(*a*) Centralization and decentralization.
(*b*) Level of penetration of policy.
(*c*) Thinking at different levels of abstraction.
(*d*) Helping subordinates to get more work done.
(*e*) Helping new subordinates to get more quickly into a job.
(*f*) Implicit policy-setting by managerial behaviour.

Underlying all I have said is the importance of *explicit recognition* by managers of the need to make clear to subordinates the policy which they require them to follow, and explicit recognition of the means they adopt to set such policy. It can be done without conscious perception of what is happening. Such an approach will leave gaps, contain contradictions and lead to uncertainty in the minds of subordinates, because they do not know fully the limits within which they can exercise their own discretion. It can, on the other hand, be done with deliberation on a planned basis. This will lead to increased fullness and consistency, and growth of confidence on the part of subordinates.

CHAPTER 7

MANAGERS AND DEVELOPMENT WORK

WHEN I became chief executive of the company, the aspect of greatest novelty was the feeling that one was 'steering' a company. Was one to propose to the board that it grew bigger or smaller? What products or new processes should we develop? Should we lay down more manufacturing capacity for this or that? Were we trading in the right markets? Above all, were we 'up to date'? This last question can induce a feeling of great anxiety at times. The urge to keep up to date is strong: and the feeling when one sees other companies doing better is very worrying. Deciding which mode of advance to pursue, and how to apportion limited resources, feels like 'steering a ship'.

It was from this vantage point that I was able to look back on the job I had vacated (sales manager) and consider what I had done in that job compared with what now seemed necessary seen from the viewpoint of my new position. My previous efforts did not look very satisfactory. I appeared to have done too little in an explicit manner to develop the job of sales manager. I could see, for example, that extension of the sale of certain products was vital, if the manufacturing resources were to be provided with sufficient volume of work to be operated at an economic level. I could see, too, that this implied the devotion of more selling resources to certain markets which hitherto had received scant attention. Many new possibilities of expanding sales in directions which were desirable for the company opened up for me. The facts of the situation had been known to me in my previous position, but I had not acted in a manner which now seemed appropriate for another person in the post of sales manager.

After the war, I set about the job of trying to make certain that our new sales manager fully appreciated his responsibility for developing his work in the way needed by the company, and in accordance with the changing position as affected by the development of new or improved products and increases in manufacturing capacity. In the course of prescribing the sales manager role, I found it necessary to set fairly precise terms of reference, and I began to realize that one of the difficulties which I had experienced in the sales manager's job before the war was the lack of explicit terms of reference.

I arranged for the sales manager to be provided, at least each month, with data on such matters as company profits, investments in finished stocks, the relationships of orders received to deliveries of goods made to customers, the changing period of delivery on each product, etc. These explicit data had not been received by me in the job, but had been conveyed in a much vaguer way simply by statement of opinion about the situation.

I found it necessary to set limits on what could be sold in terms of number of bearings, standard hours of work, delivery times, design of bearings, on the number of staff the sales manager could employ, and the expense he could commit without reference to me, and so on. Gradually, but on an increasing scale, the explicit terms of reference within which the sales manager was to work grew as a result of interaction between the needs of customers, the needs of our factories for different types of work, the work done on our products by our research and development organization and, finally, my own ideas on the situation. I had been thinking of the manner in which I had done the job without fully realizing that the terms of reference – or absence of them in explicit form – set by my superior were one of the determinants of the way I had done the job. In fact, owing to the absence of clear terms of reference, I had found it necessary constantly to refer to my superior for his decision on a wide range of subjects, where I would have much preferred to be allowed to decide off my own bat. The idea, for example, of planning different approaches to new markets, in order to sell more of some specific product and using, perhaps, additional resources, fell into the category of things on which I would have been eager to offer an opinion if asked; but I could not take the initiative, lest it should have appeared that I was trying to teach my manager how to do his own job.

Thus it is that in my experience the level of development of new ideas, methods, organization, etc., done by subordinates is very intimately connected with the prescribed terms of reference explicitly set for them by their manager.

The matter can be considered in terms of *revolution* and *evolution*. The subordinate carries the responsibility for a certain level of evolution of his task, and this potential level is a function of the prescribed content of his job. The extent to which actual performance measures up to this potential level is a function of the personal ability of the subordinate. The manager takes a revolutionary step when he materially changes the prescribed content of his subordinate's role; for such a step will change the potential level of evolution for which the role is responsible.

When a new man is appointed to a job, his terms of reference – to begin with – are usually such as to give him only very limited discretion to introduce change. As managers, we do this either explicitly or intuitively, because we cannot take the risks inherent in giving a person who is relatively inexperienced in the job the right to make mistakes for which we ourselves will be held responsible. As his experience grows, and if there is a corresponding growth in our confidence in him, we bring about one revolution after another as we change the prescribed content of his job. These revolutions go on until the evolutionary potential for which we hold him responsible is the maximum possible – short of creating a situation where he will begin making decisions which our own terms of reference from our superiors charge us to make personally.

Executive freedom to act

I wish, at this point, to deviate somewhat from the subject of work development, in order to discuss a related subject which flows out of the foregoing. I am struck by the number of occasions on which superficial assessment of a situation is almost the converse of the real situation which emerges upon analysis. Executive freedom to act, or the environment which gives a manager freedom to make decisions, is a good example of this.

Many managers feel that 'freedom' lies in the sort of situation where their superior says to them: 'There are not many regulations in this place. You will understand the job in a month or two and you make your own decisions. No red tape – you are expected to take command; make the decisions off your own bat as they arise. I am against a lot of rules or regulations, and we do not commit too much to paper.' In my experience a manager in such a situation has virtually no 'freedom to act' at all. He starts making decisions and his boss sends for him to say: 'Look here, Jones, I am sorry to tell you that you have made two rather serious mistakes in the course of reorganizing your work. You have promoted one man to supervisor who is not the next man due for promotion in the factory, and you have engaged five additional machinists, a decision you should have referred to me, because we have some surplus men in this category in an adjacent factory.' Now, Jones might well say: 'You said there were no regulations but, in fact, you have already mentioned the existence of two: one concerned with promotion and the other with increase of establishment. Please detail these regulations to me precisely, so that I can work to them in future, and let me know now of any further regulations which bear upon my work.'

In practice, Jones probably says nothing of the kind, because he does not think in this way; to him regulations are stumbling blocks in the path of those wishing to display initiative. He will proceed, over the years, to learn, by making mistakes, of the whole array of regulations which, by the very nature of executive systems, do in fact exist. His boss will have to say to him frequently: 'Yes, Jones, freedom for subordinates to act on their own is the policy here, but surely it must have been obvious that you should have seen me before doing *that*.' Jones is thus in a situation where he does not know what decisions he can or cannot make, and when in doubt he is likely to follow a course of doing nothing at all. In three years he will have got through this difficult period, he will know when he can or cannot act, because he has learnt by testing what his boss was unable to give him in writing – *the prescribed component of his job*. Thereafter Jones will be a staunch supporter of the 'no red tape' policy, and so the situation will continue.

It is much more efficient to delineate as precisely as possible to a new subordinate all of the regulations he must observe and then say:

'You must take all the decisions that seem to you to be required, so long as you keep within the bounds of that policy. If, keeping within those bounds, you take decisions which I think you should have referred to me, then I cannot criticize; for such a happening implies that some part of the policy which I wish you to operate has not been disclosed to you. I must, then, formulate that policy and add it to the prescribed content of your job.' If, in addition, the manager can give his subordinate a rounded idea of the discretionary component of his job by stating the types of decision which he must make, then that subordinate is in a real position to act on his own initiative in the prescribed area.

I have found, however, particularly in discussing jobs with external applicants, that the array of policy represented by our Policy Document, standing orders and directives, causes people to assume the precise opposite of the real situation, i.e., that this extant written policy will deprive them of the right to make decisions. In fact, it is only by delineating the area of 'freedom' in this way that a subordinate knows when he can take decisions. The absence of written policy leaves him in a position where any decision he takes, however apparently trivial, may infringe an unstated policy and produce a reprimand.

The organizational requirements of an optimum rate of development of improvements

No manager can reasonably expect his subordinates to initiate optimum improvement in their sphere of responsibility, unless the prescribed and discretionary components of their jobs are understood. This is a prerequisite of an optimum rate of sound evolutionary change.

Having done that, a manager must get his subordinates clear about their responsibility for developing their work. Many managers feel quite comfortable in their jobs if they are avoiding trouble and keeping current problems down to a level that is tolerable to their own managers. I have found in the past that a subordinate sometimes registers surprise when I point out to him that the way he does his job is static, and that I have had no development plans or proposals for change put up to me. Such people are not 'at the helm'; they are 'down in the engine room'. On the other hand, there are managers who have constantly got some plan on the move. They are training people for new jobs that are coming; ferreting out information from obscure sources or working out slicker methods. When one meets such managers there is a zest in them as they explain the latest change or the improvements to come.

Development work always implies change. This can create anxiety among one's subordinates, or even in one's superior manager. One of the most frequently used methods of forestalling development proposals is to make absolute criticism of them. Instead of comparing the shortcomings of a plan with the problems of the current position, people frequently seek to delay or abandon improvement on the grounds that the plan is not 'perfect'.

Development and change involve risks of negative results or failures. Negative results are recognized as an integral part of research work. It should be recognized that they are just as inevitable a part of any development done by a manager on the work entrusted to him. The urge to experiment; the courage to face the doubters; and the resilience to accept temporary setbacks and to try again – are all valuable qualities in a manager. They must be fostered constantly.

In one sense it is wrong to consider a manager's capacity to develop his work as a distinct phase of his work; it is a function of his whole capacity and approach and should be regarded as a basic need in a manager. One could rate all performance on a continuum. At one end is the manager who bombards his superior with details of his own *ad hoc* problems which he is unable to solve. The possibility of such a man being able to develop methods, organization, and new targets for his own command is remote. At the other end is the manager who does not seem to have current problems of any magnitude. He spends his time pressing his manager for agreement to use additional resources for change in many directions. He is, in fact, putting pressure on his own manager to think about his own policy and define it ever more exactly.

I do not think I am talking about absolute personality characteristics in setting up these two types. I am talking about one manager who has been over-promoted, or whose role has grown faster than the growth of his own personal capacity; and about another manager whose capacity is growing faster than his job. The first manager, given a role at a lower level, will probably exhibit at once the capacity to develop the simpler job. The second manager may be ready for promotion to a higher level. If he does not get it, he may leave the company or he will, in the way I have described in a previous chapter, begin taking over part of the role of his superior without either of them appreciating what is happening. This will lead to one of those complex situations where the extant situation differs markedly from the assumed.

If a manager shows inability to lead his command in such a way as to cause it to develop its techniques, its organization and its use of resources, it is the clearest sign that he does not measure up to the size of the job he has been given to do. This does not mean, however, that his immediate superior is not contributing to this inability. Here are some of the ways in which the superior manager could help subordinates to develop their own jobs.

(*a*) Make certain that the manager knows company policy in respect of his right and responsibility to have a team of subordinates acceptable to him. If a manager is hanging on to specialist subordinates in his command who are not up to their jobs – because 'they have been there a long time'; 'they know the job'; 'it is difficult to make changes without upsetting people' and so on – he is letting the company down. And in the long run he will also be letting down the specialist he is trying to protect. It is not doing a good turn to a subordinate to keep him in a job which he cannot perform at a satisfactory level. His own interests would be better served by a re-positioning in another job which he might be able to do competently.

(*b*) Make certain that he has got his work into proper focus in terms of the priority that should be given to development in various fields. In the past, work of an extensive and successful nature has frequently been done on a product, market or process which is fading in importance, while development in a more promising field has been neglected. This is an easy mistake to make if the current level and importance of the product or process is accepted as the criterion of priority for development. The type of work that best repays development is often one which is at a currently low level of activity but which, in future, is likely to become much more active. It is the job of a manager to see that his subordinates have the information on which a proper perspective can be formed.

(c) Make certain that the economic terms in which a development is considered are sound. The company is working hard at the moment to achieve a more realistic set of notions about costing, estimating, pricing, etc. These should help to avoid the many situations that have occurred when much work has been done on a process, say, to save labour hours, on the assumption that for every hour saved the company will save, say, 25s. (this being a possible total cost per hour of operating a department including the expenses pro-rated to it). In fact, the real saving may be nearer 8s. or 9s. per hour. There are many pitfalls lying in the path of a manager who seeks to calculate the savings arising from a given change unless the basis of calculation is checked periodically to ensure that its underlying conceptions are correct.

(d) Above all, a manager must continuously be watching to ensure that his subordinates know the full discretionary contents of their jobs. There is great value in the practice of a manager taking his subordinates individually and *writing down* the answer to the question: 'What decisions or choices am I charging this man to make?' It is a difficult thing to do at the first attempt. But after practice this mode of analysis of a subordinate's job becomes a vivid method of describing the work he is expected to do. Here are some samples of the choices which I expect a general manager in charge of a factory to make in determining the development phase of his job.

To decide if the level of investment in stocks, work in progress, and finished goods is the minimum achievable without drop in efficiency; and if it is not, to decide on the method of reducing, and on the category requiring attention.

To decide whether the scrap level in each type of product is optimum and, if not, to decide the priorities to be given product-wise in reducing scrap.

To decide whether the needs of his planned work-load for the next few years are to be met by existing production equipment, or whether to recommend necessary capital expenditure on new equipment.

To decide, from time to time, whether his executive organization and division of work are appropriate to the work to be done and to decide the adjustments required.

To decide whether future work-load is going to require additional skilled personnel, technicians, managers, etc., and the steps necessary to make them available when required.

To decide the kinds of development in method and techniques needed in order to meet changing and competitive demands of the factory.

I know of no surer way of failing to get development work done by subordinates than by failure to make clear what is required of them. It is fatally easy for managers to continue to accept shortcomings, because they have been accepted for a long time. Bad situations become accepted as norms on the assumption that, because previous attempts at solution have failed, further effort is not justified. The sort of problems I have in mind are, for instance, processes which throw up high scrap and low yields; apparently good products on which sales are static, although potential markets look large and so on. I have seen instances where nothing was being done about such situations, and when the question was raised: 'What are we doing about tackling that one?' the answer has been: 'We have to put up with that problem.'

In a competitive business economy, failure to improve is not 'standing still'; it is falling back *relative to competitors*. Every role has its requisite development component: nothing is more likely to advance the career of the individual, and the well-being of the company, than the ability for as many people as possible to grasp this simple fact. It is a major responsibility of all managers to make this clear to their subordinates, and themselves to set the example.

Process organization and product organization

(The differential effect of organizing managerial commands on:
    (*a*) Part of the process for a wide range of products; or
    (*b*) All the processes for a narrow range of products.)
Figures 12 and 13 depict diagrammatically the structural

choices which sometimes offer themselves in planning organization. In Figure 12 the groups of machines of the same type,

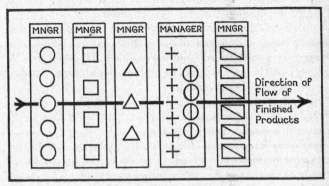

FIGURE 12. Process organization

or the processes which involve common techniques, are assembled under separate managers. Thus, in a machine shop one might give one manager command of all centre lathes and capstans, another all milling machines, a third all drills, a fourth all grinding machines, and so on. If, for completion, a product must have lathe work, milling work, drilling work and

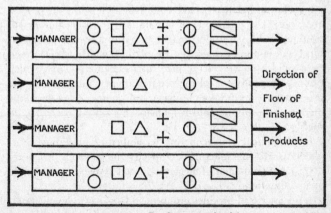

FIGURE 13. Product organization

grinding work done upon it, then none of these managers is responsible for a complete product. In such a case, the manager in charge of these process section managers is the level at which responsibility for the complete product rests.

Alternatively, it may be possible to give each of four managers a balanced command of centre lathes, capstan lathes, milling machines, drills and grinding machines. It is then possible for each of these managers to be held responsible for a restricted range of completed products.

Thus, in the latter case, the responsibility for the quantity, quality, etc., of products can be placed at a lower level in the executive system than in the former case, where the section managers carry responsibility only for a particular technique of work performed on a range of products. For brevity I shall refer to these two types of organization as *process organization* and *product organization*.

A great deal of study remains to be done on this important topic. It would appear at the moment that the placing of product responsibility at the lowest possible level is consistent with optimum level of efficiency. This statement has not got much value, however, because it leaves unanswered the question of what the 'lowest possible level' is. The criteria which appear to determine this are associated with such matters as:

(*a*) Output balance between one type of machine or process and another: e.g., in one of our units there are a number of product lines each under the command of a section manager; but there is one process, i.e., tin plating, which is performed by a single and very large piece of mechanized plant, which provides capacity for all the product lines. Thus, none of the product lines is complete in itself, and the managers in charge of them can only be held responsible for output *excluding tin plating*.

(*b*) Technical and economic feasibility of providing completeness of manufacturing capacity in a small low-level managerial command. Tin plating, cited above, is an example of this situation.

(*c*) A low-level product group postulates for its manager an ability to understand and control a wider range of technical processes than would be necessary if process organization were used instead.

(*d*) The range of technical ability required in the manager of a product group may draw forth or *elicit* the need to provide him with specialist support to encompass so wide a range of knowledge and skill. It may, however, be uneconomic to position specialists at such a low level in the executive system.

(*e*) Product managers come in direct contact with external market pressures concerned with cost, quality, delivery, etc.; the lower the level at which product responsibility exists, the lower the level at which these market pressures are felt. In view of the vital need of the executive system constantly to adapt its behaviour and aims to market requirements, this would seem to be one of the valuable results flowing out of low-level product commands.

Insufficient analysis of this subject has as yet been carried out for us to have a developed policy on the matter. I have, however, raised the matter here, because it is clear to me that a manager, placed in a job where the impact of the market bears directly upon his activities, is able to obtain a first-hand feel of the extent to which his work matches that market demand. Such a manager is in a position where he is much more likely to develop his work with requisite speed and objectivity than would otherwise be the case.

Until five or six years ago, no manager below the level of general manager in our company really carried product responsibility. It was the recognition that optimal organization is a function of the work to be done and the techniques available to do it that led us to set up, under our general managers, product units. These are, *as far as possible*, independent of manufacturing processes in other parts of the company, and the unit manager has, as will be described in a later chapter, the support of his own specialists. Within some units it has been possible to give section managers a large degree of product responsibility. I believe that it is possible to go further in this direction.

PART THREE

COMMUNICATION

CHAPTER 8

CONTRACTION OF EXECUTIVE LINES

I SHOULD first like to give the meaning which we allot to two phrases which will be much used in this chapter:

The immediate command of a manager is that group of employee members which he makes immediately accountable to him.

The extended command of a manager comprises all the employee members under his control.

I have discussed interaction and communication between a manager and his immediate subordinates in a number of different situations. I now want to consider the position when the situation puts pressure on a manager to communicate directly with his subordinates once removed, or even with the whole of his extended command. Our company policy on this matter reads as follows:

Contraction of executive lines

A manager shall, when he feels such action to be necessary, contract the executive lines in his command; i.e., make executive contact with any member or members of his extended command, either directly or indirectly, through the intermediate subordinates (E.6).

When he makes such contact in the absence of the intermediate members, he must recognize that he has removed responsibilities from his subordinates down to and including the manager of the member with whom he is making contact. He must, therefore (except where he judges that his instruction does not interfere with the existing executive relationship between a member and his immediate superior): (*a*) cause the intermediate subordinates to be informed of his action with the least possible delay, (*b*) arrange for the member to return to the command of his manager when he has completed the designated task, or by other means restore, in due course, the responsibilities he has removed from the intermediate subordinates (E.6.1).

When the contraction includes the intermediate members, no such special subsequent action is necessary (E.6.2).

There are two major forms of contraction to be considered.

The first arises when a manager gives an instruction to a single member of his extended command who is not an immediate subordinate. I will not discuss this situation at any length. The most frequent cause of such contraction is emergency of some kind. For instance, a manager finds himself using contraction when the telephone rings and a customer on the line wants information from him quickly. He contracts, and gets in touch with the individual who has the required information although this may not be his immediate subordinate. If such contact involves him in giving any further instruction beyond that of requesting the information, then he informs the relevant manager of what he has done. I frequently use contraction when I am showing a visitor round a factory and perhaps require a section manager to explain the details of some method of manufacture in his section. Such situations are common, and the policy is clear and appropriate. Its explicit introduction has avoided some troubles which used to arise when a manager became aware that one of his immediate subordinates was not 'on his job', because he was busy carrying out some instruction from 'higher up' about which he had not been informed. Such situations can be extremely irritating and, at times, lead to inefficiency. Use of this policy avoids them.

The second form of contraction arises when a manager decides to issue an instruction to a group or stratum of people in his extended command who are not, however, his immediate subordinates. Such an instruction must reach those whom it affects as coming from the manager who actually issued it.

If manager A, having given his subordinate manager B the specific terms of an instruction, then instructs B that *he* is to instruct his subordinates C_1, C_2, C_3 on the matter, A will create the false impression in the minds of C_1, C_2, C_3 that this instruction is at the initiative of B. Whereas if A says to B: 'Here is my instruction; see that it is passed on to C_1, C_2, C_3 as *my* instructions to them', then he has contracted his command.

An instruction is not an impersonal thing; it either has the authority of a person behind it, or it is not an instruction. If an attempt is made by A to create the impression that the source of the instruction and the authority behind it is that of B, then trouble will follow. People intuitively know the real source of an instruction by its content, for requisitely it can come only from one role. They will look upon any attempt to make it appear to have come from another role as dishonesty. Contraction can, therefore, be said to be a property of that particular instruction which is given by a manager both to his immediate subordinate and to subordinates at lower ranks.

In order to discover whether or not he is contracting his command, a manager must look at the nature of the instruction or communication he is issuing. Take, for example, the case of a general manager who becomes convinced that the policy he has set in the past, with regard to the care, cleaning, lubrication and day-to-day maintenance of production plant, is allowing avoidable deterioration to take place and who therefore decides to set more rigorous standards. He must decide what kind of instruction to issue. This can either be to his immediate subordinates as follows:

'I have decided, after careful review of the situation, that the factory requires to change its approach to cleaning, care and maintenance of plant in order to retard the rate of deterioration and replacement. The steps necessary may differ from one production unit to another. I require you to consider the subject very seriously, to draw up new policy, issue instructions to your subordinates and report to me when you have done so.'

This is a *non-contraction instruction*.

Or, it could be to a part of his extended command, viz.:

'After review of the situation, I have decided that this factory requires to follow a more precise and careful approach to the care, cleaning and day-to-day maintenance of production machinery. Accordingly, I require unit managers, section managers and supervisors to begin carrying out, from today, the different instructions which I have enumerated for each in the attached directive.'

This is a *contraction instruction*.

Clearly, it is inappropriate for the general manager to decide what he requires section managers and supervisors (who are not his *immediate* subordinates) to do, and then to ask his unit managers (immediate subordinates) to issue these requirements as if they were their own instructions. This would be a form of deceit. It would not, however, be deceitful if the general manager were, for instance, to issue the contraction instruction cited above to his unit managers, telling them to pass it on in the *general manager's name* to their own subordinates. This is one way of giving a contraction instruction. Other means at a manager's disposal are:

(*a*) Issuing the contraction instruction in person at a meeting of that part of his extended command to which it applies.

(*b*) Publishing the instruction in a notice under his signature.

(*c*) Stating the instruction over the public address system.

(*d*) Instructing one of his subordinates to give the contraction instruction by speaking *in his name* to his extended command.

There are some confusions about this matter of contraction in the company.

(*a*) Some managers believe that it is essential for a member to be left with the *impression* that the only source of any instruction which they receive is their immediate manager. In order to achieve this position, they therefore (with the best of intention) attempt to disguise the source of some instructions in the manner described. I believe this is always 'seen through', and that accordingly such practice – besides being inconsistent with the essence of our policy – lowers the status of managers in the eyes of their subordinates. In addition, it at times puts their immediate subordinate managers in the difficult position of likewise having to issue another person's instruction to *their* subordinates as though it were their own. This puts them in a situation where they cannot speak with sincerity and force. These are the sort of instructions which do not get carried out effectively.

(*b*) Some managers seem to be under the impression that contraction is a *mechanism* which can be used to give an instruction to people below the level of their immediate subordinates. In other words, they have decided whether or not to contract when they have decided upon the content of the instruction that they wish to give; instead of realizing that an instruction is either a contraction instruction or it is not, and that it is its content which decides the way the instruction is given.

(*c*) A manager may find it necessary to meet members of his extended command about the way they are executing some policy which he has set in the past. This is a very serious situation; for in doing so he is by implication criticizing one or more of his immediate subordinates in front of their subordinates. Here is an example to clarify the point.

A general manager has set clear policies about starting- and finishing-time discipline. He has charged his immediate subordinates with the task of seeing that his policy is effectively carried out. Observation causes him to conclude that in one of his units discipline about these matters has become lax. On several occasions he speaks to the unit manager concerned (his immediate subordinate), instructing him to see that policy already issued is observed, but without effect. He then decides to meet the unit manager and his section managers to voice his criticisms.

This is not a contraction situation. The general manager is not issuing new instructions. He is, in fact, stepping down into the role of his unit manager and doing part of his job for him, because the latter seemed unable to do it effectively himself. This sort of action invariably arouses feelings on the part of the manager who is thus being criticized in an exposed position. Such action may be necessary, particularly in an emergency, but obviously it is advisable for the manager who acts in this way to understand quite clearly what he is doing.

Contraction and the representative system

I have noted a different type of confusion about this matter among representatives. They, not infrequently, express the view that a manager's contraction of his extended command, especially when this involves the manager actually meeting face to face with those whom they represent, usurps their function of being the channel of communication between those who elected them and higher management.

This attitude is contrary to agreed company policy and the requisite needs of the situation. The confusion arises from failure to differentiate between executive roles and elector roles. It is, indeed, a representative's exclusive function to be the channel of communication between those who elected him *in their role of constituents or electors*, and managers. Equally it is exclusively the function of managers to be the channel of communication between people, *in their executive or work roles*, and higher management. It is essential that a manager be able on occasions to contract this executive channel of communication in order to issue instructions or to make clear his own attitude on any matter for which he is executively responsible. Managers must be clear on this issue in order to avoid the very serious form of managerial abdication which would arise if they were indeed to accept the idea that they could only communicate with the lower echelons of their command on executive matters through representatives.

There has been much discussion about the practice of a manager who is in negotiation with representatives of those in his own extended command, meeting his extended command in order to make clear to all his people his own point of view. Requisite organization is that a manager should be in a situation to communicate his own views in this way at any time. Clearly he cannot depend upon representatives to communicate *his* view, for that is not their function. If they choose, they can omit from the communications they convey to their constituents facts which the manager believes to be relevant, and certainly they cannot easily argue the manager's point of view on his behalf. The manager has no authority to instruct them to do so.

There are, however, certain elements in a manager's behaviour in such a situation which are requisite. He must not attempt to elicit from his subordinates their views as constituents. He must recognize that individual views expressed by a person to his representative are confidential between that person in his constituent role and his representative.

If his people start to discuss with him, during such a contraction meeting, the issue which is under negotiation between him and his people's representatives, he must remind them that it is their choice whether he is to negotiate the matter with representatives or with all of them, but that they cannot have both processes going on at once. In other words, he must say to them:

'I am here to give you my viewpoint, to persuade you that your attitude is unrealistic, to present to you the facts of the situation. You seem to want to discuss the whole issue with me and attempt to resolve it on the spot. I must remind you that you have already charged your representatives with the responsibility of negotiating the matter with me on your behalf. You have the right to insist on discussing the matter with me directly but, if you exercise that right, then your representatives cannot also carry out the negotiation for you. You must consider which course you wish to pursue, and if, after due deliberation, you still desire to discuss the issue with me directly, I will meet you for that purpose.'

The complexity of the processes of issuing orders. The foregoing on the subject of contraction, which is just one aspect of the instruction-issuing process, will suffice to show that there are many varied situations in which a manager can find himself, each possessing different properties and calling for different treatment in accordance with those properties.

Broadly speaking these properties of situations are not understood, and managers make mistakes of the types referred to. The irritation and resentment caused by these mistakes are often felt by managers to be evidence of unreasonable touchiness on the part of their subordinates. This leads to feelings of anger and frustration on the part of all concerned and, I think, results not infrequently in managers beginning to abdicate parts of their job. They prefer to refrain from issuing instructions rather than run into trouble. That is, of course, no solution. A manager who has had much experience will learn intuitively how and when and to whom to issue instructions; but he will be unable to pass on this experience unless his knowledge becomes explicit.

It is, therefore, an explicit understanding of the nature of the different situations which can arise, and explicit perception of the various ways in which a policy can be set, that is required. Complex as the matter may appear in the form in which I have written it, nevertheless, this knowledge once absorbed can save a manager from many mistakes and much waste of time.

CHAPTER 9

WRITTEN POLICY AND COMMUNICATION

UP to fifteen years ago very little *written* policy was available in the company. Changes agreed between managers and representatives were recorded in the minutes of works council meetings, but the instructions given by managers to implement those agreements were not often written; or, if written, they were not formally filed and, therefore, not easily available to those concerned with them. While some instructions and routines existed in written form, examination frequently showed that changes had taken place which had not brought about written amendments. The result was that many of them were not up to date and had ceased to be a true picture of the way the work was carried out.

In 1948 we issued the first written statement of company policy. It was the subject of extensive discussion and amendment at meetings between the management of the company and representatives of all ranks; and, after receiving the approval of the board of directors, it was issued and made available in written form on a continuous basis to all who worked in the company. The current statement of company policy is the fourth edition of this document.

The existence of this written policy proved very useful indeed to all sections of the company and set up pressures for the commitment to paper of many other policies and instructions. It became obvious that so much reliance on memory, so many discussions about just what instructions had been given, so many inconsistencies between the action taken by different managers over the same issues, were unnecessary. If we adopted the practice of committing the important decisions to paper, and keeping them in a manner that allowed quick reference or amendment, we could avoid a lot of trouble.

Difficulties have, however, arisen on deciding when policy or instructions should be written and when they should be communicated verbally. In seeking answers to this question we became involved in considerations about the time-span of the discretion which arises from the setting of a policy. For example, in the past I have made many decisions to start manufacture and sale of some new product, only to discover later, when troubles arose, that the general manager responsible for product development wanted more time to complete tests.

In order to avoid repetition of this situation, I instruct that general manager that he must, with respect to each product under development, decide when the time has arrived for him to feel sufficiently confident of the quality and performance to recommend to me that manufacture and development should be started. This recommendation must be accompanied by a full technical report detailing tests, results, designs, materials and performance.

Within a month of issuing the instruction, I receive from the general manager his first formal recommendation. After discussion with those responsible for manufacture and sale I decide to accept it and issue the necessary instructions to get the whole project on the move. It may be four or five years before I know whether my own decision to go ahead is sound or not. It may be one or two years before I know whether the general manager's recommendation that the product is ready was sound.

The delay in coming to conclusions about the soundness of decisions made is due to the fact that the criteria of soundness are such things as: (*a*) What happens when manufacture starts? (*b*) Reaction of customers to the test data; (*c*) The performance of the product; (*d*) Relative performance of competitors' products.

All the above is stated simply to demonstrate that there is a time-lag between the issue of an instruction and the assessment as to whether or not it is being carried out effectively; and, furthermore, that this time-lag may be in terms of years. Research done in the company[1] has shown that this time-lag is, in fact, a function of the nature of the work allocated to particular roles, and that it can be measured in days and

---

1. See Jaques, *Measurement of Responsibility*.

weeks at the bottom of the executive system, rising to years as we proceed from operator to managing director.

We have there, I think, the fundamental reason why a section manager, for example, relies almost entirely on verbal instructions to his operators, and why a managing director must commit so many of his instructions to paper. Observation demonstrates that a section manager's decision is implemented relatively rapidly, and that he will have a feed-back as to the soundness both of his own instruction, and of the way in which it has been carried out, within a few weeks of giving it. If troubles arise, there may be dispute as to the exact terms of the instruction. But this is unlikely, because only a period of weeks or, at the most, months has elapsed since the instruction was originally given. In the case of the managing director, however, it may prove extremely difficult to recollect the terms of an instruction, like the one I have quoted in my example, two years after it was given. It is my experience that within two years it is possible to forget completely the existence of such an instruction, if it is unwritten. If the managing director has given a complex verbal instruction, and problems arise two years later, it is very likely that the terms of the instruction will be the subject of argument; who is to say with any precision, after such a lapse of time, what they were in the first place?

I used to assume that the criteria which decided whether instructions were written or given verbally had to do with the size of the organization, the number of subordinates affected, the frequency with which one met one's subordinates in discussion and geographical distribution of subordinates. I think that such matters do, in fact, affect the decision, but only marginally. The fundamental determinant is the level of work in the roles of one's subordinates and the time-span of discretion arising from that work. In effect this means that the higher up the executive system one's role is, the greater the necessity to commit instructions to paper.

Some characteristics of written policy

It is easier to set policy verbally than in a written statement. At the moment of statement to one's subordinates, questions will be asked if the instructions are not understood. Writing instructions clearly, so that they will cater for the eventualities which they are designed to cover, takes considerable skill and time. It is for these reasons that I think there will always be a tendency to leave unwritten some policy which would benefit from being committed to paper. The benefits of the latter course tend, therefore, to need emphasis:

(i) Written policy tends to be more flexible and easily changed than unwritten policy. At first sight, this may be a surprising statement. It is, however, my experience that when problems arise and there is need to make changes, it is usually exceedingly difficult and arduous to discover just what policy has been in operation up to that point, if nothing has been committed to paper. If it has been written, one can consider its content, and usually the aspect which needs amendment will soon become clear. I have, in discussing other subjects, already frequently referred to the general principle in play here; where managers have explicit knowledge of what they are doing, then change is not difficult; but if this knowledge remains at the intuitive level, then change is both difficult and hazardous until an explicit appreciation is achieved.

(ii) If verbally established policies are in operation and difficulties appear, changes have to be made. A subordinate will approach a manager, and he will agree to some change that is clearly necessary. But if this policy applies to other people as well, and if there is not some well-established drill for making the change formally in writing and getting a secretary to circulate a copy to all concerned, then there is a danger that these others will not be informed. This leads to a situation where two inconsistent policies are in operation.

(iii) When new people are appointed to high-level vacancies, the task of initiating and training them is rendered vastly more difficult by the absence of written policies and instructions. They have almost literally to learn much of their jobs by making mistakes. Two new general managers were recently appointed in the company; their induction was made easier because they could study, in written form, the vital issues covered by such written documents as our company policy, standing orders and managing director's directives. They have both commented favourably on the help these have given them to get a quicker grasp of the job.

(iv) Many of the inevitable differences of opinion between colleagues, managers and subordinates arise out of disagreement as to what policies are in operation, what was agreed, what instructions were given. The decisions they are disputing were often made years before; such difficulties could so easily be settled if the decisions were committed to paper.

(v) During absence, managerial jobs must, from time to time and for short periods, be carried on by deputies. Written policy is very valuable at such times.

(vi) A general manager who relies too much on the giving of verbal instructions can produce a situation where his subordinate managers treat their own extended commands differently over various points of detail; for example, they vary on such matters as leave of absence, standards of light, heat, space and ventilation, quality of equipment, amount of overtime. People have a certain level of tolerance for differences over matters like these; but if it is stretched to the limit, trouble arises. Written policy not only helps to maintain consistency but serves to demonstrate that a reasonable degree of uniformity is part of the policy required by the general manager. Such evidence is generally valued by people.

I close this section with a review of the main types of written recording of policy and decisions at managing director level existing in the company.

Definitive policy circumscribes the activities of the board of directors. By law, such policy must be available in written form. It includes the Memorandum and Articles of Association of the Company, Company Law, the Factories Act, Stock Exchange regulations, etc. Normally it is the board of directors who exercise any choices open to the company in these fields.

Company Policy Document: this is a written statement – sanctioned by all works councils – laying down how the executive, representative, legislative and appeals systems shall operate.

Standing orders are the written form used for giving effect to the agreements arrived at by works councils. They refer generally to matters which affect working conditions of the members of the company, and they take two forms: Company Standing Orders (CSO) and Factory Standing Orders (FSO). The former, applying to the whole company, must be agreed by all works councils. The latter apply only to a factory or a geographical area of the company.

Here is a sample list of some current standing orders to illustrate their nature.

Alternative work	Holidays
Absence for education	Membership grading
Appointments	Nightshift
Company products supplied	Overtime
to company members	Redundancy
Expenses, advances, loans, etc.	Wage structure

Books containing these standing orders must be kept in each office and department in order to be easily available to all those affected by them. It will be noted that the standing orders quoted above cover policies which, once established, tend to endure for long periods without change. We cannot, on the other hand, reasonably draft standing orders on such matters as: When do we take annual holidays? Where do we park cars? These things are subject to constant change.

Management meeting minutes

Such meetings arise when a manager calls together his immediate subordinates to discuss issues, in order that he may make decisions and set policy. The group of subordinates may help the manager to come to these decisions and their views will certainly colour his thinking on them; but the decisions themselves are his alone.

The minutes should be essentially a record of such decisions. I notice a tendency for minutes of meetings to record matters inaccurately by stating, for example, 'It was decided that' or 'The meeting decided'. Minutes should state the facts, e.g., 'The general manager decided', and so on.

It was not until 1949 that I started keeping a written record of the decisions I took at my own management meetings. I cannot now imagine how I kept a reasonable grip of the situation without them, and the absence of the record must have caused much trouble to my subordinates. Certainly I, and others, now make constant back reference to the index and file of minutes which now exist. I recollect much hesitancy on my own part about initiating this practice, and a good deal of anxiety among my subordinates – largely based on objections like: 'It would make our meetings much too formal and inhibit reasonably free expression of opinion. The presence of my secretary would inhibit frankness'; but I never heard these anxieties referred to again after the practice of taking written minutes had got going. The practice demonstrated its own value, and this overcame the anxieties. I was interested to read later in Sir Ivor Jennings' book on Cabinet Government that it was as late as 1916 that Mr Lloyd George introduced this practice for the first time to meetings of the British Cabinet, and that he aroused very considerable anxieties among his fellow Cabinet Ministers in doing so.

Two things should be made clear:

(*a*) In referring to meetings I mean formal occasions where all my subordinates are present and not the many less formal talks which I have with one or more of my subordinates about matters which do not affect the whole of my command. I hold regular immediate-command meetings, to survey the whole field of operations, once each quarter, and another type of meeting, involving only my immediate subordinates working in London, each month. Thus the number of written minutes is limited.

(*b*) I have noted, in the company and elsewhere, a constant tendency to try and set down in written minutes a kind of précis of the discussion. I think this practice is bad. One cannot, in fairness, quote what somebody else has said in abbreviated form without getting their agreement to the precise wording, and there is never time for this. The practice is simply not valuable, because it dilutes the essence of the minutes, leads to arguments about accuracy and is unnecessary. Minutes should be a record of decisions only, with any important supporting facts which need to be represented in permanent form.

Directives

As can be seen from the above, 'Standing Orders' is the term we have rather arbitrarily chosen for contraction instructions, i.e., instructions that apply to many layers of people in the company or in a factory. In contradistinction, I have tried to reserve the term 'Directive' for instructions which will have long-term standing, will require to be fairly frequently referred to by my subordinates and which are issued to them alone, i.e., they have no element of contraction about them except in rare cases.

When the directives are issued, each of my subordinates receives a copy which he is required to file and maintain. Each year, a new index to these directives is issued, and there is a gradual but constant process going on all the time whereby new directives are issued, old ones withdrawn and a few amended. These files contain a very precise written record of a part of the prescribed content of the work of my staff officers and the general managers of the company. The following is a sample of seven titles of these directives chosen at random:

> Depreciation of fixed assets
> Foreign currency when travelling on company business
> Supply of tooling and machines to licensees
> Control of metal specifications
> Transfer of members between branches
> Responsibility for patents
> Manufacture of parts for stock in anticipation of customers'
>   delivery schedules

As far as possible these are written in a form which first states the policy and then enumerates the separate responsibilities of each member of my immediate command who is concerned in the matter.

I will quote the content of one directive as an example. The last directive in my sample list gives general managers of factories the right to manufacture products in excess of the monthly schedules sent to us by our customers; this is to enable factories to maintain the required rate of delivery without each month having to manufacture each customer's exact monthly requirement, which would sometimes be inefficient. This involves keeping stocks of parts that are individually suitable only for a single customer. But there are dangers that that customer will call for change in design which might render the part in stock obsolete. The directive, therefore, having granted discretional responsibility to general managers, goes on to condition that discretion by limiting the finance that may be so invested; and by limiting the number of parts of any particular design that may be manufactured in excess of schedule, by stating a maximum in terms of a percentage of a customer's annual usage of such parts.

Finally, with regard to directives I notice an increasing tendency for my own subordinates to point out areas where such written policy has not been issued, with the suggestion that it would help if the gap were filled. I think it is the practice of writing instructions that enables people to see the gaps that have to be filled.

It can thus be seen that we have developed some general concepts about the writing of policy and instructions, but that we are still far from having a systematic basis of thinking that would help us determine, as matters arise at different levels, whether or not the instructions and policy issued should be committed to writing, and the manner in which such written documents should be filed, kept and communicated.

Industry uses an immense amount of paper work nowadays, and most managers feel there is far too much of it. I have probably given the impression that our approach to the writing of policy gives rise to still more paper work. I have no doubt whatever that the contrary is the case. One well-drafted standing order or directive will function unaltered for years. Its absence during those years can give rise literally to hundreds of memoranda, letters, telephone calls and discussions. I strongly hold to the view that the most promising approach to the reduction of paper work is greater conceptual clarity about organization. As ideas about the structure of the executive system and of the work content of individual roles are clarified, it becomes increasingly easier to understand the function that the many forms of paper work fulfil. With this increase of clarity it becomes possible to construct a systematic basis upon which to base decisions about what should be written. This book is, for the company, a long-term statement in written form which will take the place of repeated memoranda or discussions about the subjects which it covers.

CHAPTER 10

THE MANAGER AND MEETINGS

THIS chapter discusses some aspects of verbal communication. To be able to talk more clearly on this subject it is necessary to remember the precise meaning I wish to give to two phrases. I, therefore, quote from our Policy Document:

'*Immediate command* of a manager is that group of members which he makes immediately *accountable* to him.'

'*Extended command* of a manager comprises all the members under his control.'

Immediate-command meetings

It is necessary to differentiate between meetings at which all of a manager's immediate command are present and others which involve some members only. I will call them 'full' and 'part' immediate-command meetings.

I hold full meetings at least four times a year. Greater frequency is somewhat difficult owing to the geographical distribution of my subordinates. Four full meetings seem sufficient at present. I hold a larger number of part meetings. General managers hold full meetings at periods ranging from two weeks up to two months; unit managers more frequently. In the case of section managers, the immediate-command meeting is not an established institution. I often feel that it should be possible for section managers to find themselves, at regular intervals, in face-to-face discussion with their immediate subordinates as a group. In this way they can more explicitly savour the experience of giving instructions and of forming policy at their own level. The difficulties in the way of such meetings are the interruption of production, office accommodation and a certain reluctance on the part of managers at this level to put themselves deliberately into such formal situations.

Immediate-command meetings and committee meetings contrasted

Some salient features of committee procedure are as follows:

Committee decisions are taken by a majority voting in favour of, or by other means indicating assent to, a proposition. All its members, including the minority, share the responsibility for the decision. The minority can evade responsibility only by resigning. Committees appoint a chairman to conduct the meeting; but *vis-à-vis* its decisions he carries no greater responsibility than his fellow members. His special responsibility is to conduct the meeting in accordance with committee custom, its own constitution and any standing orders it may have formulated for the conduct of its affairs. He is bound to observe these rules of procedure.

Contrast with this an immediate-command meeting. The manager calls the meeting at his own discretion, he decides the procedure to be followed, and he alone is responsible for all the decisions taken. Normally the purpose of the meeting is to enable him to get information from his subordinates, to test out the workability of his ideas with his subordinates, to give information, to clear up misunderstandings, to set policy and to give orders.

In the past, I failed to distinguish between these two quite different institutions. This gravely affected the efficiency of my own meetings. I used to attempt to get the unanimous agreement of all my subordinates to any decisions I wanted to make – as one would do at a committee meeting if taking the chair. A good deal of committee custom was used in connexion with the timing and procedure at meetings. I note this same tendency in the ideas of many managers. Such confusion wastes time by laboriously extending discussion long after the manager has made up his mind as to the decisions he must take, and it leaves his subordinates unclear as to their role in the meeting. The manager's decisions are likely to lack crispness and detailed definition, and this will lead to his orders being misunderstood subsequently.

The managing director of another company, in discussing his organization, told me that he had instituted a large number of committees to deal with various levels of policy. I suggested to him that he was not, in fact, using committees at all, but command meetings. We discussed the matter in some detail. At his 'committee meetings' there was always one manager present who was senior to the others, and he 'took the chair'. There was never any voting, and the chairman took the decisions when there was a difference of opinion. To me, he was describing command meetings, but he insisted that they were committees. I was left with the impression that confusion about the roles of those present was inevitable.

In an executive system, committees are not viable propositions for they deny the requisite reality of the manager–subordinate relationship. The reasons for this widespread confusion are, I think, mainly cultural. Committee procedure is associated in people's minds in this country with democracy and is 'good'. The manager–subordinate relationship is associated with authoritarianism and is 'bad'. Good relationships are felt to rest on not overriding the opinions of subordinates when they have been asked to give them, and vigorous attempts are made to maintain a situation where conflict is suppressed and an apparent agreement exists.[1]

Committee procedure gives scope for behaviour that accords with these underlying feelings and allows, discreetly, of abdication by the manager of his executive relationship with his subordinates. Though such unrealistic use of a non-executive institution may produce a superficial absence of conflict and supports the 'all is well; we are friends' culture, it is my opinion that, in fact, it generates precisely what it seeks to avoid. Subordinates, forced by the culture of the meeting into a situation where they either acquiesce in or delay the taking of a decision, voice their anxieties to their colleagues *after* the meeting in a situation where their doubts cannot be resolved. Real dissension is created, which the manager is unable to resolve because of the manner in which he conducts his meetings – the very place where such dissension could be cleared if the real nature of the executive roles involved is kept quite clear.

It is interesting to consider the situation of a board of directors in the light of the foregoing. The board is a *committee* elected by shareholders and is responsible to them. But, such a board can be confused with a command meeting, and I suspect that this happens not infrequently, particularly when all or the majority of its members hold executive posts in the company.

1. See Jaques, *The Changing Culture of a Factory*, Chapter 10.

If, in addition, the managing director is also chairman of the board, then role-confusion will be very difficult to avoid; for the managing director's immediate-command meeting will embrace all, or nearly all, the members of the board, and the board meeting will almost entirely consist of the managing director and some of his immediate subordinates. It is open to doubt whether those subordinates who hold their executive roles at the discretion of the managing director can effectively take up the role of director, where one of their major responsibilities is the appointment of the managing director.

The Companies Act holds directors corporately responsible; but the members of a board without any external directors have to ignore their executive relationship to their chairman during meetings, in order to take up this responsibility. In short, a board of directors composed of a managing director and his immediate subordinates alone can scarcely be regarded as conforming with the legal intention of the Companies Act.

I have been interested for many years in two contrasted aspects of the behaviour of people in industry:

(*a*) The tendency of people working in the lower levels of industry to want to turn command meetings into committee meetings; their marked familiarity with committee procedure, arising from their experience in trade unions; and their occasional resentment of what they regard as authoritarian conduct when managers reject committee procedure in a command-meeting situation.

(*b*) The relative ignorance on the part of many managers, at high level, of committee procedures, and their occasional resentment of conventional committee practices when they are sitting on committees.

On occasions, for example, I have had the experience of raising a 'point of order' at an external committee meeting chaired by an industrial manager, only to find that the essential need to give priority over any other business to such points was not recognized by the chairman.

In short, then, immediate-command meetings are not committee meetings, but an institution by means of which a manager may: (*a*) seek the views of his immediate subordinates, and get the interaction of those individual views on each other;

(*b*) test his ideas on policy by getting the reaction of his subordinates in a situation where he may also note the interaction of his subordinates' ideas on each other.

The purpose of command meetings

Sometimes, between my full-command meetings (quarterly intervals), I have to make important decisions about change of policy that affect many of my immediate subordinates. In the absence of a command meeting this can prove time-consuming, and even irritating. I send out details of the proposal in writing. One manager points out snags; the rest respond by saying that they find no difficulty. To overcome the snags I amend the policy, only to find that, as amended, it raises snags for other managers who had agreed the first proposal. This process can go on for a long time. A meeting overcomes such problems. This seems to me to be one of the prime functions of a command meeting – interaction of all concerned simultaneously instead of in series. (Examples are too long and complicated to quote lucidly.) Command meetings are one way of preventing such prolonged procedures – another way is through the intelligent use of staff officers. I shall deal with staff work in Chapter 11.

The use of immediate-command meetings to resolve a range of problems, each of which concerns only one or two of those managers present, is an inefficient use of time. If A has present at his command meeting B_1, B_2, B_3 and B_4, and raises a problem which concerns B_1 alone, then: (*a*) the time of B_2, B_3 and B_4 is being wasted and this costs money; (*b*) B_2, B_3 and B_4 will often – for lack of something to do – begin giving opinions on the matter under discussion. If the policy under discussion applies to B_1 alone, then these comments are in the strict sense of the word irresponsible. It is, however, difficult to be critical of B_2, B_3 and B_4, since the real fault lies with A in raising the matter in their presence.

Our Policy Document contains some statements bearing on the conduct of immediate-command meetings. These constitute important terms of reference for a manager, because they sum up an experience of the behaviour required in a command meeting, namely:

A member shall be accountable for the results of all his executive activities to his own immediate manager (E.2.1).

In other words, a manager is not responsible to his immediate command for his action, as would be the case, for instance, with a committee chairman.

A member shall question any instructions which he does not feel able to carry out within the policy set and with the facilities available to him. In the absence of any such query, his manager may take it that the member has accepted the instruction as being reasonable (E.2.2).

This puts the responsibility on a subordinate to raise queries about his manager's policy, or to implement the policy or instruction.

When a member raises a question with his manager, his manager shall try to give him an immediate decision. If he cannot give an immediate decision, he must commit himself to give a decision by a specified time (E.2.4).

This attempts to prevent the too common situation where a manager is hesitant and woolly, and his subordinate is left, either without terms of reference, or in a position where he risks taking his own decisions without, in fact, knowing whether he is entitled to take such decisions.

In communicating with his immediate superior, a manager shall give his own assessment, and any reservations he may have, taking into account the views of his subordinates (E.11).

At one time, I frequently used to experience the following kind of response from some of my immediate subordinates when I proposed a particular line of action:

MD: What are your views, Mr X?

MR X: I have discussed the idea with two of my subordinates who will have some responsibility for carrying out the plan. They do not think it will be an improvement. Generally, my subordinates are worried about it.

At the time, I saw nothing wrong with this type of response. But it consistently irritated me. Only after we had discussed communication at some length did the following concepts emerge. It is a manager's job to give *his own* assessment to his superior, and not merely to quote the assessment of his subordinates, or of others. In making this assessment, he should take into account the views of his extended command. Having given his own assessment, it may be wise to quote the opinion of subordinates with his own assessment of the validity of their comment.

In my more recent experience, the sort of comment made by Mr X no longer arises. Discussion of problems or of plans is therefore simplified, because I am now really getting my subordinates' *own* opinions, after they have taken into account all the relevant factors known to them, instead of their simply serving as postmen to bring some of the facts to my notice. This is the real meaning of the first sentence of Section E.11 quoted above ('In communicating with his immediate superior, . . .').

The essential point and intention of this policy require further elaboration. When a manager has made a decision and is giving instructions or information to his subordinates, he must take personal responsibility for what he transmits. We are all familiar with the constantly recurring situation in which a manager B has tried to persuade his superior A to follow a different course from that which A eventually chooses. B then

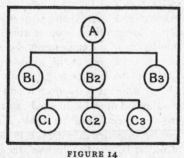

FIGURE 14

may have to issue consequential instructions to his own subordinates. What often happens can be described diagrammatically (Figure 14).

B_2 has argued against a particular plan put forward by A.

But A has decided, nevertheless, to go ahead. B_2 now has to instruct C_1, C_2 and C_3 variously in their part of the plan. They know, because B_2 has previously and quite properly discussed A's plan with them, that B_2 would have preferred a different course. If B_2 has not got a realistic perception of the real position, he is likely to give a communication to C_1, C_2 and C_3 which, 'between the lines', carries this meaning: 'I have no confidence in A's plan, but A wants it and, therefore, I must carry out my part of it by giving you these instructions. Do your best with it. I am sorry about it.' Such communications breed anxiety and inefficiency and, in the long run, reduce the status of B_2 in the eyes of his subordinates.

The perception needed is this: A is at the cross-over point. B_2 must be able to see that while A's plan may not be the best for *his* command, it may well be best if the whole field of operations, including the command of B_1 and B_3, is taken into account. B_2, by role position, knows more about his own extended command and its workings than A. But A knows about the commands of B_1 and B_3 as well and, in addition, A is responsible for the strategy of his whole extended command. B_2 is judging the plan on the basis of special knowledge of a part of the situation which A can see as a whole, and on which A must base his plan.

If B_2 perceives the reality of the situation, the communication that will 'get across' to C_1, C_2 and C_3 is something like this: 'I wanted A to follow a different course which would have been more in the interests of the efficiency and comfort of my command, but my plan does not fit the whole situation with which A has to deal. Obviously, therefore, because we are part of a greater whole for which A is responsible and because the objectives of my command must be directed as a first priority towards sustaining the objectives of the whole, A's plan must go through. It must be supported as being best in the long-term interests of all of us.' If B_2 gets that 'across', then C_1, C_2 and C_3 have been taught how to handle a similar situation when they have to deal with their subordinates at the D level.

Let me give one simple practical illustration of what happens in such situations. An extra power press is urgently required in one of our factories to meet a surge of demand. All the existing presses are running to capacity. Another factory has a lighter load on its press section; but the transfer of a press would cause extra night-shifting, more time spent in setting up, and so forth. I do, however, instruct that the transfer is to be made, because it seems to me that the interests of the company are thus best served. In this situation, it is not possible for either of the general managers in charge of the two factories to assess realistically whether the transfer should or should not be made; each has only a partial view of the situation. If they can both think of the situation in these terms, they can deal with the feelings of their subordinates. But if they cannot, then unrealistically based emotions are let loose.

Here are some points of emphasis on the subject of immediate-command meetings:

It is often necessary to experiment with the frequency of such meetings in order to discover the longest gap that can be tolerated without giving rise to difficulty. I used to hold my full meetings at monthly intervals; the gap was then extended to two months; it is now three months. It certainly cannot be a longer gap, in present circumstances; but I shall experiment if circumstances change.

They deal with the setting of policy and the giving of orders that apply to as large a proportion of those present as possible, with whom it might prove difficult to resolve such matters in separate discussions individually.

They are for the purpose of helping a manager to work out and set policy, and give instructions. Although the working through of disagreements and their resolutions is one of the purposes of the meeting, if the manager is unable to get agreement, he must still make decisions – even though at times these may contravene the views of each of his subordinates. If he is over-easily persuaded by his subordinates, he will find himself carrying responsibility for decisions that his own judgement had, in fact, rejected.

They are a valuable opportunity for assessing subordinates. In such meetings, the manager can assess the extent to which each of his subordinates is capable of conducting collateral relationships with his colleagues. If a subordinate is intolerant of the interests of any part of the company except his own extended command, this will be exposed at a command meeting.

A special point about the conduct of command meetings

Time is often wasted unwittingly in meetings by discursive comment on issues which are not requisitely the business of that particular meeting. There is need for managers to teach subordinates how to get through the work of such meetings with speed, by sticking to the requisite problems of those present. To illustrate the sort of thing that needs correction I quote an example.

We are discussing means of increasing the manufacturing capacity for a particular product to meet a growing demand. This entails consideration of factory space, plant, methods and personnel. The discussion focuses on the possibility of a new design of tool which, if feasible, will double output on certain operations and minimize the need for extra space and personnel. Enthusiasm is generated, and the pencils and paper begin to appear. Those present begin sketching ideas for tool design there and then. Various detailed ideas are debated. Our ration of time for the meeting comes to an end. What have we decided about the increase of manufacturing capacity? It can now be seen that we have developed an idea upon which a tool might be designed. But, by descending to the level of abstraction of the tool designer, we have left undone our real job. I should have said when the idea arose: 'Good, if a tool can be so designed, let it be done; by what date, Mr X, will you be able to inform me if this is workable or not? Now let us leave that as a potential contribution to our problem and explore the rest of the action required.'

I find it difficult in my own meetings to register the moment at which the discussion goes off the rails in this way, with the result that I sometimes waste a great deal of time. If, however, when a discussion takes a turn into what feels like a rather detailed sector of the subject, I can ask myself the question: 'Is this the sort of issue on which I take decisions?' If the answer is: 'No, you rely on others to take such decisions', then I call a halt to the discussion, and fix responsibility on the appropriate person present for considering the matter further and reporting back.

There is need for more explicit recognition of the different levels of abstraction at which a problem can be discussed and of the fact that operators, supervisors, section managers, unit managers, general managers, all operate at ever higher levels of abstraction. Consider again the example I have quoted. There are present, say, the managing director, a factory general manager, and two of my staff officers, one concerned with company programming and the other with company production techniques. If we talk in detail about the design of specific tools, the price at which we buy certain sizes of steel, or specific customers who need additional supplies, we are doing work which is done in detail for us at lower levels. This is what I mean by working at the wrong level of abstraction. We have to be aware of the fact that detailed work will have to be done on those issues, but we must not spend time doing it ourselves.

Extended-command meetings

Such meetings are most likely to be required when big changes are to be made, in order to get an index of people's feelings; or in times of crisis or trouble when the feelings of large numbers are running high; or when there is a need to disseminate information accurately and rapidly to a large part, or the whole, of an extended command. Such meetings always involve the notion of contraction which I have already discussed in principle.

There is a strong tendency for managers to abdicate from the responsibility of talking to their extended commands directly. This arises from a number of reasons, some of which seem to be connected with the following points:

(*a*) Speaking 'in public' is emotionally disturbing to many managers. Training may help, but no practice situation has attached to it the responsibility of the real thing. If a section manager made a practice of talking face to face with his command of twenty to thirty people whenever it seemed necessary, the experience would stand him in good stead when he became a unit manager. If, however, he fails to take advantage of the opportunity at section-manager level, then lack of experience will make the exercise look very formidable when he reaches unit-manager level. He will probably not essay the task when it is, in fact, an appropriate way of dealing with a situation.

(*b*) Many managers reach unit or general manager level by gaining experience in technical and staff jobs. Such roles do not afford much opportunity for getting accustomed to the unusual strains of talking about problems to a large number of people.

(*c*) Too many managers seem to rely upon the representative system as a means of communicating with their extended command. Thus, when a situation arises where they should present the facts to their command, they rationalize a reluctance to face a large meeting by reasoning that this would be undermining representatives. This is merely confused thinking. Their extended command is their responsibility; so long as the manager makes it quite clear that he is talking to them all in their *executive* roles, he is in no way undermining the status of the representative system.

When representatives hold a meeting with the whole of a department, unit or factory, they are talking to people in their role of constituents. Managers meet their subordinates in executive roles; representatives meet their constituents. It is important that people should become more aware of their different roles; clearly structured command meetings can help them to distinguish the differences. At this stage an example of a situation giving rise to an extended-command meeting might prove helpful.

Some years ago in our London factories there was need for women to work rather a lot of overtime. The Factories Act stipulates that a factory shall register either as a five-day or a five-and-half-day establishment for the purpose of regulating such overtime. We were registered as a five-day factory, and a change of registration seemed desirable to allow more overtime working on Saturdays. Representatives were not prepared to agree to the change, in spite of a great deal of discussion. The reasons for this resistance seemed rather confused to me at the time. I thought it essential to get the purpose of the change across to the women concerned. They were dispersed throughout the London factories. I therefore used the loudspeaker system to do so, although it was already plain that we could not implement the change at that time, because it was not agreed by representatives.

Within a matter of months, however, it became clear that, as a result of not changing the registration of the factory, some women who did not wish to work overtime in the evenings were having to do so, while others who would have liked to work on Saturday mornings could not be allowed to because of the Factories Act. A second discussion with representatives at a council meeting took place, and the change was agreed. I believe that the statement of facts on this complex situation, made by me to the women concerned in their executive roles, contributed greatly to the changed terms of reference given by those women to their representatives.

Extended-command meetings are necessary for the following reasons:

(*a*) They are usually the best way of issuing contraction instructions.

(*b*) A manager must, by some means, expose some facets of his personality to all those subordinate to him. Unless he does so his people have no objective means of forming an opinion of the sort of manager to whom they are ultimately responsible. In default of real opportunities for making an assessment, they will project imaginary feelings on to that manager. These may be anxious, or hostile, or the reverse; but they will not be very objective and will lead them to make erroneous assumptions about their manager and his actions. Usually these assumptions set up tensions that cause suspicion about any proposals for change that the manager puts forward. Such suspicion makes for inflexibility of attitude, and prevents adaptation of custom and practice taking place when it is required.

(*c*) There are situations, especially where feelings are running high, when it is essential both for the extended-command manager to hear at first-hand what his people feel, and for these people to hear the manager's comments directly from him. The manager involved is in a very difficult position at such times; for he has to make decisions which may lead to loss of morale or even strikes, or to accept situations which he feels are not in the interests of the company. At such times, he should have as much *first-hand* information as possible. He should make quite certain that the high feelings are not, in fact, a product of confusion that has arisen from relying upon communication through different levels of managers, or through the representative system. Both such results can be obtained by contraction.

My own experience impresses me with the extent to which sheer misunderstanding can cause high feelings. It is always difficult to trace the causes. I have sometimes wondered whether the confusion is perhaps motivated by a wish to bring senior managers 'out into the open' and in face-to-face contact with their people. I do not know if this is right. But to the extent that it is true, it suggests that such situations may be prevented if managers took more advantage of opportunities for 'showing themselves', and did not shrink from the task.

PART FOUR

SPECIALIST WORK

CHAPTER 11

ANALYSIS OF SPECIALIST WORK

MANAGERS in industry often attempt to analyse executive work into 'line work' and 'staff work'. They talk about 'line managers' and 'functional managers'. On an increasing scale they talk about 'staff officers' and 'staff assistants'; but in my opinion the definitions given do not lead to any systematic elucidation of the work to be done. The basis of the difficulty in getting down to clarification is the lack of conceptual clarity about the content of business work.

The content of business activity

It may be observed that the owners of every business carry out the following:

(a) *They decide what goods or services they seek to provide.* If their company is making a product, they may decide that to safeguard the future, or to ensure full use of productive capacity, they want to have new or additional products. This, in turn, leads to a decision either to develop new products within the company, or to arrange with some other company to develop products for them for payment. In other words, there is a product- or service-development function to be performed.

(b) *They arrange for the provision of some goods or services.* They may decide to employ people, plant, buildings, etc., to produce the product or service, or they may decide to sub-contract the manufacture to some other company. There is, however, a producing function to be carried out either by employing people or by sub-contracting.

(c) *They arrange for the sale of goods or services* which they have brought into being. Again, they may do so by employing people to sell, or by arranging for some other company to sell their output on a commission basis. The chief executive has to arrange for this selling function to be performed.

The economic conception of business activity always comprises the development, production and sale of some commodity or service. The business does not always carry out these functions directly by the employment of people. It does so at times by arranging for the function to be discharged for it by some other business. Every business using this sub-contracting arrangement has, however, to organize the sub-contracting, and in that sense carries out the function. The usefulness of this generalization can be tested by observing a large number of businesses in operation.

Consider the case of just one rather difficult example, a retail shop, to illustrate the notion. The owner has to decide, from time to time, what he shall sell. Shall he add newspapers to the existing tobacco business; shall he stop selling confectionery; ought he to visit trade exhibitions to look for new lines; shall he decide to open a small lending library, a need for which appears to exist in the locality, etc. In thinking and investigating along these lines he is performing the *development* function. He rents a shop, buys storage racks, buys stocks, attends to customers, packs goods, delivers goods, etc. In so doing, he is *producing* the service. He thinks about attracting more customers, rearranges his window display, decides to buy better display counters, sends out advertising material, etc. In so doing, he is performing the *selling* function.

According to the emphasis or energy which he applies to such different work, the success of his business will wax or wane, but he cannot leave any of these functions undone completely or he will cease to have a business. The more explicitly he can think of these three functions separately, the more likely he will be to give them appropriate balanced attention.

I have never seen a business whose work is not describable in these terms. We use the term 'operational work' to describe these three functions, and in our company we use the separate symbols D (development), M (manufacture) and S (sales) to refer to them.

Operational work of the company

Requisite organization is a function of the fact that we exist to develop, manufacture and sell bearings. It would be equally possible to take as an example a company set up merely to develop bearings; but consider just what such a company would have to do. One would likewise get, in this company, the basic notions of developing ideas as to what developments should be undertaken (development), doing the actual development work (production) and selling the result (sales).

Consider a company manifestly set up to sell only. One would have to *develop* ideas on how to go about selling. These ideas would have to be worked up into the production of a selling service, and this service would have to be 'sold' to somebody who developed and manufactured bearings. In other words, the product of the firm would be the selling service, and such a service has to be developed, produced and sold.

If we, as a company, decided to employ the services of another firm to carry out one of these functions for us on the basis of some fee or commission, then the structure of our executive system undergoes basic change. If we made an arrangement for another company to carry out for us all work on the development of new types of bearings, then the structure of our research and development organization would require radical alteration. Similarly, if we in this company subcontracted all manufacture of bearings, retaining only the development and sales activities, the executive structure of the company would be greatly altered.

An *operational manager* is one who carries out the whole (the managing director is responsible for the development, manufacture and sale of bearings), or some part, of the operational work of the company. When people refer to line managers, I think that generally they are referring to what I have defined as an operational manager. All people employed in our company, except specialists, can be said to be engaged on developing, or manufacturing, or selling bearings, or some part of those activities. Having defined operational work, we are now able to proceed to a consideration of the nature of specialist work. It will become clear as I proceed that it is not possible to discuss specialist work in conceptual terms until operational work has been defined, because the former is a phase of the latter.

Analysis of specialist work

Specialist work is the work performed by people in roles where they are held responsible for having particular concentrated knowledge appertaining to one or other of the phases under which operational work can be analysed.

I have already defined the content of work as having two components, prescribed and discretionary, but employment work can also be described along another 'dimension' as: a person, in a role in an executive system, using a technique on a timed and balanced programme of activity, all set by a manager. *No instruction given by a manager is complete unless, in fact, or by implication, it specifies who shall carry it out, what technique shall be used and the timing and quantity of activity which are demanded.*

This can be put in another way; all work activity implies a manning of activity, a technique of activity and a chosen quantified and timed deployment of activity on a particular operational task. The contention is, therefore, that operational work is a three-dimensional activity and that it can be analysed under three headings: (*a*) organizational and personnel work; (*b*) work concerned with the techniques used in production; and (*c*) programming work concerned with balancing, timing and quantification of operations. Thus, all specialist work in the company falls into one of three specialist divisions: Personnel Division (P); Technical Division (T); and Programming Division (Pr). The specialists in these divisions are concerned, respectively, with the optimization of profit by the use of:

(*a*) the optimum organizational and personnel practices;
(*b*) the optimum production techniques;
(*c*) the optimum balance and timing of the pattern of operations.

Is this analysis valid?

The foregoing is not an hypothesis which can be validated by experiment. It is a conceptual idea which arises out of observation of what happens in one industrial company. My experience is that the concept fits the daily circumstances of my managerial job, and that this experience is supported by that of many other managers in the company.

Take any situation that requires a managerial decision; for example, whether or not to provide additional manufacturing capacity. If the concept is useful, then it should be possible to analyse and allot any consideration that arises from the taking of that decision to one of the three specialist phases named. Here is a typical assortment, culled from personal experience, of the kind of considerations that do arise on such an issue.

(*a*) For which type of bearing is the additional capacity required and is such deployment of activity and resources optimum from the economic point of view? (Pr)

(*b*) What competing demands for such capacity exist in the company and what economic return will these others yield us? (Pr)

(*c*) What programme of activity, in terms of timing or quantity of work, on the part of the general managers in charge of development, manufacture and selling is this going to involve, and will this interfere with other urgent work which has to go on? (Pr)

(*d*) Can we afford the higher stocks necessary to support this additional capacity, without depleting our finances in such a way as to force us to deflate some other activity which is economically more important to us? (Pr)

(*e*) If we increase capacity, can we foresee keeping that capacity reasonably fully loaded in the future with work from customers at an economic price? (Pr)

(*f*) What type of plant will we need? Are we going to use existing types or new types to get higher production rates? (T)

(*g*) If we decide to lay down a new type of plant, what space will be required in which to house it; will the floors take it; have we sufficient electric power laid on; will it pay us to do so? (T)

(*h*) Can we so arrange plant, conveyors, storage facilities, packing and dispatch in the available space to get an economically efficient flow of work? (T)

(*i*) Can we, in planning the production methods on this additional capacity, get a degree of serviceability, accuracy or finish of the product that will give us a bigger competitive advantage? (T)

(*j*) Can we organize this additional production under the command of an existing unit manager; or have we got to go to the considerable expense of setting up a new unit, complete with a manager, specialists, section managers, and is it economic to do so? (P)

(*k*) Can we get the additional operators, craftsmen, managers, for manning this new production, who will have the skills required to produce at economic levels within a reasonable space of time; or is this going to be a case of low output and high scrap over a very long bedding-in process? What are the economic effects from this point of view? (P)

(*l*) If, instead of using existing factory space, we put up a new building, then this will relieve overcrowding at a number of other points and, by the creation of better working conditions, help to increase the satisfaction and efficiency of a large number of operators, managers, etc. (P)

Clearly, one could go on almost endlessly throwing up points to be considered in coming to such a decision; but however many these are, I find that, subject sometimes to considerable and prolonged thought, any cogent point concerned with the internal coordination of such a plan can be subsumed under one of these three phases.

Consider the case of a section manager who has work to do for customer A and customer B. He has to decide whether to put job A on line 1 and job B on line 2, or vice versa. There will be programme considerations, such as which arrangement will best meet the delivery times asked? There will be technique considerations, such as are the machines and tools on line 1 suitable for job A, or not? There will be personnel and organizational considerations, such as are the supervisor and operators on line 1 sufficiently used to job A to be given the job, or will putting job B on line 2 involve increase of the existing operator strength on that line?

A general manager may have to decide whether or not to limit the amount of overtime worked in his command. He has, let us suppose, three staff officers, P, T and Pr. P will be worried about the effect that limitation of overtime will have on wages, but also worried about the effect that continuance will have on health, efficiency and scrap. His labour turnover will be affected; reduction of overtime may mean more new people, more training, reduced output from new people for a time, and so on. T may say: 'If you are prepared to spend all that on overtime premiums, then for a small expenditure on new machines I can increase output and get rid of overtime in that way.' Pr is concerned whether new techniques or intake of additional operators will effectively safeguard deliveries; or whether, on the other hand, continuance of overtime with its high premiums is not already so reducing the economic return on the job as to make it desirable to reduce the intake of orders for such work.

These three dimensions of activity can be demonstrated also in manual work. A turner on a lathe considers whether he shall, within prescribed limits, increase the speed of rotation of his chuck which holds the job he is machining. The following sorts of considerations must arise, albeit perhaps intuitively: 'Can I maintain finish and accuracy at the higher speed; am I skilful enough for that (P)? I shall have to alter the speed of traverse of the tool in order to maintain finish (T). Unless I do increase chuck speed, this job will take longer and be late on delivery for the next operation. It is behind time now (Pr).' These are just three considerations that arise, but the others fall into place with equal rationality.

Is this analysis useful?

I have not the basic technical training to keep up to date on everything; and if I am to get assistance in making new policy, I need people who have specialized knowledge in advance of my own. If I have to have such specialized assistance, I must specify in what fields of knowledge, and this analysis does that for me.

If I am to be able to exercise more detailed control over the interaction of my operational subordinates, then I must in some way be able to split up this coordinative work in order that I can delegate some of it. This analysis enables me to do so.

If, having set policies, I have not got the time to follow them up and see that they are properly implemented, or discover the difficulties which are preventing this from happening, then again I must have some way of splitting up this staff work in order to get it done.

Work in the company seems inevitably to require personnel officers, engineers, production control personnel, specialist planning people, chemists, metallurgists, experts in devising routines, statisticians and so on; and it is more than useful to discover that all these different specialist skills can be grouped into three discrete divisions, the work of which can be differentiated one from another on the basis of apparently realistic general statements.

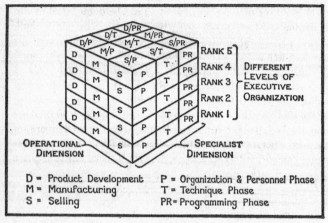

FIGURE 15

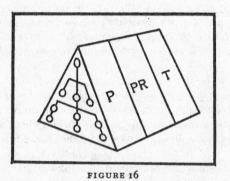

FIGURE 16

Figure 15 is a diagrammatic presentation in three dimensions of the interrelation of operational and specialist work at five levels of executive organization. Figure 16 demonstrates another way of presenting the idea of the specialist dimension in a conventional organization chart.

CHAPTER 12

HISTORY OF OUR SPECIALIST
PROBLEMS

ONE of the difficulties which we in the company felt for a number of years was in holding managers (below the level of general manager) fully accountable for the price, quality and delivery of goods; in spite of the fact, be it noted, that these matters comprise the whole *raison d'être* of our concern. One of the causes of this was the existence of what one may call a 'specialist barrier' between factory managers and departmental superintendents. The way in which we used to look at our executive system is illustrated in Figure 17.

This diagram gives no guidance in understanding what the nature of the relationship is between those roles concerned with carrying out the 'operational' tasks of the company – to make, develop and sell its products – and those which are concerned with matters, for example, of manufacturing techniques or personnel. We tended to say that a specialist (such as a production engineer or a production controller) had no authority at all over the process of production; so far as he had any contact with operators or managers, it was to offer advice or to give services. When, however, we came to look at just how our system worked, we found that these so-called advices or services that specialists gave were not only felt to be instructions by those who received them, but that they had in fact to be instructions if the company was to get its work done efficiently. Thus production engineering and production control specialists (among others) carried what we came to call 'staff authority' – i.e., they issued instructions on layout, prices, priorities, delivery, etc. – and moreover, this staff authority impinged on the shop floor from junior specialist levels and in many cases bypassed line managers. An impression of how this unrecognized authority worked, and of the relationships concealed in the organizational chart shown in Figure 17, can be obtained from Figure 18.

Two points may be stressed here: firstly, that the company

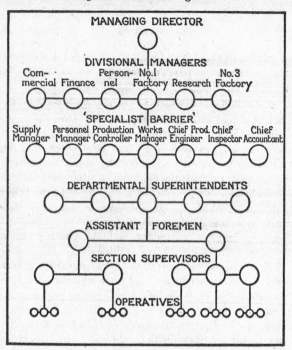

FIGURE 17. The executive system as we used to look at it

had to incorporate this staff authority into its system in order to get its work done; and secondly, that it did so in a concealed manner without recognizing the fact. As a result of research these points became apparent to us. In order to attempt to deal with the confusion and inefficiency we experienced, we began slowly to develop a different kind of organization which recognized the underlying nature of what was observed to be, in fact, in existence (Figure 19).

The main features of this organization may be enumerated as follows: (i) We differentiated operational from specialist organization. (ii) We organized the company into units not exceeding some 300 to 350 members. This is the maximum size which allows personal leadership by a unit manager, since all his subordinates can know him and can also recognize each

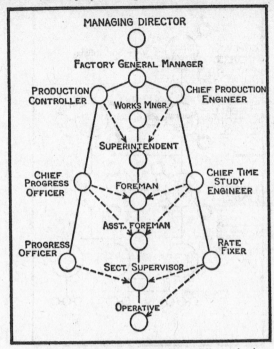

FIURGE 18. The hidden pattern of specialist authority

No one below the level of general manager could be said to be fully in charge of production. Dotted lines represent so-called services given by specialists, but which were in fact felt to be instructions by those who received them.

other. (iii) We organized shop-floor work into sections of from ten to seventy members each, under a full-scale manager fully accountable for work and for personal leadership. (iv) Supervisory roles were set up to assist managers, and these roles carried specifically designed supervisory authority. (v) Specialists were attached as necessary at any level to assist each operational manager to discharge his responsibilities. These specialists carry recognized staff authority within their own fields, in relation to their manager's subordinates.

Such a set-up means that responsibility is more clearly placed squarely on operational managers for such work as:

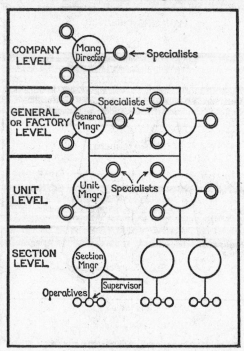

FIGURE 19. Our current form of organization

Each manager is fully in charge of operations carried out
under him and has his own specialist staff to assist him.

(*a*) Deliveries to schedule – because they have their own
specialist staff responsible to them. (*b*) Development work and
methods engineering – because they have the requisite engineering specialists. (*c*) Appropriate organization and manning
roles – because they have undivided control within company
policy.

It can be seen that a further result is to reduce the total
number of levels in the organization, facilitating communications up and down the line.

CHAPTER 13

SPECIALIST ORGANIZATION

MY experience of industry suggests that the relation of BS_1 to B_1 and B_2, as shown in Figure 20, is the subject of great confusion. I am convinced that failure to analyse these relationships really does contribute greatly to social friction, loss of efficiency, failure of specialists to keep their organization up to date, and failure of managers to be able fully to take on responsibility. Some description of the general situation surrounding the issue will help to highlight the importance of our policy on this particular relationship.

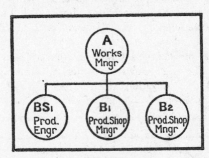

FIGURE 20

If BS_1 is described simply as a colleague of B_1 and B_2, then all sorts of questions are left unresolved. I have had a great deal of painful experience of this unclarified position. I can remember meetings at which there were present production superintendents, on the one hand, and the chief production engineer, on the other. The superintendent claimed that the manufacturing layouts which they had to follow were often wasteful effort, involved too much tooling and, at times, gave rise to unnecessary scrap. Given discretion to alter these layouts, the superintendents claimed they could bring about substantial increase of output and a reduction in scrap. The chief production engineer claimed that he and his staff produced new manufacturing layouts only after real appraisal of the situation in the machine shops, and after discussion with superintendents, foremen and others. While there was seldom dispute on paper, there was far too much unauthorized departure from layout without any reference to the production engineering department. I could quote many such examples.

We attempted to resolve the problem of authority by the idea of the 'prescription'. This was defined as the experts' way of tackling a problem or overcoming a difficulty. But it was not an order given to an operational manager; it was offered to him, or asked for by him. Like a doctor's prescription, it could be refused by the patient but, of course, at his own peril. This idea tended to increase the authority of the superintendents, because it left them in command of the situation even though the turning down of a prescription had its risks. On paper, however, it deprived the specialist of authority. It left him with the job of persuading operational managers to accept his 'prescription'.

Figure 21 depicts the assumed organization as it was seen at one time; Figure 22 shows the extant organization as it really was, and the organization which is requisite to the optimum execution of work.

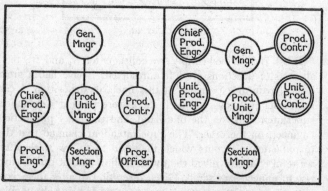

FIGURE 21.
Assumed organization

FIGURE 22.
Extant and requisite organization

Specialist Organization

A specialist became recognized to be one of a constellation of roles around the manager. This specialist role carried responsibility for being expert in a particular phase of the manager's job, for advising the manager on what policies he should follow, for helping the manager to plan the implementation of new policies and for coordinating the actions of the manager's subordinates in carrying the new plans into effect. Looked at in this way, it could be seen that the specialist was doing work in a particular phase at the same level as his own manager. Our Policy Document defines a specialist as follows:

Specialist role. A role in which the occupant is accountable for assisting a manager through the discharge of one or more of the following responsibilities:

(*a*) *Advisory responsibility* – for giving technical advice and assistance to his manager (or operational co-manager).

(*b*) *Service-providing responsibility* – that of providing service or prescriptions.

(*c*) *Staff responsibility* – that of assisting a manager in the coordination of the work of that manager's immediate subordinates in a particular field by exercising authority and issuing instructions on his behalf.

(*d*) *Technical coordination responsibility* – that of operating one or more of the following mechanisms (as instructed) for the coordination of the technical aspects of specialist work:

(i) *Technical guidance:* Where a specialist is accountable for giving advice and guidance to other specified members.

(ii) *Inspection:* Where a member is instructed to review, assess and report upon the effectiveness of work which is in his specialist field but which is not directly under his executive control.

(iii) *Attachment or secondment: Attachment* – the process of deploying a specialist from a Specialist Division to an established position under a manager. *Secondment* – the temporary deployment of a specialist to a position under a manager.

Staff responsibility

I wish first to set up a convention about diagrams. If I designate a manager by the symbol of A_1 or B_1, etc., I shall designate his specialist subordinate by the symbols A_1S_1, A_1S_2, B_1S_1, B_1S_2, etc.

The relationship of AS_1 to B in Figure 23 is one within which AS_1 gives instructions to B, so long as these instructions are for the purpose of implementing a policy made known to B

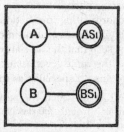

FIGURE 23

by A. AS_1, a staff officer, is responsible to A for seeing to it that A's operational subordinates carry out his policy. B, at all times, has the right and duty to see A, if he wishes to question A on the policy he has set. If B feels that the policy which AS_1 is implementing is not A's, he will say so and query this with A if he wishes to. Paragraph E.2.2 of our Policy Document is quite explicit on this point:

A member shall question any instructions which he does not feel able to carry out within the policy set and with the facilities available to him. In the absence of any such query, his manager may take it that the member has accepted the instruction as being reasonable.

This situation gives the appearance of being one within which B has two managers; or, if we consider the situation when A has three staff officers, then B might be considered to have four managers. If one were to define a manager as 'someone who gives instructions', then this statement would be true. But, in point of fact, I hope I have already demonstrated in Chapter 4 the usefulness and realism of the idea that a manager, minimally, is the person who selects, appoints, assesses, rewards and disciplines subordinates and sets the main work targets. In this sense, AS_1, AS_2 and AS_3 are not B's managers; they do not select, assess or discipline. A alone has that relationship to

B. According, therefore, to the definitions used in our company, this is not a dual-manager situation. My experience indicates that it is not felt to be so; for despite the fact that AS_1, AS_2 and AS_3 give instructions to B, these instructions are given on A's behalf and must be within A's policy.

AS and B, in our company, are of the same rank. AS is responsible for deciding whether his manager's policy and instructions are being carried out by B_1, B_2, B_3. He will not be regarded by A as having discharged his responsibility, unless *in extremis* he is prepared to issue warnings to B_1, B_2, B_3, and, failing compliance, to report back this failure to A. Notwithstanding, AS is not responsible for assessing B managerially.

I know this is difficult to grasp and that the first reaction to the idea is the assumption that staff officers will inevitably discuss with their own manager the personality, ability, etc., of that manager's operational subordinate. In practice, however, this does not happen. There are barriers to such comment. To some extent these are psychological and cultural. AS and B are both subordinates of the same manager and thus share, to some extent, the same frustrations and the same executive leadership. But that is not the whole story. If AS and B are correctly positioned in the executive system, then, within limits, they are people of roughly the same personal capacity to do work – though it is work of a different kind. B is doing a part of his manager's work in all its phases within his manager's policy. AS is looking after one phase of his manager's work by helping him to set and implement part of the policy within which the manager's operational subordinates do their work. AS is not responsible for the totality of what B does, only for seeing to it that one phase of B's work is carried out within the policy of manager A. Thus AS cannot see the whole of B's work and is incapable of making a total assessment of B.

This colleague relationship, based on consonance of capacity of AS and B, possesses the merit that it allows a freedom of speech between the two that is not possible between a manager and his subordinate, because the *assessment* component of the former's responsibility inhibits such complete frankness. Here is a typical scene:

B: The whole situation is crazy. I am asked to produce to higher standards than ever before in less time. I do not trust the new casting technique and I think we are in for trouble!!

AS: You did not say so to A when all this was discussed two weeks ago. It is a tight time target, but you have not even started yet – why lose two weeks? You agreed that quality must be raised. I know you argued the point initially, but you shut up pretty quickly when it was made plain that either quality had to improve or you lost the whole contract. You cannot achieve a satisfactory standard with your current methods, and you have been very difficult all along about trying out the new methods.

B: I must have another month, and I want Mr X put at my disposal to help with the new casting methods. Our sales people have been weak about this. The quality point should not have been accepted so easily from the customer – it is easy for them, they have not got to make the things.

AS: Strictly speaking, that is not your business. A has accepted sales' point that we must do better – it is your job to get on with it. You have got a new method which, on quite a large pilot-scale run, has worked very well. You have got time if you get cracking now. I will try and get the date put forward, but I cannot promise. You know it is almost impossible to release X to help you. Now are you going to get on with it or do you want to raise the whole issue again with A? I must know. . . .

and so on. Such a conversation could not easily take place between a manager and his subordinates, because B would not feel free to be so frank; he has got to think of his long-term career. If a clearly structured staff relationship does not exist, B will quite probably make these remarks to some colleague who can do nothing constructive about them and will merely feel uncomfortable. But when B makes such frank comment to AS, the latter can use these comments. After such a conversation, he is completely in role in going to A and saying:

'There is trouble over the plan on contract Y. B is really worried and not getting on too well. I suggest we get sales to do their utmost to get more time from the customer, before we are committed to the change of quality. I have seen our development people, and although X cannot be released entirely, he can spend a good deal of time helping B to get the new casting technique going. Do you agree that I fix it?'

A pitfall for managers which must be avoided

The relationship I have just described puts B in a position where he may receive instructions from his boss and any one of three staff officers. This makes it essential that the A–B relationship is clearly and unequivocally a manager–subordinate one. Any weakness or abdication on the part of A will cause trouble. B will begin to feel that his real boss is AS_1, AS_2, or AS_3, not A. This, in turn, stresses how essential it is for A to make his policy clear personally to B and to give B the opportunity to comment on it, or to object before it is implemented. If A allows a position to grow up where his staff officers are promulgating his policy to his own subordinates, then he is abdicating his own role.

When we first considered setting up these staff officer roles, I, and I think others, felt anxious lest their staff authority should be resented by the managers who were subject to it, and lest some of the staff officers should perhaps be inclined to be officious. This anxiety, on the whole, proved to be unfounded. The opposite, in fact, was true. Many specialists finding themselves, for the first time, in a role with clear-cut staff authority refused to use it. They preferred tact and persuasion, which I was prepared to tolerate provided it did not take too long. But it was not at all acceptable if it involved delay. I had many conversations of this type at the time:

AS: I am worried. We are now doing quite an excessive amount of overtime in many parts of the company. It is costing the earth, scrap is rising, and I put the current high sick-absence figure partially down to the fact that there are some people who are regularly trying to work ridiculous hours. We must take on some more people instead of coping with the load by overtime. I think you should raise the matter again most sharply at your next meeting.

A: I did at the last meeting. I instructed managers to cut overtime by taking on more people where required. There is a minute on the subject.

AS: Well, it is not happening, and I thought you ought to be aware of it.

A: Do you mean that my managers are refusing to act?

AS: No, of course not, but they are not getting on with it.

A: Well, make them, give instructions, use your authority. You are trying to get me to do your job for you. You are a staff officer responsible for seeing that my policy goes, get cracking, your authority is clear. If they are in real difficulties, find out and let me know, but otherwise see that they get on with it quickly.

Attachment of specialists

Even before the analysis of organization which enabled us to develop our current conception of staff specialist roles, it had been observed that if A and his subordinate manager B both had in their respective immediate commands engineers (AS and BS) who assisted them with production techniques, then the following pattern would often emerge:

(a) If manager B's engineer left the company, he would not appoint another engineer without consulting AS.

(b) If B was worried about the performance of BS, he would very often discuss BS with AS.

(c) If AS had some new ideas about technical matters he would, with the agreement of B, see BS and explain these ideas to him.

(d) If B was puzzled about production methods and could not get elucidation from BS he might ask BS to see AS and find out more about the subject, etc.

In other words, there was an observable and important relationship between AS and BS which, however, lacked a coherent and explicit structure. Such lack of structure leaves the relationship an informal one, and this results in inconsistent use of it. B might, for instance, at times appoint an engineer BS, without reference to AS. This would seem wrong to both A and AS; but B could not be criticized, for he was not explicitly held responsible for consulting AS about the type of person required for the role BS. The same comments apply, of course, to the relationship of BS to CS.

One of the consequences of this situation was to bring into being organization of the type where BS and CS became direct subordinates of AS; though this results, as already described, in an unstructured relationship of BS and CS to managers B and C. The requisite needs of the work situation are met, however, by the notion of attachment which is defined in the Policy Document as follows:

Attachment. Managerial authority and accountability with regard to attached specialists shall be shared between the operational co-manager and the specialist co-manager in the following manner (DD.3):

The two co-managers shall be jointly accountable for the selection of the attached specialist and for his merit assessment (DD.3.1).

Only the operational co-manager shall assign operational responsibilities to attached specialists, and he shall be accountable for:

(*a*) informing the specialist co-manager of any major changes he introduces in the operational use of the attached specialist;

(*b*) the type of responsibility he assigns; and

(*c*) the discipline of the attached specialist in the discharge of these responsibilities (DD.3.2).

The specialist co-manager shall set the terms of reference governing the techniques which an attached specialist uses in the discharge of his responsibilities, and he shall be accountable for:

(*a*) informing the operational co-manager of any major changes which he makes in the technical terms of reference which he sets;

(*b*) ensuring that his specialist subordinates are technically equipped to carry out the requirements of the roles which they occupy; and

(*c*) the technical discipline of specialist subordinates (DD.3.3).

Such a policy appears to me not only inevitable but to have been in practice, in a hidden way, in our company for as long as we have had specialists to assist us.

B is a manager. He wants, say, engineering specialist assistance. AS is the chief production engineer of the company. B's own engineering is the sort acquired by practical work in engineering shops for many years, but he has never had much theoretical background. Would he, in any circumstances, appoint without any reference to AS? A must keep some grip

on such an appointment, but will A personally interest himself
if he has AS, an engineering specialist, as his own staff officer?

When it comes to a question of assessing BS, can AS's
opinion be left out? If BS needs training, who is to give it? B?
No, surely, AS. If BS proves unsuitable for the job in B's command, that does not mean he may not be suitable in some other
post. Who should consider this? AS surely. Finally, in the matter of assessment of BS's work, B himself can, as a manager, do
much of this; but the technical component of BS's performance
may be something that B cannot assess. (My experience of this
situation is that where a manager has difficulty in assessing the
technical component of a subordinate's job, because he is himself unfamiliar with the technical field, then almost invariably
he overrates the work of that subordinate.)

Looped instructions from AS to BS

AS is thus responsible for BS to the extent of helping to select
him, educate him, keep him informed of changing technical
policy; he also is responsible for helping B to assess his progress and merit, and for playing a co-managerial part in his
promotion or demotion should the occasion arise. But AS does
not give task instructions or orders to BS. Experience shows
that communication of a particular kind between AS and BS
does develop in some parts of the company but not in others.
For example:

AS TO B: Re the four boring machines you have on hand, I must
also remind you that A has decided that, whether or not you
specifically require gauging equipment on the machines for
your own use, they are in any case to have it, so that the
machines will be interchangeable in future.
B: What gauging equipment?
AS: According to specification already issued.
B: Look, will you see BS? I do not want to handle it personally.
Tell him what to do and to get on with it.

A manager will, on occasions, generalize this request to a
staff officer by saying: 'In future, AS, will you contact BS on
all issues of this kind, sending me a copy of any written note to
keep me in the picture, and let me know personally if anything

unusually important arises in this area.' This mechanism, whereby B allows AS, on specific issues, to give instructions to BS, is depicted in Figure 24. We refer to the instructions so given as 'looped instructions'. B can withdraw his permission at will.

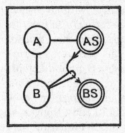

FIGURE 24

The specialist division

The mechanism of attachment links all specialist roles of a particular type together, and we refer to this linked system as a 'Specialist Division'. The specialist division is an organizational form which has to be capable of providing specialist technical assistance to any operational role where it is required.

The emerging divisions in our company provide great hope for the future. I say *emerging*, because I do not think that they are fully grown yet. It takes time to knit all the specialist roles of a particular phase in the company into a division with a feeling of corporate existence and a shared body of technical knowledge relevant to the problems of the company. It will require, I think more mobility on the part of our divisional managers in getting around the company, holding technical conferences, reviewing the job being done by members of their division, organizing training, and so on. Only then can we hope to reap the full fruits of this idea. It is important that our three divisions (personnel, technical and programming) become the sort of organization within which technical interchange and communication can take place with ease and rapidity.

For years I have watched with dismay the repeated spectacle

of a technical problem being solved in one part of the company, followed by a complete inability to transfer that solution to another part of the company where an apparently similar problem exists. I have seen machines designed, built, tested, and working with efficiency in the factory where they were built, apparently quite unable to perform the identical operation in another factory without major modification. Well-thought-out labour-saving routines for administration of stores, wages, production control will work in one part of the company; but, in other parts, to perform almost identical work it is necessary to employ quite different techniques involving more expense and, very often, with worse results.

I know that these are the ordinary problems that plague any managing director. But I know from experience that the growth of camaraderie within divisions and the sense of carrying out a combined technical operation could help such problems.

Figure 25 depicts diagrammatically the technical channel of communication of one division. These channels are quite distinct from, and an addition to, operational manager-subordinate channels. They are needed – in these times of rapid

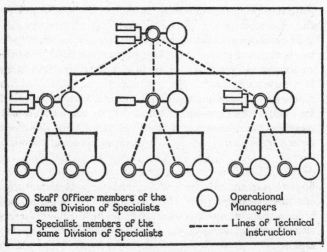

FIGURE 25

technical change – to alleviate the pressure of traffic of communication of instructions, policy, etc., that builds up in the operational lines of communication.

The work of the three specialist divisions

I will now state as briefly as possible the requisite work of the personnel, technical and programming divisions in terms of the specific responsibilities of the divisional manager in each case. It is not possible, without going into immense detail, to set out the responsibilities of each division in depth, for this would entail, for instance in the case of the technical division, describing not only the work of the technical divisional manager, but of his immediate subordinates, of his co-subordinates at factory level, of unit engineers attached at unit level, and so on.

It should be borne in mind, when reading these three staff officer job specifications, that the work of a group of staff officers around one manager interacts on every issue that arises. Thus, a technical staff officer, who is considering improved methods of producing a particular product, must know and take into account the programme of production of that product (Pr), and the organizational arrangements which exist to get that product made (P); likewise, a P staff officer can only consider the organization and man power required to do a job in the light of the programme of work to be done (Pr), and the techniques which will be used (T). In detailing the tasks of my own three staff officers, I have made very little reference to this continuous interaction, because it would have to be stated with reference to every point of their responsibility; but it is, however, to be understood as the background to the whole description of each job given in the passages which follow.

Programming divisional manager's responsibility

In general terms, he is responsible for working out and presenting to the managing director, the timing, quantification and balancing of that pattern of product development, manufacture and sale, which he considers will make an optimum contribution to the managing director's general plan of operations. In order to discharge this general responsibility he will constantly require to advise the managing director on the following matters:

(*a*) He will continuously need to take account of at least four main sets of interconnected variables and base his advice on his observations. These variables are as follows:

(i) *The company's target of manufacturing activity.*
He must, from this statement of activity, derive the product development and selling programmes which he considers necessary to maintain manufacturing activity at an optimum economic level.

(ii) *The company's target of financial recovery from the market.*
He must work out policies on product mix and sales prices which, within the terms of target manufacturing activity, will maximize profitability.

(iii) *The company's target on minimum investment.*
He must continuously advise the managing director on the changing policies required to minimize the level of stocks, investments in plant, buildings, raw materials, work in progress, finished goods, etc., in a manner consistent with targets on manufacturing activity and financial recovery.

(iv) *Company continuity of business into the future.*
He must continuously advise the managing director of those levels of production capacity, financial recovery from the market and stock levels which will best safeguard the future, and allow the continuation of a profitable programme of future operations.

(*b*) In brief, the programming divisional manager is responsible for advising the managing director how to achieve an optimally balanced level of activities, comprising such mixture of work as will keep the company's manufacturing capacity continuously loaded at a level at which optimum financial recovery can be obtained, optimum stocks held and optimum continuity of business achieved.

(*c*) Programming divisional manager is responsible for using techniques by which the balance of operations is controlled, namely:

Operations research which is concerned with the modelling of multiple factor situations, predicting the effects of altering controllable factors and indicating those changes most likely to result in the optimum.

Routines control which is concerned with designing, refining, altering and simplifying the routines which control:

(i) the flow of inquiries, orders, materials, work in progress, finished goods, etc., from outside the company, through it, and out again;

(ii) the flow of data, analyses, etc., from the financial division to managers;

(iii) any other subsidiary activities concerned with service-providing, purchasing, sub-contracting, etc.

(*d*) The programming divisional manager is responsible for coordinating the balancing, timing, mix and quantity of work done by the managing director's subordinates in the execution of his programme of work, and for controlling, by means of attachment, the programming division of the company.

Responsibilities of the technical divisional manager

In the most general terms, he is responsible for working out, and for presenting to the managing director, those policies for the development, modification and exploitation of manufacturing techniques which, in the light of the company's product development, manufacturing and selling operations, will make an optimum contribution to the managing director's total plan of operations. These responsibilities will involve the technical divisional manager in constantly advising the managing director on the following matters:

(*a*) The production methods required to optimize volume of output and minimize cost, at given standards of quality, accuracy, finish, etc.

(*b*) The manner in which available capital resources shall be spent in order to optimize production techniques.

(*c*) The specification of materials most suited to given techniques to optimize volume and minimize cost of output at given standards of quality.

(*d*) The production techniques in which members of the

company have to be trained in order that optimum output at minimal cost may be achieved.

(*e*) The desirability of developing one new technique as against another in the light of economic results which will be obtained.

(*f*) The optimum standards of quality, accuracy, finish, etc., which are attainable with a given level of equipment and organization. The techniques and equipment required if standards of quality are to be raised.

(*g*) The range of products which are capable of being manufactured with the equipment and resources available in the company, and what further techniques or equipment are needed to produce new products when they are required.

(*h*) The technical divisional manager is also responsible for coordinating the managing director's subordinates in the execution of his production technique policy and for controlling, by means of attachment, the technical division of the company.

Responsibilities of the personnel divisional manager

In general terms, he is responsible for advising the managing director on those policies for the structuring, manning and operation of the executive organization of the company which, in the light of its product development, manufacturing and selling activities, will make an optimum contribution to the managing director's total plan of operations. In order to discharge this general responsibility, he will continuously require to advise the managing director on the following matters:

(*a*) The appropriateness of the current organization and its manning as a means of helping to achieve the current planned programme of activity.

(*b*) Recommendations for organizational change which constantly endeavour to align the structure of the executive system to the requisite requirements of a changing company workload and forward planning.

(*c*) Policies for the manning of roles in the executive system which take account not only of current, but also of future requirements.

The foregoing responsibilities require:

(1) analysis of work content and the level of work in roles;

(2) development of systematic payment techniques which take account of level of work in roles and the developing capacity of individuals;

(3) constant review of techniques for recruitment, selection, training and progression of people that will lead to optimum filling of roles;

(4) planning for future manpower needs by maintaining a continuous scrutiny of the personnel employed, and by consideration of availability of people from external sources;

(5) arranging for a constant feed-back of information (through such institutions as assessment boards) on the effectiveness of:

  (i) current organization,

  (ii) allocation of work between roles,

  (iii) performance of individuals in roles.

(*d*) Changes in personnel policy made necessary by changing programmes of work, changing production techniques, legal requirements, etc.

(*e*) Changes required to conditions of work arising out of national agreements and contact with managers, representatives, trade union officers, etc. This will involve assisting the managing director to take part in works council discussions, implementing new policy arising out of such discussions, keeping written company policy up to date, drafting new standing orders, etc.

(*f*) Following up personnel policies including welfare policies which the managing director sets for general managers, discussing difficulties as they arise, reporting back to the managing director if necessary, and coordinating and progressing the implementation of these policies.

(*g*) Attaching personnel specialists to managers as specified, for maintaining the necessary flow of technical instructions to these specialists, for assessing their technical effectiveness and for ensuring that the personnel division, as a whole, maintains a clear perspective of its specialist duties.

Accounting in relation to specialist work

At one stage we ran into great difficulty over the sorting out of the role of specialists in our company. This centred on the lack of clarity about the role of the accountant and the resultant confusion of this role with that of what we now call the programming divisional manager, but who at that time was called the commercial divisional manager.

It is easy to assume that because chief accountants are concerned so much with money matters they are, in fact, the specialist custodians of the economy of the company. I believe that there is, in fact, a good deal of confusion of this kind generally in industry. This confusion over the role of chief accountants is, I think, one of the reasons for difficulty in analysing the work of specialists in an executive system. As long as accountants are seen as the people responsible for advising managers on economic and commercial matters, it will be difficult to see the role of specialists in realistic terms.

The chief accountant's function is intimately connected with that of secretary to the board. This combined role has very special responsibilities set out in the Companies Act. It puts the secretary in a position where he must report on the activities of the managing director and his subordinates to the board, and even to the shareholders in certain circumstances. He also has special responsibilities laid upon him by law with regard to income tax: reports to Somerset House, and so forth. These indicate that the secretary–chief-accountant role lies, in one sense, outside the executive system proper, since it consists of a financial inspectorate which reports in financial terms on the results achieved in the executive system to the board of directors and others. In order to carry out this role, accountants have been required to grow a hierarchy of their own, extending downwards parallel with the executive system. This hierarchy has, in course of time, also taken on such tasks as paying wages, keeping records, analysis of costs. The result is that today it carries not only its inspecting and financial-reporting function, but is a complete data-processing service to the executive system. It reports to managers (usually in terms of finance) the result of their activities. Costing systems are, in fact, mechanisms for analysing and classifying the quantified result of managers' actions in terms of money results.

Accountants do not, in our experience, advise their managers on commercial matters; for example, whether to invest available finance in more plant, bigger stocks, new buildings; what prices to charge the market for different products; whether the buying policy is sound; or how best to ensure the most economic use of the company's resources. Accountants, in general, have never been put in a position where they would be able to advise on and take decisions about such questions; although there used to be, in our company at any rate, a tacit assumption that they were responsible for many of these decisions.

Programming work is concerned with working out the timing, balancing and quantification pattern of product development, manufacture and selling which contributes in an optimum manner to the achievement of the chief executive's plan of operations. In the absence of a specialist role specifically set up to do such work, it gravitates by default into the accounting sphere. It is thus that we arrive at a situation where it is almost customary for cost-accounting departments to set up the budgets of activity, take decisions about the proration of overhead expense between the different production units of the company and generally, in a superficial way, to do that part of programming work associated with production. (I use the term superficial not as a criticism of cost accountants but as a description of the only way in which it is possible for them to do such work.)

Cost accounting is, in the main, concerned with production work. It is highly unusual, for instance, to find such people attached to or working within the product development or selling sectors of a company. They are normally based on manufacturing organizations and are not in a situation where they can budget an optimum pattern of development, manufacture and sale, because they are not in touch with product development or selling. Because they appear to be carrying out budgeting activities, the programming of sales and product development activities tend to get left uncoordinated with each other and with manufacturing. The result is that coordinated planning of activity simply does not get done.

It is for these sorts of reasons, and many others which I shall not attempt to discuss, that it is very important that accounting work should be as sharply differentiated as possible from Pr,

T and P. The functions of our financial division are concerned with auditing the entire operations of the company on behalf of the board, keeping the executive system within the law, and providing a wide range of services to the executive system, such as paying wages, keeping personnel records, analysing and processing data, recording and reporting credit given. These are extremely important and necessary functions; but such work, in spite of its consistent association with money terms, is not concerned with the economic direction of the company's activities.

PART FIVE

THE GAP AT THE
BOTTOM OF
THE EXECUTIVE SYSTEM

CHAPTER 14

THE SUPERVISOR

WE all know that, ultimately, the entire executive system depends for its effectiveness on the coordination that exists at the bottom where, in fact, the actual work of developing, testing, making and dispatching, etc., goes on. That is why we are so continuously preoccupied with the question of supervisors. Their job is inextricably bound up with the relationships that exist at the bottom of the executive system. The history of our attempts to study this question is important to the solution of the remaining problems.

Historical review of our thinking about supervisors

Up to 1944 we had a large number of roles in our production shops and offices, variously entitled charge-hand, leading hand, setter, supervisor, assistant foreman. What was clear, even at that time, was that there was little consistency between the job title and the job done. Thus, for example, some setters were clearly managers and some supervisors were supervising nobody.

In an attempt to simplify a very complex situation, we abolished the terms charge-hand, leading hand, supervisor and setter. We subdivided our production shops into small machine sections, and placed a section supervisor in 'full managerial command' of each. (We had not, at that stage, defined the managerial role, and the real meaning of 'full managerial command' was, therefore, obscure.) This role also carried the responsibility for doing any machine-setting required, and for supervising closely the work of any operator where this was necessary. The sections were quite small, ranging from about six operators to a maximum of fifteen.

A group of from three to seven sections was under the charge either of an assistant foreman, in the case of a department with a superintendent in charge; or a foreman, where there was no superintendent in the department. Thus, in theory, operators were responsible to their managers, the section supervisors; and *on paper* the section supervisors had the job of selecting, disciplining, assessing and, if necessary, discharging operators. There is little doubt that these section supervisors had sanction from 'high up' to take command.

This step was taken because, at that time, the turnover of supervisors, charge-hands, etc., was very high, due to the call-up to the armed forces. New appointments were having to be made all the time. We were also facing the post-war situation, and were beginning to concern ourselves about reinstatement of people who had been called up. The need for more job clarity was obvious. But these manifestations, though they existed, were superficial compared to the underlying reasons that concerned me and others. The fact was that, after five years' experience of running an engineering company during a war, I had come to realize that managers were not in command of events. Some of the more obvious indices to me of the extent to which a situation is, or is not, under control in a factory is the discipline at stopping and starting time, tidiness and care of machinery. (While these are not necessarily the most important in their effect, they are the most obvious to higher management.) I found that carefully thought-out orders and instructions on these questions had no effect. You could be in the shops at twenty minutes before stopping time and see men closing down work. If you got hold of the foreman and told him to stop that happening, he would blame his charge-hand or setter. They would blame it on the men, or on general indiscipline in the country, or on anything they could think up. Apparently, nobody was really prepared to take command and to give instructions. Some managers argued that it was not necessary; for the wages office 'fined' a man on the basis of his clockings if he was late, and the piece-work system 'fined' him if he did not work hard enough. There were all sorts of ideas around at that time for special bonuses and enticements of one sort and another to get men to do the job which was part of their contract, and which should have been the subject of straight instruction. We continued to suffer such problems as:

(*a*) Unresolved production difficulties arising from tooling which, while it appeared correct to an engineer, would not produce efficiently in the hands of operators. And yet, the matter was never taken up executively as between the operator and his manager. It appeared as a 'grievance' to be ventilated by a representative. There were so many issues of this kind – where straight problems which operators should have raised with their supervisors or foremen came up instead as part of a fabric of complaint in the representative system – that it gave grounds for assumptions that there was very real difficulty in communicating across the operator–manager gap.

(*b*) Large numbers of complaints about individual rates of pay, pay brackets for jobs, etc., floated around year after year without our being able to get the facts and work out solutions. As soon as we tried to grapple with the problem it faded out only to appear in another form later. I remember one situation – where lines making flanged bearings made very low bonuses, while lines making plain bearings made very high bonuses – and all the consequent jealousy between the various teams. This situation, in three swings of the pendulum over as many years, completely reversed itself; the low bonus type of work became high bonus, and vice versa. This seemed to occur without change in piece-work prices or methods, and constituted one of the type of nebulous problems which defied solution.

(*c*) There were disciplinary problems that seemed to arise out of uncertainty about responsibility and authority; this situation led to lost work, scrapped work, damage to tools and damage to plant. At higher level we could see things happening in the shops which were wrong; but in spite of orders given, even though accompanied by threats, these things continued in a manner suggesting organizational unclarity rather than original sin.

The 1944 changes helped a little with the appointment and reinstatement problems. We were at least able to talk about the jobs we were manning with more clarity than had been the case. Despite the changes, we were still unable to get the facts at shop floor level, and to get instructions carried out. The real nature of the cause of our problems began to come to light after the Tavistock team started working with us.

Many of the section supervisors were not managers. They had small but continually changing commands. They could not assess their 'subordinates' at rate reviews, because, during the period of time covered, these operators had their time divided up between half a dozen section supervisors. They could not do much planning of their section because they were too busy trouble-shooting and setting; operators were posted to their sections or sent elsewhere by the foreman, and those operators looked on the foreman as their manager, even though they had to approach him through the section supervisor. The foremen themselves were often not in a full managerial role and were uncertain about their authority. It was difficult for anybody in close touch with the production force to issue clear instructions.

Split at the bottom of the executive chain

The Tavistock team began to dig into this subject. It came up with a general idea of what is still called 'the split at the bottom of the executive system'. They were impressed with the confusion surrounding the role of section supervisor, and the failure of the company to sort it out.

In 1950 they reported deep-seated resistance both in management and hourly rated workers to interference with this split, and suggested that the split itself was a reflection of the current culture in industry in general. Managers were afraid that free communication of problems through executive channels would interfere with their ability to carry on with their own jobs, and that it was better to leave things as they were; workers found it an advantage to have a management which remained split off, because it gave them a scapegoat upon which to vent hostile feelings, and as long as these feelings existed, it enabled them to avoid facing differences between each other. The creation of a coherent executive system at shop level meant giving up this subconscious collusion to keep matters as they were.

The team, however, noted a growing recognition on the part of all concerned: (a) that problems not tackled directly do not disappear but grow; (b) that difficulties in group relationships can be worked through if approached with a real wish to discover solutions; and (c) that because of the split in the executive system, higher management were out of contact with production and hourly rated workers, who, while on the job, were almost a leaderless group.

In 1953, Dr Jaques (who had led the Tavistock team and later became a consultant to the company on social issues), in reporting some of the findings of his research into organization, suggested that clarification of the role of section supervisor might go far to resolve the split at the bottom of the executive system. If this could be achieved it would mean a clear-cut line of command from the top to the bottom of the system. This would have two important effects: it would set up precise *managerial* accountability for morale and attitudes of operators, thus obviating the complaints of managers that shop stewards tended to usurp their function; and it would overcome the oft-stated complaint of shop stewards that they were forced, by the circumstances, to accept far too heavy responsibilities. Dr Jaques went on to point out:

(*a*) That the precise responsibility and authority of section supervisors was the most strongly felt and widely raised problem met in the analysis of company organization.

(*b*) That while the notion that the section supervisor was a manager with equivalent authority and responsibility was considered to be a kind of myth, the demand for clarification was not an attempt to gain authority to 'wield the big stick', but a straightforward anxiety on the part of section supervisors to find out just where they stood.

(*c*) That, in fact, the term section supervisor appeared to cover a variety of roles that differed greatly. Some had large sections, had setters to assist them, were able to requisition all supplies they required, take part in the selection of operators and could have them removed from their teams in extreme cases. Some had nearly full authority, but did not take part in selection, could not have operators removed from their teams, and referred matters of discipline to their superiors. Some considered themselves managerial assistants to the foreman and responsible merely for the quality and quantity of work done by their operators. Many section supervisors worked under conditions where the operators they controlled were frequently changing, so that they could do little other than control them while they were on the job.

(*d*) That, in short, the then current conception of section supervisor ranged all the way from what we today regard as a full managerial role to a role we now call machine-tool setter.

Supervision of work

The most troublesome aspect of the confused situation described in the analysis was the lack of clarity as to who was a manager. If the section supervisor was assumed to be a manager, whereas, extantly, the superintendent alone had the managerial authority, then we were in a position where the section supervisor was being given responsibility without authority – an obviously impossible situation. Consequent upon the greater insight obtained into the problem, we defined supervisors and their work in the following terms in our Policy Document:

A member who assists his manager by assigning appropriate work to those members of his manager's immediate command allocated to him, and seeing that this work gets done.

A supervisor shall apportion and assign work to those of his manager's subordinates allocated to him (E.5.1).

A supervisor shall judge whether his manager's subordinates are performing executively at a satisfactory level and conforming to general conduct requirements. When in his estimation they are not doing so, he shall inform them of this fact, and shall give them the necessary instructions to ensure that the required results are achieved (E.5.2).

A supervisor shall report to his manager his assessment of the quality of the work and conduct of his manager's subordinates, recommending advancement or discipline whenever he considers this to be appropriate (E.5.3).

Supervisors and section managers

Having defined supervisors and having by now also worked out a definition of the managerial role, we then set about the re-organization of the executive structure in the production shops. We abolished the titles section supervisor, assistant foreman, foreman and superintendent, because it was felt that these terms, even if used by the company within the confines of a precise definition, would still continue to carry along with them all the varied meanings which other companies in industry gave to them. We decided to use the terms Machine Tool Setter, Supervisor, Section Manager and Unit Manager.

It became clear, as soon as we started the task of deciding which of these roles previously titled 'section supervisor' were managerial roles and which were supervisor roles, that the definitions which we had set up were not completely adequate. We had to do our best, and although this reorganization has helped considerably, problems still remain.

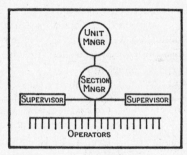

FIGURE 26

Figure 26 depicts the manifest situation today in the company. It is very doubtful if in all cases it is the extant situation. Evidence continually crops up to suggest that:

(*a*) Some supervisors are exercising practically the whole of the managerial function. Some section managers, for instance, rely on one or more of their supervisors to assess operators, and accept these assessments without themselves knowing their 'subordinates' in a proper managerial way. Such supervisors are carrying managerial responsibilities without managerial authority.

(*b*) Some supervisors apparently are confined to work which we regard either as part of the machine tool setter role or of the moveman role. They do very little real supervisory work in terms of our definition. Such supervisors are carrying supervisory authority without supervisory responsibility.

(*c*) Some section managers are not fully taking up their managerial role, with the result that operators come to regard unit managers as their real managers. Such section managers are thus carrying managerial authority without managerial responsibility.

It is clear to me that if one considers the nature of the managerial–subordinate relationships – as between, say, general managers and unit managers, or as between unit managers and section managers – they have a quality at these levels which is different from the relationship between most section managers and operators. The differences appear (perhaps superficially) to be of the following kind:

(*a*) Most managers talk of their subordinates in warm personal terms. They know their personal idiosyncrasies, their strong points and their weak points. They exhibit along with criticism a noticeable tolerance. In short, they have established a person-to-person relationship.

Such opportunities as I get to judge, suggest that relations between section managers and operators are different. The deep personal knowledge seems to be lacking. The relationship is a sort of bridge across a gulf in many cases. Neither party in the relationship seems, at this level, to understand each other as fully as is the case at higher levels.

(*b*) Subordinates of general or unit managers seem generally to respect their managers, and exhibit considerable tolerance where they feel there are some shortcomings. They are protective. Over the years I observed many instances of subordinates taking great trouble to cover up what they felt to be a poor decision by their manager.

At operator–section manager level, on the other hand, operators in some cases seem to get pleasure out of exposing a section manager's mistake. They do not give the impression of feeling that they are part of their manager's team. I do not suggest that subordinate–manager relations at the higher levels are perfect, or anything of the sort. But I do feel that were we able to establish at section manager–operator level the same sort of psychological relationship, we should make a most substantial contribution to reducing social friction and increasing work effectiveness.

My conclusion, therefore, is that in many cases a gap remains at the bottom of the executive system; that operators still do not feel they are clearly answerable to a manager to whom they have access, whom they know and who knows them, and who is constantly assessing them. The consequence of this is that authority and responsibility become dispersed between section managers, supervisors and shop stewards. More work needs to be done by our company on this important issue. We are certainly not alone in this problem. I find in discussion with managers in other companies that they have the feeling that the chain of authority and responsibility that extends downwards from the top breaks down at shop-floor level. As a visitor to other factories and offices I have frequently discerned the effects of this in terms of timekeeping, untidiness, inattention to work, and so on. There seems to be a remarkable lack of clarity about managerial authority at the lower levels in large sectors of British industry.

I am impressed, for instance, by the oft-repeated view that the purpose of Whitley Committees, Joint Consultative Committees and Representative Committees of all kinds, is to enable workers to make suggestions about work to management. This, indeed, was the basis upon which the Government itself launched its campaigns for joint consultation during the war. Workers have good ideas which must be tapped; workers know things which need correction; they must have channels through which such matters can be aired. All this thinking is subconsciously postulated on a belief in the existence of the 'split at the bottom of the executive system'. Why should peripatetic contact between high-level managers and representatives achieve so much that daily and hourly contact between operators and their managers cannot do – unless there is a barrier at that level? Why has the immediate manager got to be by-passed in this way? Why cannot this knowledge be tapped through the executive system?

Our inability to make more progress in overcoming this split throws a heavy burden on to the representative system. So long as operators feel difficulty about raising problems with managers, these executive matters find their way into the representative system. This means that we shall continue to get generalized complaints about pay (which may possibly arise out of the failure of the operator–manager relationship to agree about the pay of one individual only), or complaints about ventilation, tooling, etc. (which might readily be solved by an executive discussion), routed via the representatives; instead of being dealt with in terms of the first-hand experience of the individual affected. Such complaints gather an unwarranted emotional pressure behind them when routed in this way, and make for difficulty in solving them on a rational basis.

There is a strong tendency to blame representatives for this situation. But I think management must take the responsibility for getting a solution, by making changes in the social structure which will bring about a different manager–subordinate relationship at the bottom of the executive system.

Some emerging thoughts on the problem

Recent observations and discussion have thrown more light on to the nature of the role of the supervisor, and if these thoughts are correct, then our current definition of the supervisor is inadequate. The clearance of confusion about this role would, I am sure, help the problem of relationship on the shop floor.

In so far as supervisory work continues to be seen as the carrying out of duties which a manager would perform himself if he had no supervisors to assist him (and our definition biases one to look at supervisory work in this way), then it will be difficult for all concerned to distinguish the boundaries of supervising and managerial roles. The great need is to be able to make statements about the unique component of the supervisor's role, and thus be in a position to distinguish it sharply from the managerial role; recent analysis points the way.

The clue lies in the fact that the role of supervisor exists only on the shop floor, where production work is going on.[1] The entire economy of the factory rests on that production work; thus, if a single operator stops work, a part of the cost of plant, buildings, services and the entire organization of the company ceases to be recovered from the market; for all expense is re-

1. I know that the term 'supervisor' is used in other parts of the company also; but I think that analysis would show that these non-production supervisor roles have quite different work content from those in the production departments, i.e., one word for two quite different roles.

covered by including a portion of it in each item of production which is sold. Everybody knows this, either explicitly or intuitively, and we all know that to stop a machine or a production line working, by withdrawing an operator from it, creates loss.

If production stopped every time I held an immediate command meeting or met a general manager in my office, then we should have an enormous problem to face – which we might conceivably solve by having two men in each general manager role: one who would leave his work to sort out troubles or meet his superior, and one who would continue on the job and keep production running. Fortunately, this situation does not arise, but *it does arise on the floor of the production shop*. An operator who requires to take away turnings from his machine, to move work to it or away from it, to obtain special tools, to get a drawing, to take up a quality query with an inspector, or to go and arrange a repair to his machine, etc., *may* have to stop his machine in order to do so. I say 'may', because if he is on the type of machine where once he has got the cut started there is nothing to do for the next ten minutes, he may be able to do at least some of these things.

This idea can be posed in a different way. Mental work goes on wherever the person who is responsible for that work is. A manager's responsibility is to think; he does much of this work at his desk, but his work does not stop when he leaves his desk. We are not anxious about 'percentage desk utilization'! Manual production work is concerned with keeping a machine running, and the machine stops when the operator leaves it. We are, indeed, anxious about 'percentage machine utilization'!

Because an operator cannot leave his machine, a series of roles designed to allow him to remain at his machine are forced into existence. Auxiliaries to handle swarf, turnings, cutting oil, etc.; movemen to bring work to machines and take it away; machine tool setters to make machines ready for the next job; and supervisors who:

(*a*) Find out what work is coming forward for each machine;

(*b*) Discover which work has priority to go on to a machine;

(*c*) Make certain that a specific type of work is within the capacity of a specific operator, or within the capacity of that operator's machine;

(*d*) Arrange a study of a particular job to improve output or quality;

(*e*) Organize running repairs to a machine;

(*f*) Improvise methods of production to overcome *ad hoc* difficulties;

(*g*) Discuss quality and finish with the inspector when difficulties arise;

(*h*) Check up availability of tools for the next job.

Thus, the essential basis of the supervisor's work arises from the need to have somebody available to do that component of the production job which the machine operator is unable to do without stopping his machine.

It is notable that many craftsmen, particularly those working the heavier and slower types of plant, carry out the *mental* activities listed under (*a*) to (*h*) above themselves, but when they do so their manager has not got supervisors to help them with this work. Operators do only that mental work which is capable of being done on the machine – the other mental work involving contact with other people must be done for them if machines are to be kept running.

The term supervisor is a most unfortunate one. Its Latin foundation *super videre* means to overlook, and as I now see it, so-called supervisor jobs are not uniquely concerned with overlooking. Every managerial job has a component of overlooking; but the use of the term supervisor biases us towards the thought that people with this title do the overlooking for managers, who are thus spared to do other things! The supervisor is essentially an 'off-the-machine direct producer of the product'.

Once this discrete role has been pushed into existence by the nature of production work, further work, which would otherwise have to be done by a section manager, gets added to its responsibilities as a means of releasing the manager from the more detailed components of his work, and enabling him both to handle a larger command and to do more forward-planning work. This further work, which is often added to a supervisor's role, is concerned with:

(*i*) Assigning work and seeing that it gets done;

(*j*) Apportioning work between operators;

(*k*) Judging whether operators are performing at a satisfactory level and conforming to general policies or conduct;

(*l*) Reporting to his manager his assessment of performance, and recommending advancement or criticism when he considers this appropriate;

(*m*) Training operators on the job.

According to this analysis, a supervisor's job thus has two components. The first is the unique component, and is characterized by the type of work described in (*a*) to (*h*) on pp. 207-8. This is the 'machine stopping' component of the operator's job. The second, (*i*) to (*m*) listed above, is the component which a manager would do himself if the supervisor role did not exist. Such a description of the supervisor's job does two things: it corrects the false bias given to thinking by the unfortunate term 'supervisor';[1] and it differentiates quite sharply the supervisor role from that of the section manager.

The second point arising from this analysis is that, just as the operator cannot leave his machine to do mental work, so he and his manager have great difficulty in finding time to establish a relationship without stopping production. This, no doubt, seems an extraordinarily obvious conclusion at which to arrive – especially after so much study of the matter. The fact remains, however, that only recently has this thought obtruded itself as being a component of the problem. It could certainly seem to be an explanation of why so much of the relationship of operators to managers is substituted by a relationship between managers and shop stewards who, as representatives, can get permission to leave their machines.

The final point I wish to make on this subject is that until we can establish in the company a fully grown technical branch of

---

1. It is interesting to note what has happened in our Thin Walled Unit when, as a result of mechanization, many of the operator roles on a production line were rendered unnecessary. The 'supervisory' role was still essential. We initially regarded it as something different, because it was not associated with 'supervising operators', for there were none on a major part of the line. We, therefore, produced a new term, 'line technician'. I notice now, however, that this new term has disappeared and has been replaced with 'supervisor', in spite of the fact that those in these roles may not have any operators to supervise! Such is the pressure of convention in the use of words.

P specialists, who are able to focus attention on to problems such as I have discussed in this chapter, make analyses of the work being done, formulate recommendations for organizational change, and implement those changes when sanctioned, then problems such as the split at the bottom of the executive system, with all the social friction which they generate, will remain with us.

CHAPTER 15

SUMMARY OF RELATIONSHIPS

THROUGHOUT the previous chapters I have been discussing the working of the executive system. In fact, it seems possible to sum up much of what has been said in a brief definition of several role relationships and a definition of 'instruction'. This chapter, therefore, sets out in condensed form the different kinds of relationship which exist in the executive system.

Superior–subordinate relationship

This concerns the relationship of a manager to his subordinates. These subordinates' roles are of different types, as shown in Figures 27, 28 and 29.

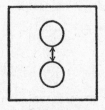

FIGURE 27
Operational manager
and managerial
subordinate

FIGURE 28
Operational manager
and non-managerial
subordinate

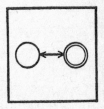

FIGURE 29
Operational manager
and staff officer
subordinate

In the relationship illustrated in Figure 29, the staff officer gives specialized advice to his manager and helps his manager in the implementation of his policies by the use of staff authority *vis-à-vis* his manager's operational subordinates. I know of no role in the company which allots a subordinate the responsibility of advising his manager only. Such an advisory role seems always, in our company, to carry staff authority also. Clearly, however, other roles which are purely advisory are also a possibility.

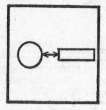

FIGURE 30

Manager and secretary,
supervisor, technical
assistant, etc.

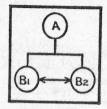

FIGURE 31

A collateral relationship arises when the
efficiency with which one person can
perform his job is dependent to some
extent on the manner in which a colleague performs his task and vice versa

Staff relationship

This arises when a manager has the assistance of a staff officer
in the coordination and control of the work of his operational
subordinates. In this relationship the staff officer gives orders

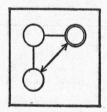

FIGURE 32

to his manager's operational subordinates, although he is not
their manager. These orders must be in implementation of, and
consistent with, the manager's policy. The staff officer carries
responsibility for ensuring that his manager's policy is applied,
or for proposing changes in policy to his manager. Because the
staff officer and the operational subordinates share the same
manager, they are of the same status and are, therefore, colleagues. This colleague relationship enables frank discussion
about their manager's policy to take place, which is helpful in
sorting out difficulties. Thus the staff officer is able to feed back
to his manager information about difficulties arising from the
policies which he sets.

Conjoint relationship

This exists when a manager has more than one staff officer. It is complex because it involves interaction between three roles, and ranges over the whole field of those roles. If a manager has

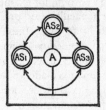

FIGURE 33

no specialists, he sorts out on his own any considerations that arise from the relationship between the P, T and Pr phases of his work. Where he has staff officers, responsibility for ensuring interaction must be carried by the staff officers AS_1 AS_2 and AS_3. In such a situation there is a paramount need for staff officers to be so placed that communication between them can occur easily and rapidly.

Attachment relationships

These are the relationships between staff officer BS and his co-managers B and AS. AS is responsible for seeing to it that the

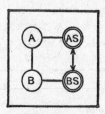

FIGURE 34

technical knowledge of BS is up to date; it could be described as an educational responsibility. AS and BS are, of course, members of the same division, but manager B is responsible for giving BS instructions. AS and B choose the candidate to fill the role BS, if it falls vacant. Both are responsible for assessing BS. In the event of disagreement between BS and either of his co-managers, the matter must be referred to A.

Service-giving relationship

This relationship arises when, for example, manager A decides to position a source of facilities or prescriptions in B_2's command, and instructs B_2 to make these available to specified members of his (A's) extended command, e.g., to B_1 and C. D is responsible for the quality of service provided, and for deciding the priorities of demands made upon him. B_1 is responsible for getting the service he considers necessary to discharge the work required of him by manager A.

In the event of disagreement between B_1 and D, B_1 must inform D that the service is insufficient, and must see his colleague B_2. If he is still dissatisfied, he must see his manager A to inform him that the services he is providing within his extended command are not adequate for the work he is delegating. If C disagrees with D, C must inform D that he is taking the matter up with his superior B.

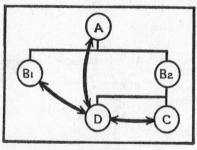

FIGURE 35

Supervisory relationship

This relationship arises when a section manager is provided with a supervisor to help him allocate work; to give technical assistance to his subordinates; and to control them at work. The supervisor is not in a managerial relationship with those whom he supervises; for he is not entirely responsible for assessing their performance, nor for their selection, promotion, etc. The relationship imposes on the supervisor responsibilities for exercising 'on the job' discipline, for making technical decisions, and for making recommendations about those of his subordinates whom he supervises.

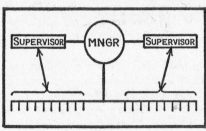

FIGURE 36

Instructions

The executive relationships so far described in this book are greatly concerned with the subject of giving and receiving instructions. In Chapter 2 I have given the definition of an instruction as we use it in the company, and have commented on it. A more detailed consideration, however, reveals that there are a number of categories of instruction which it is useful to separate, and I shall now go on to do this.

Policy and policy instructions. Policy,[1] as the term is used

---

1. The word 'policy' is defined in the Company Policy Document, as follows: 'Any statement adopted by a Council or laid down by a manager, or any established practice or custom, which specifies the behaviour required of members in given situations. It will be noted that policy so defined does not include the Definitive Policy which circumscribes the activities of the Board of Directors (i.e., the Memorandum and Articles of Association of the Company, Company Law or other legislation, and Stock Exchange Regulations)'. I think that this definition can be validly criticized on two counts – on the one hand, it can be seen that the attempt has been made to define policy largely by reference to its source, rather than to its inherent nature; and, on the other hand, the definition is, in any case, incorrect, since policy emanates also from the board of directors.

in this book, means the prescribed part of a role, or group of roles. This prescribed part of a role, or roles, sets out the physical, temporal, administrative or procedural limits, or targets, by which a role is bounded. This reference to boundaries should not be taken to imply that all policy is restrictive.

Aims and objects, too, are the subject of policy; and as well as such statements as, 'It is our policy to award grants only where the circumstances are so and so', there are also statements of policy like, 'We must promote the sales of such and such a product'.

A policy instruction is quite simply a communication from a manager to any or all of his subordinates, stating the policies which they must observe. It should be noted that policy statements define the boundaries within which a subordinate will be expected to exercise his own judgement, and the aims to which he must orient his decisions. So far as a subordinate has subordinated himself, then part of his discretion lies in what policy to set them.

Task and task instructions. A task is a specific job of work, and a task instruction a communication from a manager to a subordinate giving him that specific job of work to do. Task instructions may thus range from 'Post this letter' to 'Place the order for a million pounds' worth of new plant'. Such task instructions are always by definition given within a framework of policy already set.

Staff instructions. A staff instruction is an instruction given by a staff officer within his own manager's policy to any other of that manager's immediate subordinates. In giving such an instruction, a staff officer is implementing his manager's policy, which his manager should already have stated. If the staff officer's instructions lie outside his manager's stated policy, then they should not be given.

Technical instructions. This is the term used in the company to refer to instructions given by a staff officer to another staff officer attached by him to one of his manager's subordinates. Such technical instructions are confined to communicating the techniques which the subordinate staff officer is required to use when performing tasks for his own operational manager. It should be noted that, with one exception, a staff officer will give no other type of instruction to those specialists whom he attaches at lower levels. The only exception is where the manager of the lower-level specialist either asks, or agrees, that staff instructions which should be given to him (the manager) shall instead be communicated to his staff officer for implementation (looped instruction).

PART SIX

SOURCES OF MANAGERIAL AUTHORITY

CHAPTER 16

THE REPRESENTATIVE SYSTEM

ONE of the problems in writing this book has been the constant temptation to break into the discussion dealing with the executive system in order to describe its interaction with the representative and legislative systems. I resisted this temptation to avoid confusion. But by doing so I may have given the impression that the only constraint placed upon the decisions of managers is that set by their superior managers. This chapter and the next will explain why this is not so. The representative system is the social mechanism which makes it possible for a manager to negotiate with his whole extended command at one time. Without such an institution, negotiation, bargaining, compromise or agreement on innovations is often very difficult. The representative system is defined as follows in our Policy Document: 'Comprises constituents, elected representatives and elected committees, electoral units and constituencies.' This definition is by content rather than by function. It is the function and operation of the system that I propose to discuss next.

The inevitability of a representative system

I believe it is true to say that wherever an executive system exists, you will find operating within it, or alongside it, a representative system as well. The question is not 'Shall we have a representative system?' but rather 'Shall we recognize the existence of it or not?' This is capable of being misunderstood. In using the phrase 'recognize the existence of', I am not referring to the practice of agreeing to meet, say, shop stewards for discussion. What I am referring to is the recognition of the existence of a separate social system, with its own series of roles and role relationships.

Of the existence of this separate social system there can be no doubt. I have written about the executive system at length. Contrast the following Policy Document definitions with what we already know about our executive system, and the existence of a distinct representative system becomes clear:

Constituency: A body within an electoral unit whose members have the right to be represented by a common representative or representatives.

Elector: A member of a constituency who has the right to vote.

Representative role: Any role in the representative system which a member takes up by election and in which he acts on behalf of the constituency . . . which elected him.

True, there may be no explicit recognition of the existence of these social phenomena; but they exist nevertheless. In large parts of British industry there is no explicit recognition among managers and technicians of constituencies, electors and representatives. It is not common for foremen, senior managers, technicians, accountants, salesmen, explicitly to elect representatives or to form committees. The more frequent practice is for this to happen informally as required. If a managing director attempts to introduce change of a radical nature, which affects people at these levels, a 'deputation' will contact him. This deputation is a manifestation of the existence of a representative system. People with feelings about current issues in a company will get together and express those feelings; if their feelings are sufficiently strong, some spokesman will communicate their views to the appropriate manager.

Electing, representing and forming committees is not part of the responsibilities of any executive role. Nor is it part of the operational job of the company to do such things. These matters belong to a distinct social system.

The executive and representative systems contrasted

The relationships in such a system are quite different from those in the executive system. It is instructive to contrast them. When a person states an opinion in his executive role, it will be regarded as his own, and he will be held responsible for this opinion by his manager. If he makes precisely the same statement in a representative role, the viewpoint cannot be assumed to be his own. He will feel, and will be, responsible to his electors; for he is stating their views, and not necessarily his own.

A person can be discharged from his executive role by his manager. But the latter cannot tell a group of electors that they must elect somebody else to represent them because he is dismissing a representative. Only the electors can discharge a person from a representative role.

A manager can criticize or praise a person in an executive role for the way he performs his job. But he cannot criticize a representative for his performance, unless the latter goes outside the bounds of company policy. A manager who, for instance, criticizes a representative because he had left his work without permission is, in fact, criticizing him executively, and not for the way he does his representative job. If a group of people instruct their representative to leave his work in defiance of his executive work contract, a manager's criticism should be directed not only against the representative, but also against the group itself. All are open to criticism, or disciplinary action; but in their executive roles, not as electors or representatives.

If a manager learns from a representative that members of his command wish to pursue a course of action which he considers detrimental to the interests of his command or of the company, it is his duty to make sure that they have the facts of the situation correct, and if necessary, to persuade them to follow some other course of action. But he cannot *instruct* the representative to argue with, or persuade, his electors. The only courses open to the manager are either (*a*) to instruct his subordinate managers to see the members of their commands, or (*b*) to contract, and talk to them himself. If he meets them for this purpose, it is an executive meeting. The manager must keep this in the forefront of his mind; for any comment about representatives is out of order. For instance, he might say to his command: 'Your representatives want this or that, or have done this or that.' Such comment is out of order; for the information that has reached him is that his people, the members of his command, want this or that. Representatives are a channel of communication; reference to them personally is, therefore, not only factually incorrect, but will sound like a threat. If criticism or argument is required, it should be directed at its sources, i.e., those on behalf of whom the representatives speak.

When a representative communicates with a manager, there

is no individual name attached to that communication. The representative speaks on behalf of an unnamed person or persons. All that the manager knows is that this communication comes from the whole or part of his command. This anonymous property of all communications reaching managers from representatives is in contrast to the opposite feature of communications from the executive system – where the manager can insist on knowing the individual source of each message. He would not be able to do his executive job without this information. The representative, on the other hand, would be unable to do his job if he had to disclose the names of those expressing particular views.

These properties of the situations which we face almost daily in industry are, perhaps, a sufficient demonstration of the existence of a social system which has roles and relationships separately distinguishable from the executive system. Furthermore, such a system exists, whether we recognize it or not.

Some advantages of explicit recognition of representative systems

Much friction is caused in industry by behaviour that is not consistent with the inherent properties of the situation. This is nowhere more common than in a situation where managers and representatives are involved. There is so much ground for real conflict of ideas over such matters as pay, conditions and hours of work, that it seems a pity to add unnecessary disagreement; especially when it really arises from non-recognition of the role relationships that are requisitely part of any interaction between people in executive roles and people in representative roles. For example, a manager who asks representatives to meet him in order to criticize, through them, the conduct of his subordinates, will cause offence. This is so because, implicit in his comments, is the idea that it is the job of the representatives to go back to those who elected them, and to criticize their conduct. It is a manager's job to criticize subordinates, and it is certainly not a job for which a representative can be held responsible.

People, through their representative, often put great pressure on managers; sometimes accompanying it by veiled threats, in order to get arrangements that are inconsistent with the efficient conduct of the manager's task, e.g., no evening overtime, or objection to new production methods. When such demands are unrealistic, irritation on the part of the manager is only human; but if this irritation is vented on the representatives, they will naturally feel it is unfair to them. They may even themselves feel that the demands are unrealistic. The requisite properties of the situation demand that the 'irritation' should be vented on subordinates, not on those who speak these views.

Representatives who get 'out of role', and make personal criticism of managers, or make assumptions on situations about which they have no knowledge, cause unnecessary conflict. Many such conflicts can be avoided if representatives have insight into the real nature of a representative system. Just as conflict in the executive system so often tends to be seen in terms of personal shortcomings, when the cause may, in fact, be due to role confusion, so conflict between managers and representatives may often be due to lack of explicit recognition of the different behaviours required by the two systems.

We have in the company a highly developed representative system which embraces the formal election of representatives, even for the most senior staff. This is uncommon. At the time when such formal arrangements were explicitly set up, I think many senior staff felt them to be inappropriate. Time has, I believe, changed this view. Hourly rated workers and junior staff are not the only members of the company who have views and feelings which they prefer to voice through representatives.

In the absence of an explicit institution, more devious and less satisfactory representation of views takes place. Again, role confusion can easily enter the situation with unfortunate effects. I once attended a week-end conference at which were assembled the senior staff of another company. Certain subjects were discussed in a series of groups; each selected a 'rapporteur' (i.e., a representative) to report back to a plenary session. The managing director of the company was present at the plenary session, and took exception to the comments of one rapporteur. He defended himself by pointing out that he was representing the views of others, and that these were not necessarily shared by him. It was clear, however, that the managing director regarded this as a 'mere defence'. The affair created the most unfortunate atmosphere.

Once there is explicit recognition of the existence of a separate system, it becomes possible to work out some of the responsibilities attaching to the distinct roles within it. Our Policy Document has a complete section on this subject. The duties of representatives are defined as follows:

A representative is accountable to that constituent group or electoral unit which elects him; and it is his responsibility (F.4):

To make himself aware of the main interests of all in his constituency (F.4.1).

To represent the point of view of his constituents in committees and Councils, even where this may mean presenting a point of view contrary to his own personal opinion or his view in his executive role (F.4.2).

To allow Councils or committees to work with the greatest possible realism by judging when to state any views held by minorities within his constituency or committee (F.4.3).

To judge when reference to constituents is necessary, and when to accept responsibility for acting without such reference (F.4.4).

To initiate proposals for change which would be in the best interests of his constituents (F.4.5).

To take appropriate steps when in his judgement executive actions or the actions of his constituents are inconsistent with policy (F.4.6).

To assist his constituents to understand the executive implications of the agreements he has accepted on their behalf (F.4.7).

To familiarize himself with the Constitution and Standing Orders of those bodies of which he is a member and with established rules of procedure (F.4.8).

To know policy, and in particular to understand those aspects of policy which are of most immediate concern to his constituents (F.4.9).

To ensure, before taking up an appeal with and on behalf of a constituent, that the constituent has in the first instance taken the matter up with the manager concerned (F.4.10).

To act as adviser to any of his constituents in cases of appeal when requested to do so. (F.4.11).

Types of communication that take place through the representative system

The representative system communicates ideas and feelings

that may not otherwise travel up the executive system to the appropriate level, so that decisions can be made. The main functions of a representative system can be summed up as follows:[1]

(*a*) There are groups of people in an extended command who share common ideas without sharing a common immediate manager. It would be very difficult for them to communicate, except through representatives.

(*b*) Sometimes communication upwards in the executive system breaks down. I have already cited the gap at the bottom caused by unclarity about roles of supervisors and section managers. Other cases of non-communication through the executive system occur when the representative system acts as a sort of safety valve, and exposes important feelings which require discussion.

(*c*) Frank speaking is not always possible in the executive system; there are constraints upon it which are part of the manager–subordinate relationship. A subordinate, on occasions, feels that frank comment to his immediate superior is not possible. Unsupported by the views of others, it will, he is sure, be ignored. He knows that his manager is working within policies which disallow him from taking the desired action. He feels that to raise the matter in an executive relationship will irritate his manager and do him no good, and so on.

I remember lecturing to a group of senior industrial managers. In the discussion that followed, one manager was highly critical of 'industrial workers' in general, because so often they failed to speak frankly to their superior. This failure, he went on, led to imperfect communication, and many of our industrial ills could be attributed to this imperfection. He received a great deal of support from the audience. I asked each member of the audience to think of his own manager, and to make a mental frank assessment of that manager's more recent decisions and actions. After a short lapse, while they thought, I asked them whether they had already communicated, or

1. I am dealing with the representative system from an executive point of view. There are of course, other very important functions from the point of view of those who elect representatives: 'Unity in Strength'; protection of interests, and so on.

whether they were prepared to communicate, these frank thoughts to their manager. Loud laughter was the response.

(*d*) Discovery of the degree of sanction for change that exists is perhaps the most important function of representative systems, at any rate from the point of view of a manager. I shall discuss this aspect of the question at greater length in the chapter on the legislative system.

The effect on the representative system of faulty structuring in the executive system

A representative job is certainly one calling for understanding, for statesmanship and for tolerance. Long-term considerations have to be weighed against short-term ones. Interests of constituents have to be looked at in the light of trade-union policy, and of the reactions of management. If, however, there is lack of clear managerial authority and responsibility at shop-floor level – leading to a situation where constituents constantly have recourse to a representative to sort out what, in a different situation, should have been resolved in face-to-face discussion between an individual and his manager – the representative's job may become much more difficult than it should be.

Figure 37 indicates the work of such a representative in dis-

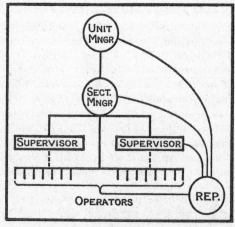

FIGURE 37

cussion with his constituents' supervisor, his manager, and his manager once removed. When there is unclarity about authority at the supervisor and section manager level, the representative will often have to seek to raise issues with the unit manager. Many of the issues will look very detailed and trivial to the unit manager, as indeed they are, when compared with the more normal responsibilities of a Rank 3 manager. It may thus very easily result in a unit manager feeling that a representative is being pernickety and trying to make trouble over small issues. The job of a representative becomes difficult in these circumstances; much of such work is really compensating for unresolved organizational difficulties in the executive system. But if this is not recognized by supervisors or section managers, hostility is bred; then the more settled personalities among operators will not take on such representative jobs. These will then tend to be filled by people who, to some extent, want to be able to retreat from work into the confused situation described where there is a good deal of hostility lying around.

Thus it is that unclear structuring of managerial roles, especially at the bottom of the executive system, leading to a failure to develop sound managerial–subordinate relationships, can impinge on the representative system and cause difficulties, hostility and irritations. We have not solved this problem of the 'gap at the bottom' of the executive system in all areas yet.

The results of breakdown of communication

The situation can arise in a factory that – perhaps because of lack of suitable people to accept the role of representatives, or because of faulty structuring of the executive system – communication about the real feelings of people breaks down. Most managers know what is likely to happen in such situations. A management devoid of a feed-back of representative or executive information can go ahead making changes, without realizing how much resentment is being built up, until, suddenly, it is faced with a strike or some other severely damaging reaction. Such a situation is represented diagrammatically in Figure 38.

The top graph represents a situation where the representative system is insensitive, and executive channels of information are blocked. Important feelings do not get communicated to a level where action can be taken. Pressure of feeling, built up over long periods of apparent quiet, bursts forth as depicted. The lower graph might be said to represent a situation where

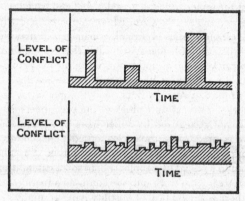

FIGURE 38. Extent of hatched areas intended to be about the same in each diagram

the representative system was formalized and sensitive; as a result, feelings were constantly being fed to appropriate levels of management, where they were receiving attention. In this latter situation, the manager might have the feeling that he was continually dealing with problems arising from the representative system; but while he could not get free of them, at least major conflict was avoided.

These two graphs represent the opposite ends of a continuum. It presents us with two choices. We can either have our trouble in large 'dollops' and, having dealt with it, settle down to apparent quiet for long periods, during which time the problems which will give rise to the next conflict are gradually building up underneath. Or else, we can set up mechanisms through which we are continually dealing with issues as they arise. Although the resultant feeling may be that we are in continual trouble, the fact is that we never really reach a stage of open hostility and breakdown. The latter situation is much to be preferred from an economic standpoint.

The Representative System

Should representative comment be accepted at its face value?

One hears managers commenting about the views put forward by representatives in the following terms. 'I know the people in my own extended command, and they are nothing like so concerned about this problem as their representatives suggest.' This comment raises important issues that require to be clearly understood. Obviously, representatives may not report accurately the views of those who elected them. They are just as capable of doing a poor job as anybody else. In any case, the difficulties of a representative in discovering the real views of his constituents are, at times, very great. Nevertheless, although a manager may have doubts about the accuracy of the reports made to him by representatives, it is essential that he should deal with such reports at their face value. If there is real inconsistency between his communications from the executive and from the representative systems, he may have to contract, and meet his extended command as a whole, in order to discuss with them their view as he understands it from their representatives. Such a meeting may prove helpful in enabling him to gauge the real situation more accurately.

I remember vividly a particular situation in one of our factories some years ago. A small group of representatives regularly reported in alarming terms the feelings of their large body of constituents on various issues. After a time, the managers concluded that these representatives consistently exaggerated the views of their constituents, and so tended to apply a sort of reduction factor to all that the representatives had to say. If the representatives said that strike action was imminent, managers assumed that there was some real anxiety among people. If representatives merely said people were worried, managers postponed any action and usually heard nothing more of the matter. The managers felt this was a realistic approach which avoided constant attention to phoney crises. I insisted, however, on managers taking the communications from these representatives literally. The result was that the constituents found themselves constantly faced by managers who wanted to discuss with them problems which they regarded as being very worrying. Soon people began to comment with frequency to their managers that they were 'fedup' with being called together to discuss problems that did not really exist. Managers responded by pointing out that if there was inconsistency between real feelings and representatives' reports to managers, that was a problem for electors and not for managers. Over a period there was some change in representatives, and the problem disappeared.

On the other hand I have, on many occasions over the years, not believed what representatives have conveyed as the view of their constituents, and instead relied on executive channel comments that their reports were exaggerated, e.g., 'The department is not really worried about the matter – it is only a few people who, for some obscure reason, are trying to stir up a fuss.' But I have found later that the representatives were right and the executive reports on the matter wrong.

Managers, in contrasting the different messages which reach them by these two channels, must bear in mind several important features of the situation:

(*a*) That human beings do exhibit ambivalent feelings. They both want and do not want certain courses to be followed. I take a very simple illustration by way of example. Manager Jones wants to change the hours of work in a department. The change will suit Smith personally, and if asked by manager Jones if he objects to the change, he will say no. But Smith agrees with the majority in the department that the change is very inconvenient for most people, and will be prepared to join with them in briefing their representative to voice their objections. In this sense, he *has* objections to the change. Ambivalent feelings can, of course, lie much deeper and be more complex than this.

(*b*) That the relationships which are structured into the executive system result in biases against completely frank speaking. It is a fact that subordinates do not always tell their managers exactly what they think; the properties of the subordinate manager relationship are such that this is frequently not possible.

(*c*) A representative's relationship to a manager is such that he can speak quite frankly; for, while he is speaking on behalf of other people, he is not that manager's subordinate. In addition, he is giving the communication in the name of a group, and it is, therefore, anonymous.

This is not to say that the reports from subordinates are always inaccurate and reports from representatives always factual. There is always human error and misunderstanding to be taken into account, and in addition there is the fact that electors' communication of views to representatives is not anonymous (except in the case of secret ballots), and there may, in this relationship too, be bias against free speaking; e.g., a man may feel one thing and say another, because he feels that the latter view is what is expected of a loyal trade-union member.

What I do want to make clear is that inconsistency in the content of communication reaching a manager from his subordinates, on the one hand, and from representatives, on the other, is quite natural, and it does not necessarily indicate a lack of integrity or even of inaccurate communication by any of the parties involved. This inconsistency, of course, makes the situation difficult for managers; *but if they act on the assumption that the communication which indicates the most anxiety or opposition in their extended command is correct, then they will rapidly establish the true facts of the position*; whereas if they act on the opposite assumption, they will increase the anxiety and opposition to a point where they will have to take account of it. Because the representative system has the more sensitive ear for anxiety and hostility, this will usually mean that a manager should act on the *assumption* that what is said by representatives about people's views is correct.

Managers must not rely on the representative system to report views and facts to their extended commands

A representative is responsible to those who elected him and one of his major responsibilities is to look after their interests. It is to be expected that he will construe anything that a manager says in the light of its possible effect on his constituents; anything said that he feels might, on close examination, contain a potential threat to their interests will be highlighted when he reports back; factual information that might tend to allay anxiety contains no threat, needs no careful thought, and will quite likely not be reported back at all. This is part of the culture of representative systems.

Managers must face the fact, therefore, that representatives listen to what they say, consider the new situation brought about by what they hear, and report their value judgements of that situation to their constituents. The expectation that representatives should give a *verbatim* report of what a manager says to their constituents seems to me to be quite unreal and inconsistent with the representative's role.

Managers cannot therefore instruct representatives to report particular opinions or facts to their electors; and therefore the representative system is not a means whereby managers can communicate with their own extended commands. This is not fully realized by many managers; consequently one quite often hears these managers complaining that 'what they have said has been distorted by representatives'. This reliance on the representative system by managers is requisitely inconsistent with their executive responsibilities. When a manager decides that it is necessary for his views to be understood in his extended command, he must communicate them through executive channels. In so doing he has choices open to him: he can instruct his subordinates to make known his views; he can distribute them in written form; he can meet his extended command in person. I want to comment on such meetings.

It takes considerable experience to be able to talk about problems in a frank manner with a large group of people. Nevertheless, I think the capacity to talk to a large group of people is one that must be acquired by any manager who aspires to high responsibility. It is the difficulty and anxiety felt by many people about 'talking in public', or 'speech-making', which often gives rise to the executive sin of trying to rely upon representatives to convey one's views back to one's own extended command. Managers must learn to overcome their diffidence about talking to groups.

I have often heard it suggested by representatives that for a manager to talk directly to his extended command was inappropriate. This view was based on the argument that the representatives were negotiating on behalf of their constituents, and that all communications should, therefore, be canalized through them. If a manager were in a situation where he could hold representatives responsible for the way in which his own views were communicated, and if he could take steps to remedy the situation where a faulty job was done, there might conceivably be cogency in such a request. But the essential features of a representative system make direct communication by a manager correct and essential in certain circumstances.

Within what framework are such communications to be made? 'Your representatives have told me that you feel this, and I doubt if that is accurate.' This approach is clearly wrong; for a manager has no way of making such an assessment. 'Your representatives feel so and so, and want such and such changes.' How can the manager know what representatives, as individuals, want, since they speak for others and do not necessarily speak their own minds? 'I want to persuade you to instruct your representatives to change their attitude.' This will not do, because, so far as a manager is concerned, representatives merely reflect the consensus of opinion of the people they represent. Relations between constituents and representatives are not the concern of a manager. The only comment he can make is: 'I understand that your views or wishes are as follows'; and then quote what representatives have told him. The manager's job is to convince his people, in their executive roles, of the soundness of any course he chooses; and to use all the mechanisms and relationships available to him for this purpose by communication through the executive system, e.g., displayed notice, broadcast, or face-to-face meeting.

The right of constituents to alter the structure of the representative system

I have come across situations where groups of people refuse to elect representatives; or refuse to allow their representatives to sit on committees with other representatives; or refuse to allow representatives to meet managers. They are perfectly within their rights in behaving in this way. I have never really known why such acts are taken. One has, of course, theories; but, essentially, the manager is denied real information on issues of this sort. I think that these acts are sometimes an attempt to 'discipline' managers by refusing cooperation. In so far as this is the case, it would seem that representatives are stepping out of role by taking such action. A manager's attitude to such manoeuvring must be a completely neutral one: 'It is not my business.' He is, of course, deprived of a mechanism through which he learns about feelings in his extended command. He may make mistakes because of this. But if his people have deliberately refused to convey their feelings by failing to elect representatives, they will also not be in a position to make solid criticism.

Sometimes, people may wish to elect representatives in ways which clash with precedent and which may be less convenient to managers. Suppose that Grade 1, 2 and 3 staff in our company decided that, instead of representatives being elected for each grade respectively, all the engineering staff, cost and accounts staff, production control staff, etc., in the factory, should elect their own representatives, thus replacing the present grade representative committees with functional committees. Such a representative structure would be very cumbersome; but managers cannot stop such moves. They are out of role if they try. They must, of course, express their opinions about any difficulties they can see arising from such changes. But they would be out of role if they made some such comment as, 'With the new type of representative structure people in my command will not be properly represented, and I will not know their true feelings.' The manager has no way of knowing whether this is true or not.

Pay and promotion of people who take on representative roles

Representatives are both inevitable and important to industry. They can become unpopular with managers, particularly where they are dealing with matters that should be dealt with in an executive relationship. A representative who is constantly, but properly, away from his executive job is simply not as valuable to a manager as he would otherwise be. Both these situations can result in the occupant of a representative role having his executive pay and promotion unfairly affected.

A major difficulty could be avoided if it were possible to plot a person's rate of advance of ability during the non-representative part of his career, and extrapolate this during the time when he is also in a representative role. If a man's pay and promotion are based on such a curve, unfair bias is excluded from the assessment of his executive work. Work on this problem is at the moment going on in the company. The earning level of a few representatives has already been looked at in this way. The approach seems a hopeful one. I feel that the more fully the potential unfairness of assessments of representatives is discussed and faced, the more objectively will the manager be able to view the position. The experience that many senior managers get in our company as elected representatives of Grade 1 or Grade 2 staff is, I suspect, useful in helping them to understand some of the difficulties of others filling representative roles. I recollect an occasion when a superintendent in one of our factories graphically described the conduct of a representative with whom he had had a recent discussion. He spoke of him in critical terms: that he was argumentative, lacking in reasonableness. A few days later I met a staff committee on which this superintendent himself sat as a representative. I thought at the time that the critical description he gave of the representative's behaviour fitted him very well, too. There is a similarity of conduct between people in representative roles, whatever their executive roles may be.

Retaining people in executive jobs because they are representatives

I think that sometimes people are retained in their executive jobs, although this is not warranted on the basis of their performance at work, because they also have a representative role. This may arise from the fact that, as already discussed, it is difficult for a manager to assess objectively a representative who, because he holds important committee office, is constantly away from his executive job. It may be obvious to many people close to the situation that a particular individual, who also happens to be a representative, is not good enough to be retained in his executive job. But a manager may be leaning over backwards to avoid rejecting him from his command, in case his act is construed as victimization. There have thus unquestionably been cases of people quite inappropriately being retained in their executive jobs because they had become representatives.

A representative in this situation knows it. His colleagues know it too. They become aware that his work is not up to a reasonable standard. If a representative is left on his executive job when not entitled to retain it, the guilt feelings engendered turn to hostility and anger, and one can expect trouble to follow. I must make my meaning quite clear.

(*a*) If a man has a representative role, but during the periods when he is on his executive job his performance is of an unacceptable standard, then his manager must consider ejecting him from the job, despite the fact that he is a representative also.

(*b*) If a man has a representative role, has to spend a considerable time away from his executive job, but does the executive job to an acceptable standard while he is at work, then a manager is not entitled to eject him from the job merely because, due to his *absence* on representative duties, the executive job he holds is not carried out satisfactorily. This is not the fault of the individual, but arises because representatives are required by the company.

Such problems as I have outlined are not irresolvable, and should in the first place be exposed and discussed by a manager with his superior. Moreover, managers must be resolute about such situations. A decision to take action obviously requires deep consideration and discussion. There may be accusations and arguments, but these can be worked through. The long-term effects are much too serious to allow of stalemate in such matters.

Granting leave of absence from work to a representative

If a representative's absence from his normal executive work is to meet a manager, no difficulty arises, because ordinary executive mechanisms exist to handle such exigencies. If a representative committee wishes to meet a general manager A, who agrees to the meeting, then B_1, B_2, etc., who are the managers of those representatives, should make no difficulties in agreeing absence from work to meet A, so long as A behaves appropriately and informs B_1, B_2, of his decision to meet the committee; such information from A is an instruction to B_1, B_2, to release them from executive duty. It is A's duty to see that his instructions reach the immediate managers of those representatives in an appropriate manner.

When representatives wish to meet together, several different kinds of problems may arise:

(*a*) If a representative approaches his manager and asks for leave to absent himself, the manager is entitled to ask: 'Do you need this time in order to meet others in my command?' If the answer is yes, the manager must decide whether he thinks it is in the interests of his extended command that the representative should be given time off from his executive work. This is probably easier for the manager to decide than it seems; for he will probably be aware that, in fact, there are at the moment problems in his command, and this knowledge will help him to come to a considered decision. If he is not aware of any particular problem, the representative may volunteer information. If the manager feels the situation does not warrant it, he may decide not to grant time off.

(*b*) If, in answer to a section manager's question, the representative informs him that the time off is to attend, say, a works committee meeting, the manager's appropriate action is to insist that one of the officers of the committee must obtain permission from the managerial cross-over point of the area represented by that committee. If that manager grants permission, he can instruct his subordinate managers to release representatives from their executive work to attend such a meeting.

(*c*) If the representative has been asked by somebody in another command to help him, and this is likely to happen if the representative is also perhaps a convenor of a particular union, or an officer of a representative committee, the section manager may be in real difficulty. He must ask the representative the purpose of his absence from work – if he gets an answer he will be able to judge whether or not to grant permission for absence. The representative may, however, have been charged by his constituents or by a committee of representatives to keep the matter confidential. In spite of this, the manager may be able to get sufficient general idea of the matter to enable him to come to a decision. If, however, he can gain no impression at all and fears that the purpose is frivolous or not connected with the proper affairs of the company, then he can either refuse, or refer the representative to the unit manager. But it should be noted that such difficulties arise only when the representative occupies, in the representative system, an additional role concerned with the factory or a particular union's affairs. Such problems arise from this other role, and this properly makes it the concern of the unit or general manager; for he generally knows more about the time needs of such a representative than his own immediate manager, because this kind of representative is dealing with 'factory or unit' representative matters rather than section matters.

I have gone into the underlying principles behind the granting of permission, not because I would want to insist that managers consistently adhere to the very detailed procedures implied by what I have said, but because I think it is essential that managers should know the underlying principles that *can* guide their conduct when difficulties do arise. Often the problems are not as formidable as they sound, because of the tacit understanding between managers that eliminates a lot of the protocol.

Reducing time spent by managers and representatives in negotiation

Just before this book went to press, discussions were in progress with representatives and union officers on this subject. Representatives had raised the suggestion that some executive action was required to obviate the situation where they took a matter to a manager whom they knew by experience had not the necessary discretionary authority to make a decision, because the procedure was that all such matters should proceed up the executive system step by step. It was agreed that this step-by-step procedure was wasteful of time. Measures have now been taken to redraft certain sections of the Policy Document, so that questions raised by representatives, or appeals by individuals, can be presented as rapidly as possible to that manager who has the clear authority to make a decision on the matter.

CHAPTER 17

THE LEGISLATIVE SYSTEM

ONE of the major components in the task of managing a company is the constant planning and initiation of the changes that are required to optimize its position in the market. It is the responsibility of the chief executive and his staff officers to size up the position, and to match changes in the market and the rest of the external environment of the company with appropriate adjustments to its products, volume of manufacturing capacity, methods of marketing, organization, techniques of production and the way it uses its resources.

A chief executive has wide discretion in these matters, so that when plans have been evolved the changes can proceed rapidly. On many occasions he will want to have appropriate discussions in the executive system with his subordinates, in order to discover how far his plans are practicable, what additional resources are required, the time in which specific work can be accomplished, the likely reactions of customers, and so on; but the bulk of the necessary change is initiated without a great deal of what is described as 'joint consultation'. I should like to emphasize this point. It is a matter of practical observation that this is so. Most changes are a matter of decision by an appropriate manager, and do not involve discussions with the board of directors or with representatives of those employed in the company. This is the nature of executive systems.

Again, however, it is a matter of observation that some changes cannot proceed on that basis. The chief executive who desires, for example, to invest large sums of money in buildings or new plant, to develop and market entirely new products, takes his plans to the board of directors for sanction before proceeding. If he wants to make a radical change in the design or price of the product, he will probably take some prudent soundings with his customers before doing so, and will change his plans if the reaction is clearly unfavourable. Likewise, if he wishes to make serious alterations to such things as methods of payment, holidays, organization of work, hours of work, he will discuss the matter with representatives of those affected before attempting to proceed. Indeed, if the board of directors, the customers, or the representatives of people in the company express deep interest or resistance to any change, then the chief executive will either require to work through the difficulties before initiating the change; or else, he will only find that he has to do so later, at a time when his attempt to introduce the change fully exposes the resistance which exists.

This whole matter, commonly referred to as 'joint consultation' or, when the employees of the company are concerned, 'negotiation', is a highly controversial subject. Managers discuss the subject in terms which presuppose that the question of whether or not they work through resistances to change with those concerned is a matter of choice. One manager will express a 'belief in' joint consultation, another will be opposed. Trade union leaders, politicians, industrial philosophers and others discuss the subject in moral or political terms. One will claim that workers have a right to take part in such discussions; another will discuss the benefits arising from the introduction of joint consultation, and so on.

The statements I have made are an attempt to avoid this controversy altogether by pointing to the facts: managing directors cannot avoid discussing resistance to change with shareholders and boards, customers and representatives, if any of these bodies of people choose to resist them, *because such bodies can prevent the introduction of change*. This is one of the facts of industrial life.

It is clear that many of those managers who think they have a choice in such matters, and criticize the idea of discussing resistance to their plans with their own people, in fact spend much time doing precisely what they so vehemently oppose. They attempt to initiate change of some sort that gives rise to great anxieties and precipitate strike action. Then they get down to the discussions which might have been so much easier to conduct if held before the trouble arose.

Some trade union officials and leaders are equally lacking in objectivity on this subject. For example, they express anxiety lest their members 'become involved in managerial decisions';

they want their members to abstain from being a party to managerial plans, lest it limit their freedom of action, when the time comes, to negotiate with management. They overlook the fact that the negotiations with managers are, indeed, discussions about what plan management should follow, and that, in agreeing as a settlement of a conflict that certain things be done, they are deeply involved in managerial decisions.

When, for instance, the Coal Board was formed, no union official, as a union official, could sit on it. Thus, apparently, the unions avoided involvement in Coal Board plans; but the public has seen what happens. The Board promulgate their intentions, and if these are not to the liking of, say, the National Union of Mineworkers, then discussions with that union take place. The plan may be modified, and the union is then committed to attempt to enforce its provisions on its members.

There is substantial denial of the facts among large sectors of industry. The subject is usually debated with considerable emotion and a great absence of clarity. Many managers and union officials see a distinction between what is called 'joint consultation', on the one hand, and 'negotiation', on the other, but there is no precise definition of the meaning of these phrases, and it is usually quite clear, when one gets into a debate on the subject, that most of those present give quite different meanings to these words. The confusion of discussion which results is most disturbing in the light of the great importance of the topic.

This chapter is an attempt to state the analysis of the subject which we have arrived at in the company. The institutions and practices described have, in the main, been practised in the company since 1941; though the picture which we have formed of them has, from time to time, undergone considerable change as analysis proceeded. Firstly, I give a definition of the meaning which we in the company attach to some words.

Power is an attribute of an *individual or group*. The term connotes the strength or intensity of influence that a given body or individual is potentially capable of exerting.

Authority is an attribute of a role. The authority of a role is the discretionary content of that role. The only description of the authority of a role that has content is a statement of what the person (or body) occupying the role can do, whom he can instruct, what resources he can use, what he can authorize to be done by others.

To give sanction to, is the act of a person or body with power, when they agree the attachment of a certain degree of authority to a role.

The legislative system. Our Policy Document definition reads as follows: 'comprises councils . . . in which the Executive and Representative Systems meet and by means of which every member can participate in formulating policy and in assessing the results of the implementation of that policy.'

This definition needs expansion for the sake of clearer understanding. The legislative system is not, as in the case of the executive or representative system, a series of inter-related roles occupied by people, but is composed of four related role systems. One of the features of each of these role systems is that they possess very considerable power *vis-à-vis* the company. The four systems are as follows:

A group of shareholders, who elect directors to represent them, who in turn appoint the chief executive and set policies within which he can operate the company.

A group of customers. It may seem far-fetched to refer to to them as a role system, but I think an analysis would show that it is justified. Individually they certainly possess considerable power *vis-à-vis* the company. They can, in fact, close it down if they dislike, say, its products, prices, delivery dates, by withdrawing their custom.

The representative system, comprising everybody in the company in their elector and representative roles. They possess great power and can, *in extremis*, close the company down by going on strike.

These three power groups exist. Their interaction one with another and with the *executive system* takes place. I am making observations, not presenting theories. We refer to the interaction of these systems as the Legislative System. It can be seen that, in the sense in which I am using the phrase legislative system, it exists willy-nilly. If our definition is accepted then it is meaningless for a manager to say: 'We have no legislative system in our company.' The appropriate questions are:

(*a*) Is its existence explicitly recognized or not? (*b*) Has an explicit social institution been set up, into which these interactions can be canalized, and within which they can be controlled?

The London Factories Council

We have set up these institutions and I will describe the London Factories Council as an example. The London Factories is a term which covers the geographical grouping of our company comprising: Company headquarters; Research and development organization; Sales organization; Stock products organization, Service group headquarters and No. 1 Factory (a manufacturing organization). This council comprises the management member (in this case, the managing director), seven representatives of hourly paid members, three representing Grade 3 staff, two representing Grade 2 staff and one representing Grade 1 staff (the most senior staff of the company).

The important function of this council, from my point of view as managing director (representatives would, no doubt, from their different role, emphasize other functions), is to provide an institution from which I can obtain sanction to make changes for which I do not think I already have sufficient authority. It is difficult, in writing about this issue, to avoid giving the impression that as every idea for change arises I turn to this body and say: 'Will you agree that I do this thing?' This is, of course, not the situation; for any chief executive who found it necessary to behave in such a manner would be unable to run the company effectively.

Every company has a whole series of established customs and practices. These practices arise from (*a*) agreements between employers and trade unions meeting at national level, (*b*) agreements at company level, (*c*) agreements at factory level, (*d*) agreements at department level, and so on. A chief executive who desires to make changes will consider, whether he recognizes explicitly what he is doing or not, the following points:

(*a*) Is this change within board of directors' policy? If he feels the board may not tolerate the change, he will be ill advised to try and proceed without getting their sanction.

(*b*) Is this change of a sort which will be acceptable to most of the company's customers? If he is doubtful he will undoubtedly try to find out through his sales organization, before he initiates it.

(*c*) Is this change in accord with established agreements, custom, or practice, and will it be tolerated by those who work in the company?

Chief executives are quite familiar with the process of getting authority from a board of directors, or a group of customers, for the initiation of change of a radical nature; but when they come to the necessity for getting authority in the same circumstances for some change for which there is no established custom or agreement, and which they feel may cause anxiety among employees, they tend to evade facing the reality of the situation. They talk of joint consultation as a means of getting *advice* from employees. Most so-called joint consultative bodies are set up with 'advisory' terms of reference. They talk about *negotiations* with unions. The fact is that they are obtaining authority to make changes.

In the London Factories Works Council we deal with change not in detail, but in principle. The agreements at which we arrive are embodied by management in what are called 'Standing Orders'. One of these sets out, for example, that every member of the company who is physically fit shall be prepared to work so much overtime, shall be prepared to take his turn on night shift; it lays down exceptions, hours of overtime, conditions of night work, etc. Once such a standing order has been legislated by the council, I have the authority to instruct managers to instruct others to do overtime, to work night shift, etc. It is only when I consider that the terms of the order require amendment that a resort to council on this subject is again required. Thus the explicit existence of such a council, and the 'legislation' which emerges from its deliberation, instead of causing constant reference to representatives, or constant resistance by members of the company to company plans, in fact greatly reduces the amount of 'joint consultation', and puts me in a position to know what the bounds of my authority are, and enables me to get on with the job. If individuals object to the imposition upon them of the provisions of a standing order, they will not get support from their colleagues or their representatives, because they have collectively, through the deliberations of the council, already explicitly sanctioned management to impose these conditions, and managers thereby have clear authority to do so.

On the other hand, if people in the London factories begin to feel that change in existing customs or standing orders are desirable from their point of view, then the way to set about the attempt to get such a change made is clear. If it is a matter which affects the whole geographical area represented at the London Factories Council, and if representatives of all those people discover that a consensus of opinion in the area desires such a change, then the matter is taken *directly* to the London Factories Council. It was not always so; I can remember in the early days of the war the time consumed when the members in one department wanted a change in hours of work and put the matter up to the superintendent of that department. The change, however, was one that was either made for the whole area, or it was not possible. The matter, having been debated at length at that level, was then raised with the general manager No. 1 Factory. He had no knowledge of the desire of other departments, and had to find out. Having discovered eventually that his whole extended command supported the idea, it came to me. By this time the members of No. 1 Factory were expecting the change to come about; but I discovered that most of the members of the other organizations on the site were against the change. By then there had been much delay, much expenditure of time, and no agreement on what to do. Now, in effect, I had to call into being a London Factories Works Council, although at that period no such institution formally existed.

How do the four systems interact?

I have stated that the legislative system embraces the interaction of four other systems – shareholders and board of directors, the customers, the representative system and the executive system. My description of the London Factories Council describes the interaction only of the executive system – through the management member and the representative system. In fact, further analysis of what actually happens is needed.

Nevertheless, I am satisfied that, through my own participation in that council, the power of these other systems plays upon the situation. Here are some of my reasons for this statement:

(*a*) The proposals for change which I make to the council may already have been referred to the board or to some customers, and reflect their attitude. In most instances this is not the case; but even then I have had to formulate them in the light of my intuitive perception of what these other groups will agree, or within a policy already set by the board of directors.

(*b*) As discussion arises, alternative proposals are put forward. Each of these has to be considered in the light of its effect on the executive system, the board and the customers.

(*c*) When representatives put forward, for example, proposals for longer holidays, one considers almost as a reflex action: (i) The difficulties arising in maintaining scheduled deliveries to customers; (ii) the cost, its effect on profits and the reactions of the board; (iii) executive difficulties arising out of longer holidays, etc. If one feels that these reactions are of a very moderate order, one may be able to agree, but if the results of accepting such a proposal are likely to cause difficulties in any of the areas mentioned, then one rejects the proposal. It is possible to regard this as a personal rejection of a proposal, but I do not think that is the whole story.

We have, within the legislative system, other councils, e.g. Kilmarnock Factory Council, Research and Development Organization Council, etc. Such councils do not exist, however, as explicit institutions, below the level at which a general manager sits on the body as management member. Nevertheless, meetings between unit managers and representatives of their extended commands take place frequently, and although no formal institution exists, legislation, in our sense of the word, does emerge.

Can it be said that in a council where the managing director is *not* present, the interests of the other groups are interacting on the situation? I think the answer is yes. The manager present is almost certainly not thinking of the board of directors and of customers; but he is working within a policy set by the managing director, which is itself a function of these interactions. Thus the other groups are indirectly affecting the situation at all levels.

An analytical statement on the legislative system

I believe that there is value in making the simplest possible generalized statement about a complex matter such as I have been discussing, because the more general it is, the easier to test its validity in the circumstances of other companies. I think what follows is correct; but I am aware that it may be incomplete, because some factors which are important may, so far, have escaped recognition.

Executive systems exist in a field controlled by three power groups, namely, shareholders, consumers and employees. These power groups invest the executive system with authority to develop, manufacture and sell products. The executive system thus carries responsibility for planning these operations, and the initiation of such a rate of change as is appropriate to the changes which take place in the environment in which it exists. When such changes are felt by the chief executive to exceed the bounds of the authority which has already been invested in his role, he must seek an extension of that authority. In order to do this, he brings into play certain social mechanisms, e.g., meetings of boards of directors or meetings of shareholders, testing of customers' reactions through a sales organization, meetings with representatives of employees. In so doing, he is precipitating interaction of the executive system with these power groups and interaction between the power groups. This interaction is legislative by nature.

The power of these groups varies according to circumstances. In times of deflation, the consumer becomes more powerful, and the employees less powerful; in times of inflation the situation is reversed. The shareholders in a large public company are a less coherent group than those in a family business and are accordingly less powerful than the latter.

The value of this analysis from my point of view is the ability it confers on me to make clear statements to those employed in the company about my own role. This can be very important when, because of some impending change of a fairly far-reaching kind, anxiety is running at high level. I have on many occasions made statements of the following type to representatives, and I think they have helped them to regard matters more objectively.

'You can, as a body, stop any change I wish to initiate, for you have the power to do so if you avail yourself of it. If I initiate change to which you object, but which fails to arouse sufficient objection to cause you to resort to the use of your power to stop me, I have, nevertheless, reduced morale and thereby reduced the level of efficiency. As it is my task to run the company as effectively as possible, I must do everything possible to avoid such situations arising. Nevertheless, shareholders and customers also possess power in the situation. They can refuse me the necessary authority to initiate change, even though you are prepared to use your power to try to push that change through. Thus I am an active initiator of new policies which, however, can be implemented only if I have sufficient authority. I will go as far in initiating change – which seems to me likely to help this company to increase its effectiveness – as the authority which I derive from these power groups will allow me to go.'

The salient feature of the statement is that it gives expression to a series of facts.

Here are some examples to demonstrate the need to get sanction for change:

(1) We want to expand production, which involves buildings and plant. I take specific proposals to the board of directors, who decide to approach shareholders with a proposal that they invest additional money in the company by the purchase of additional shares. Meetings are called, and it is sanctioned. The money comes in, and I am given authority to spend it appropriately. But if the customers refuse to buy, or if members of the company refuse to work in the new buildings on the plant, production will not start. One needs sanction from all groups. Normally, one can assume it for most matters if one has had sufficient experience of managing. But it is easy to make erroneous assumptions.

(2) Some years ago our engineers came to the conclusion that if certain types of tools (which were used in considerable quantities) were, up to a certain stage, to be quantity-produced

in our machine shops by production methods, and then accurately finished by one of our tool rooms to the separate final accurate dimensions required by different new production orders for bearings as they were received, the results would be these:

(*a*) the cost of these tools would be reduced;

(*b*) they would be available more quickly when needed, because semi-finished tools could be taken from stock and rapidly finished to the necessary accurate dimensions.

We could not, however, get agreement from the tool room concerned that these tools should be partially made in our own machine shops; and this in spite of the fact that there was a shortage of work in those machine shops and a very heavy overload of work in the tool room.

Here was a case of an excellent idea not being able to be put into effect, because I was not authorized to give the necessary instruction since one of the power groups did not agree. In fact, a compromise of sorts was worked out, but it was not as satisfactory as the original idea.

(3) About five years ago we had a long discussion about the introduction of a greatly increased degree of mechanization into our thin-walled bearing production units. Council agreed in principle. The board had already agreed the capital investment. Customers were pressing for the increased output and the reduced prices which would result. If, however, representatives of operators, supervisors and managers had decided at that point that the career changes implied by this mechanization were such a threat to them as to cause them not to give their support, then those important changes could not have been made at that time. The results of delay would have been very damaging to the company.

(4) We have, in the London factories of the company, some bad policy which I have been unable to get changed. An example is one facet of the policy governing the selection of redundant people to leave the company. Those who are not British citizens go first. I claim that the use of this criterion is based on prejudice and fear. It has already resulted in the loss of a number of people who were serving the company extremely well. I have little doubt that the loss of those men has, over the

years, deprived the company of revenue which would have helped to provide the improvement in working conditions that is constantly being sought by the same people whose anxieties perpetuate this unfortunate policy. I will continue to raise this subject and argue it at intervals. But clearly I am not authorized unilaterally to change a policy which was at one time underwritten by the Ministry of Labour, and is still backed by many trade unions, unless I wish to initiate a costly trial of strength between the three power groups.

The broad sense of what I have written so far is summed up in Paragraph A.4 of the preamble to the Company Policy Document, which reads as follows:

It is realized that when, after a serious attempt to reach unanimous agreement has been made, differences of viewpoint prove irreconcilable, action may be forced by the section which has the power. The use of power in this way shall be regarded not as a normal alternative to the methods of legislation laid down in this document, but as the inevitable consequence of a breakdown in these methods (A.4).

The salient features of the basis upon which our legislative bodies are built is set forth in the following terms in our Company Policy Document:

Legislated Policy governing all the Operating Organizations shall be decided by agreement between the Chief Executive of the Company and the representative members of the appropriate Factory Councils, and shall be built up from:

(*a*) the decisions of the Legislative System;

(*b*) policy arising out of established practice and custom, until amended by the Legislative System;

(*c*) precedents arising out of management's interpretation of policy (unless challenged) until amended by the Legislative System (G.1.1).

Legislated Policy governing any sector of the Operating Organizations (e.g., Factory Policy, Unit Policy, Section Policy) shall be built up as above, but shall be decided between the chief executive of that sector and the representatives of the members of his command (G.1.2).

Any member employed by the Company shall have the right

to propose amendments to existing policy, through either the Executive or Representative System (G.1.3).

The salient features of a manager's legislative responsibilities are defined thus:

A manager's executive action shall be within the terms of the agreed policy, or, where there is no agreed policy, in line with precedent or custom in his extended command. (Note: It must be clear that there is a difference between policy and actions implementing policy. Managers carry responsibility for making decisions in the implementation of policy, and must make such decisions as seem appropriate to them, whether or not they have the full support of their subordinates.) Where he finds it necessary to make a decision which he feels is not covered by existing policy or precedent, he shall decide whether or not it is sufficiently important to report to his manager or to bring before the appropriate council (E.21.1).

A manager, when getting a workable policy agreed by means of the legislative system, shall take into account:

(*a*) the effect on his executive subordinates;

(*b*) the policy of his manager;

(*c*) whether there is any likelihood of a given decision having effects outside his extended command (E.21.2).

A manager shall review his executive decisions where these are questioned by representatives, and shall ensure that they are in line with policy or precedent (E.21.3).

A manager shall report newly agreed local policies to his manager (E.21.4).

Unanimous voting at a council meeting

The term 'unanimous voting' is somewhat misleading. It gives rise to the following false impressions:

(*a*) That every member voting for a motion positively wants that change. Actually, it may indicate the mere minimum degree of tolerance for such a proposition.

(*b*) It carries the implication that all who are represented at a council meeting are in favour of the change. In effect, it must be clear that representatives have to assess, perhaps intuitively, the feelings of those who elected them. On most occasions, their positive vote merely signifies that they believe that a majority of their electors will accept the proposal.

(*c*) When the management member of a council votes in favour of a proposition, some may assume that such an act signifies that the whole executive system supports the change. In fact, he may, *in extremis*, be the only person in an executive role who is in favour. He is not there as a representative but as a manager, working within a policy set executively from 'above', not from 'below'.

Committees and a Glacier council differentiated

A committee is a body which carries collective responsibility for its decisions. It reaches these by majority voting. It is responsible entirely to those who elected its members. A Glacier legislative council is not a committee in the sense of this definition. It is a mechanism through which people can make a contribution to policy-making, and by means of which a manager can discover the degree of sanction existing in the representative system for particular changes. It is a forum in which differences of viewpoint can be discussed, and agreement on change worked out. It has no executive authority, and relies on its management member to give effect to any agreed changes arrived at. Therefore, it carries no collective responsibility. Representative members are individually responsible to the bodies which elected them to council for what they say, or the way they vote. The decisions arising out of council meetings are taken by the management member as a manager; he alone is responsible for them to his superior or, in the case of the managing director, to the board.

The term 'vote' has many connotations which connect it with committee procedure and majority voting. In a council meeting, however, the real significance of the 'vote' is the power to withhold it. It is much more akin to the veto of the United Nations Assembly.

A committee seeks to discover whether it can act, by counting the number of its members in favour of a motion. Our councils, on the other hand, seek to discover whether sufficient sanction exists for a change by discovering whether there is a single representative who is in sufficient doubt about the question to *withhold his vote*. It is only in matters of procedure or election of officers that the normal 'vote' is used.

Effects of 'unanimous voting' procedure

There are some important effects of this 'unanimous voting' procedure:

(1) It avoids the council compulsorily separating into two pre-existing camps for and against the proposal – regardless of the issue – as is the tendency in committees where motions are adopted by a mere majority vote. This is because any member of a council can individually prevent any motion being adopted. Thus, nobody need be under pressure to oppose a motion on the grounds of feelings of loyalty to some other member: for that other member can inhibit the motion single-handed. 'Loyalty pressure' to support or to criticize motions is, therefore, reduced markedly, and this produces a situation where the real views of members are more likely to emerge.

(2) This positive atmosphere produces a large number of suggestions, amendments and alternative proposals with a lively exchange of widely diverse views. This, coupled with the realization (explicitly stated in the Policy Document) that failure to agree means either stalemate or, worse, resort to power, stimulates people to great effort to work out some policy that can obtain unanimous support. In seventeen years of operation of this mechanism, the number of occasions when we have reached stalemate is trifling. This does not mean that most management proposals for change have been agreed, but that after amendment – sometimes extensive – agreement about some degree of change has nearly always been possible.

(3) Every representative has to make up his mind, on each issue, as to what point of view best represents the attitude of his constituents. He is involved in a sort of intuitive averaging procedure. He may know of a minority group in his constituency that is opposed to the viewpoint he has expressed on behalf of the majority. Therefore, even if every representative votes in favour of a particular course being followed, it does not mean that all their constituents are in favour of such a course. Experience has shown us that a unanimous vote of all representatives present at a council meeting is an indication of a sufficient sanction to clothe the responsible manager with the necessary authority for implementing that course. If one

representative is unable to vote for a particular change, it is our experience that it would be impractical to attempt to implement the change. A single vote against could mean that a whole unit, or department, or stratum of the command is opposed to the course proposed. If, say, a department is opposed, it is probable that there are strong minorities in the constituencies of other representatives also.

If the management member of a council votes against a particular change, it is clear that he feels the change is inconsistent with the needs of the executive system, or with the policy set by his own manager. In the case of the managing director voting against it, it would indicate that he felt personally that it was not in the interest of the company – it could also indicate that he did not feel authorized by the board to vote in favour.

(4) The power of veto carried by every member of a council has an individually disciplining effect which is valuable. One sometimes observes new members of council at first taking up somewhat intransigent attitudes to various proposals, and then changing as they come to realize the position they are in. I suppose the thoughts that occur to people at such a juncture may be something like these: 'I am against this because I doubt if my constituents want it. I am still against it, even with that amendment. That further adjustment improves it. Am I still against it? How important are the objections which may be raised by my people? Not too important really. I think we will have to swallow this one. Those changes do improve it. One of them was specially introduced to meet my objections. . . .'

(5) The chairman possessed with appropriate authority will prevent the passing of a negative proposal, e.g., 'that we shall cease as a factory to operate the existing policy . . .', because this proposal leaves no method of carrying on. Thus, whatever subjects are raised at council, the current procedure is left undisturbed, unless some positive change is substituted. This, from a manager's point of view, makes the whole procedure a viable one, because it allows executive work to proceed whilst the working through of resistance to new proposals is taking place.

The avoidance of 'detailed' problems at council meetings

Most discussion about joint consultation makes some reference to the problem of how to avoid 'detailed' and irrelevant matters which confuse meetings and waste time. There are some simple principles which, if recognized by managers and representatives alike, overcome this problem.

Our council meetings are so constructed that they essentially consist of a manager meeting representatives *of those who work in his own extended command*. If a matter arises in discussion calling for a council decision that would affect managers and people outside their extended command, then the management member of that council has no authority to allow such a decision to be taken; he must attempt to exclude matters outside his own jurisdiction. A representative may, however, raise a matter affecting one department only of the management member's extended command. This is a matter within the authority of the manager *of that department*, and the management member must insist that it be discussed with the manager of the department concerned. If the departmental manager cannot agree with representatives of those in the department, then he will have to take it to his superior; but this does not necessarily make it a matter for the superior manager to debate at his own council meeting, unless discussion of the issue has extended the area of interest to other departments also.

Thus the problem is not to exclude 'detailed' matters from council meetings – for a 'detailed' change may, in fact, have relevance to the whole of the management member's command – but to exclude matters for which the cross-over point is a manager subordinate to the management member of the council. Clearly, if decisions are taken by a manager's superior at a council meeting at which he is not present and of a sort which he could take himself, then the council has spent its time unnecessarily on a subject which is more appropriately discussed elsewhere.

At first, when our formal councils were started, we did have a certain amount of time wasted because matters raised were not always appropriate to the meeting; but today it is only new members of council who introduce these lower-level problems, and I note particularly that it is not only the management member of the council, but others also, who explain the reasons why such matters should be dealt with elsewhere and insist on council sticking to its proper business.

Preserving the status of the legislative system

Our councils have been in existence for many years now. Nevertheless, their status and integrity as institutions require constant safeguarding. Most personal differences of opinion in our organization are solved within the executive system itself, in discussion between manager and subordinate or in the appeals procedure. Those which cannot be solved in this way often become the subject of discussion between a committee representing perhaps hourly rated members, or some other grade of staff, and the appropriate manager at the cross-over point. It is essential that a legislative council should not be used as a substitute for these more appropriate means of dealing with personal disputes. A council should, so far as possible, remain a place where change of policy is debated.

It is equally necessary that if there is any doubt about the acceptability of ideas involving changes of policy, they should be raised within the legislative system at the earliest possible moment. On some occasions I have felt that long discussions and arguments between representatives and managers about important changes which were, in fact, matters for a legislative body were not treated as such at a sufficiently early stage. As a consequence, they gave rise to tensions and hostilities which might not have arisen had they been immediately dealt with in the formal setting of a council.

It is essential that as many members of the company as possible should be made consciously aware of the existence of a legislative system, so that they may be encouraged to canalize ideas for change through that system, and so that they may develop confidence in the ability of such a system to handle problems of change. A great deal can be done by managers to impress on their extended commands the vital importance that attaches to these councils. When people are worried about some proposed change of policy, a suitable opportunity will always occur to convey to them the real facts of the situation: that it is a manager's job to plan change and to use his authority and his personality to the full to try and get such changes implemented as soon as possible; but that if people are not ready to sanction such change, it cannot be implemented and managers in our company will not attempt to do so. We accept that it is better to delay, to amend or even for a time to forgo change, than attempt to impose it on an anxious and unwilling majority. This is not a piece of sentimentality, but the consequence of an objective appraisal of what is in the best interests of the company as a whole. The guarantee that this attitude will be adopted is contained in the Policy Document and in the constitution of our legislative councils.

This really gives a council the status it must have in order to do its job. Also it is reassuring to people who have dangerous fantasy notions about the 'menacing power of managers'. Such communications help to destroy these fantasies, and produce a reasonable setting for discussion.

In our society, people do not ordinarily use group or individual power to set aside the law when it seems unfair. They start organizing themselves to get it changed by the constitutional procedures of Parliament. This innate respect for the law can be aroused in support of the company's internal legislation only if the process and the policies arising from it are most clearly understood.

We had a one week's strike in one of our factories. Its origins were very confused, but one of the major factors was the need to reduce the strength of the factory by about fifteen per cent because of work shortage. There existed, at the time, a standing order on redundancy which had been duly passed by the factory council some years earlier. It was a sound piece of legislation and had been accepted by representatives, duly accredited not only by their electors, but by their unions as well. Copies of the standing order had been received by union officials at the time of passage through council without critical reaction. The need for the redundancy was discussed and accepted at a council meeting, and the assurance given that it would be carried out strictly in accordance with the procedure laid down. There had, however, since the passing of the order, been a large expansion in the numbers of people in the factory. It was clear, from the comments made during the strike which ensued, that the operation of the legislative system was not understood and was, therefore, mistrusted. A great deal of effort was expended by management *during the strike* to explain the legislative system. I think this made a substantial contribution to the return to work on a basis which was little different from that existing before the strike.

On the other hand, I remember visiting one of our small factories some years ago and finding the manager in trouble. He urgently required to run a night shift to cope with a heavy increase in work. His people had refused to agree unless changes in rates of pay, etc., were introduced forthwith. I asked that work be stopped and spoke to everybody in meeting, pointing out:

(*a*) That through the legislative system they were parties to the standing order on night shift. According to this order each man had agreed (subject to no medical disability) to do his turn on night shift. After debate, they agreed that this was so and that they were parties to the agreement;

(*b*) That if they felt free to breach one piece of legislation, no manager would know in future what other policy they might choose to break unilaterally at any time, and that this would bring our whole legislative system into disrepute;

(*c*) That if they chose *not* to work a night shift, we had not the power to make them do so. But if legislation was going to be flouted in this way, on what basis could the company be run in the future? That if they expected the manager zealously to adhere to agreed policy, they must obviously follow suit.

There was sincere acceptance, in principle, of the importance of upholding the legislative process, and of the importance of abiding by standing orders. This recognition of the principle led to acceptance of their duty to man a night shift immediately in terms of the standing order. There were other issues raised in their discussion which had nothing to do with a night shift. These issues were discussed by the appropriate manager subsequently. I was left with the impression that non-manning of the night shift was being used to influence the manager on other issues, and that the real contribution of the discussions had been to expose to the factory the danger to our whole legislative system of ignoring a single standing order.

After many years of operating within the conceptual framework of our legislative system, which has remained unchanged in principle for many years, and of discussing with managers what happens in other companies, I am convinced that legislation as a process requisitely exists in any business.

We are a sophisticated society and cannot live without laws, agreements, policies and contracts. If no explicit institution exists for bringing them into being, then unperceived institutions grow up, and we do the legislative job willy-nilly. There is, however, a profound difference between the explicit and the intuitive approach to these matters. By denying the existence of legislative systems, we deny ourselves insight into the sources of managerial authority. This leads to a tendency to talk about 'innate' managerial prerogatives, and the need for managers to have 'power' to act unilaterally.

Society will not support such claims. It is anxious about the role of managers now, because of general lack of insight into their role. Decisions by managers properly made within agreed policy can still *look* autocratic. Thus it is that industry is talked about as being 'autocratic'. Managers are often seen as dictators; sometimes their behaviour supports the notion; but although a manager can behave autocratically, he cannot continue to do so for very long, and the cost of such behaviour is very high. The power position of consumers, trade unions, staff groups and boards of directors is real; in the long run it effectively prevents unilateral decisions being taken by managers, except within agreed policies. We must face the reality of what exists.

It is doubly important that we do so, for, corresponding to the false picture of the dictatorial manager, is the other false picture of the 'weak' worker. I submit that the situation is dangerous when those who in their organized bodies are strong, continue to believe in their own weakness. People with power, who remain unaware of the fact, can unwittingly use their power irresponsibly. Scared people follow emotional and irresponsible leaders in an attempt to get greater security. The proper concomitant of power is a healthy sense of the fact of its possession and of the dangers inherent in its use. This cannot arise unless people are prepared to face the fact that, as members of trade unions, they possess very real power.

A powerful group that does not realize its own strength, that persists in believing that it is weak, and menaced by something more powerful, can be an anxious and irresponsible group. A group that feels secure in the knowledge of its own ability to protect its interests is much more likely to be able to examine the objective need for change when it is proposed, and to act responsibly.

Failure to analyse the real situation, and to build explicit institutions to mediate change, results in people in industry continuing to hold unreal fantasy pictures of industry. This gives rise to constant fear of 'being bossed', and fear of change. This leads to opposition to plans put forward by managers; not always because of their content, but often on account of their source. So long as managers themselves maintain the current collusion with representatives to evade facing the facts of their respective situations, we shall have failed to take one step forward which might help to reduce social friction in industry.

By way of summarizing the contents of this chapter, I close by quoting from Training Memorandum No. 2, which was issued by the company in June 1955. This memorandum is concerned with: (*a*) the executive processes which should be used in arriving at decisions to introduce change; (*b*) some representative and legislative processes involved in the innovation of change; and (*c*) the response by managers to proposals from subordinates to introduce change. The document is, therefore, divided into three parts under these headings.

(1) *Executive processes used in arriving at decisions to introduce change*

Making decisions. The manager who is considering making a change should ask himself the following questions:

(*a*) Is it within the terms of company policy?

(*b*) Is it within the standards set by my superior?

(*c*) Am I sure that it will not set new precedents which might raise problems elsewhere in the organization?

(*d*) Has my superior placed at my command the resources necessary to implement the change?

(*e*) Will the proposal work to the benefit of my part of the organization?

(*f*) Will my subordinates find it technically possible to implement the change?

(*g*) Do I feel that in my extended command there is at least a consensus of opinion that will tolerate this change?

If the answer to these questions is 'Yes', then the manager should give the necessary instructions *without delay*. Those seeking to become managers have to acquire a consistent habit of asking such questions of themselves. Such consistency is not easy to achieve.

In the majority of instances managers find it unnecessary to discuss ideas for change with others (apart from their own specialists), because, given experience, they know the answers to the questions listed. Reference to their own superior manager, to their immediate command, or to the legislative system seems to arise, therefore, in the case of a small minority of proposed actions where there is a feeling of real change of direction.

The first four questions concern the terms of reference set for a manager by his superior. If the answer to any of these four is 'No', a manager will see his superior because he cannot go further on his own. Assuming, however, that the answer to the first four questions is 'Yes', and that the answer to questions (*e*), (*f*) and (*g*) is not a confident 'Yes', then the manager will require to discuss the proposal with his subordinates.

Discussions with subordinates. If, in order to give a firm opinion, they want time to consider it or to discuss it in turn with their own immediate commands, give them as much time as is reasonable in the light of the circumstances. This may often mean giving the subject a precise degree of priority.

If it clearly involves one or two of his subordinates alone and is of little concern to the others generally, a manager should not waste their time in discussion but see the subordinates affected alone, and inform the others later.

Once the manager has gone through this process, he must make up his mind as to what he wants and instruct his subordinates accordingly. Remember, that if the decision does not work out successfully, the manager's superior will hold him totally responsible, even if he claims that his immediate command persuaded him to take the action he took. A manager must make his own decision, even if at the time it has to be contrary to the views of all his subordinates.

At this stage, however, he will have to make up his mind whether these discussions have revealed sufficient evidence of sanction, in his *extended* command, to enable him to go ahead and issue the necessary instructions, or whether he must seek further sanction through his representative system – in whatever form it exists. Consider, now, the process by which a manager may seek to obtain this further sanction where he judges it to be necessary.

(2) *Representative and legislative processes involved in the innovation of change*

Before meeting his council or other representative body, a manager should take the following steps:

Try to visualize the course that discussion at council may take and consider how far he might be able to amend his proposal in the light of such discussion. Such thoughts may throw up ideas which lie outside his superior manager's terms of reference to him. This may cause him to discuss such ideas with his superior manager, so that he is clear on how far he can go before the council meeting.

Give the representatives on his council as much notice as possible of his proposals.

If he is not quite certain of the meaning and content of company policy, standing orders or directives given in the past which may have a bearing on the proposal, this should be cleared either by himself or by his specialist, who should attend the council meeting with him. It is an unfortunate experience for the responsible manager at a council meeting to find his proposition is *ultra vires*.

When a manager meets a representative body. He should, if there is dispute about facts, figures, data, etc., attempt to establish whether or not his own 'facts' are correct before proceeding with the discussion. If he is quoting 'facts', he should make clear the source of his data, and offer to let representatives examine these sources if he can do so without detriment to the company.

He, in common with other members of his council, can veto any proposal, but, as management member, he alone is responsible to his executive superior for seeing to it that no decisions are taken at his extended-command council which, in his view, are against the interests of the company. Other members of council, as representatives, are responsible to their constituents.

Once his council has agreed an innovation, the manager is responsible for implementing it. He may have to hear appeals, grounded on the allegation that the innovation has not been faithfully implemented, and if he has agreed at a council meeting too hastily, he will still have to judge appeals in the light of what was legislated by council and not in the light of his own second thoughts on the matter.

Amendments to proposals. A manager may go to a council meeting with proposal A, having expended much thought upon it. Discussion at council may produce amending proposals B, C and D, and eventually E. He, in discussion, makes it clear that he will not be able to approve E. Representatives make it equally clear that they cannot commit their constituents to A or B. Perhaps everyone falls to considering C. The manager has done all that advocacy and explanation can do to persuade his fellow councillors that A or B is better than C. They equally and variously have tried to persuade him and each other that either D or E is better than C. The stage may be reached where the manager must either vote against C, in which case he is back where he started with no change at all; or, on the other hand, C, though only 'half a loaf', may in his judgement represent a worth-while move forward. The thing that may make him pause here is this other feeling about C – it is an unfortunate compromise and its acceptance has in it the taste of 'defeat'.

It is useful to consider such situations in the following manner. Suppose a manager had the power: (i) to start trying to put A, unsanctioned, into effect, meeting with all the resistance which failure to get agreement at council indicates that he will find in his extended command; or (ii) to put C (the compromise) into effect with the authority which he has as a result of the sanction of his council. Which course is likely to bring most success to his task of managing the sector of the company for which he is responsible?

There is nothing wrong in wanting to introduce innovations which cannot yet be introduced, because of lack of sanction from a superior manager or from representatives. It is the job of a manager to go on trying to get these innovations sanctioned, if he believes they are valuable. One day, if they are really sound and he can present the case properly, he will get sanction, particularly if he raises them at appropriate intervals in the future. On the other hand, the competent manager will not put off the lesser steps forward, the compromises – the 'C' proposals – merely because he cannot immediately achieve the major ones.

(3) *Response by managers to proposals from subordinates to introduce change*

Some unnecessary conflicts and loss of time arise from failure on the part of managers, when approached by a subordinate or representatives, to make clear what they think and what they are going to do. The most common cause of such failure is the misconception that there are really only two possible answers to such proposals – either 'Yes' or 'No' – and that, as in many cases it is not possible to be decisive in that way, the best that can be done is to prevaricate.

There is a necessity for managers, in response to such approaches, to be decisive, but not necessarily in these terms. Being decisive merely means making some decisions, and there are a large number which a manager may appropriately make lying between the extremes of 'Yes, I agree and will implement your proposal' and 'No, I do not agree and cannot do so'. Listed below are a series of decisions, one of which a manager should be able to make in response to most approaches from his subordinates:

(*a*) *Yes*. I accept the proposal or the criticism and will make the necessary change; or (*b*) Authority to say 'Yes' or 'No' is outside my discretion. *I will raise this matter with my manager* and will endeavour to give a reply by a named date. If by that time I am still unable to give you a reply, I will inform you of the delay at that time, and fix another date; or

(*c*) *The proposal is not a matter for the executive system* to deal with at all; it refers to the representative or legislative system, and should be raised through the appropriate channels; or

(*d*) I require time to consider this matter personally, and *I will contact you again by a named date;* or

(*e*) I do not know what will be the full effect of implementing your proposal in terms of cost or time, or its practicability, etc. *I will, therefore, collect the facts and try and make an assessment* which will enable me to give you my answer by a named date. If by that date I am still unable to assess the matter, I will see you, explain my situation, and name a later date; or

(*f*) *No, I do not accept the proposal* or the criticism and, therefore, will not make any change. Does the proposer wish to appeal?

The points brought out are in no way exhaustive; but sufficient is stated to demonstrate that there is no situation in which a manager can find himself, *vis-à-vis* his subordinate, when it is impossible for him to be decisive – so long as the word 'decisive' is not narrowed down to mean either rejecting the proposal or accepting it.

CHAPTER 18

THE APPEALS PROCEDURE

DIFFERENCES of opinion between people, and particularly between managers and subordinates, are inevitable in an executive system. Means of ventilating these differences, and of seeking redress from a higher level of authority, come into being willy-nilly. If these means are allowed to grow haphazardly, they take on forms which are inefficient and damaging to the company. The chief danger of an unrecognized and, therefore, unformulated appeals mechanism is that it may informally institute by-passing of managerial levels. Decisions are then made without data on the full situation being available. The hearing of a grievance by a high-level manager, without the presence of the manager whose decision is being questioned, or of the intervening managers, undermines the whole managerial–subordinate relationship.

History of appeals in our company

Our appeals mechanism was established in writing in 1949, when works councils adopted the first statement on company policy. It had, however, existed in recognized but unwritten form for some eight years previous to this formal step, on the basis of various statements about the subject by management.

In the earliest stages, foremen, superintendents and other managers at similar levels expressed great anxiety about the introduction of such a procedure. The fears expressed at the time touched on the following points:

(a) The great expenditure of time that would result and the inevitably large number of appeals that would arise.

(b) That it was higher management's duty to uphold the decisions of their managerial subordinates, not to assess their validity in front of their subordinates.

(c) That the judging manager would be exposed to threats of strike, etc., and that he would, therefore, be unable to operate in an impartial executive manner consistent with policy.

In the light of the fact that at that time there was very little company policy in written form and our current standing orders did not exist, this anxiety was understandable. In retrospect, I can now see that what was being said indirectly was something like the following: 'You do not set clear policies within which we can make decisions. In their absence, we have no knowledge as to whether our decisions will or will not be upheld. If a large number of our decisions are deemed by a higher manager to be wrong (because, in fact, we are not aware of the policy which the company wishes us to operate), then we shall lose status and authority in the eyes of our subordinates.'

The appeals system was introduced without formal discussion or agreement with representatives. It did not seem to excite much attention among non-managerial members of the company. Very few appeals indeed were made in the first year or two. Many people were not prepared to go through the rather trying process of stating a case to managers whom they did not know, in front of their own manager.

I think that most people distrusted the idea, and felt that a higher manager was bound to 'back up his own side', and that therefore they could not hope for impartiality. A few people, too, have subsequently told me that at that time they regarded the act of appealing as being one which would certainly lead to their being noted by managers as 'trouble-makers' and, later, to subtle victimization.

I think there was also a feeling that either one lost (which would not be satisfying), or one won (and got one's manager into trouble and that this was not 'cricket'); and so better to try and resolve the difference at low level in the department, rather than involve senior managers in the matter, with all the unfortunate repercussions that the exposure – that would inevitably occur during an appeal hearing – of practices and customs might produce. Thus, the system grew into practice only gradually, and fear dissipated slowly. A number of things helped to reassure managers: there was not an immediate big volume of appeals; written policy began to grow in volume so that the appeals, instead of being a process of wordy recrimination, often turned out to be a search for the real intention behind some statement of policy; frequently, when an appellant won his appeal it was not because his immediate manager had made a foolish decision, but because the company itself had not sufficiently clarified the policy which it wanted him to follow. These, and other insights into the operation of the procedure, proved reassuring.

Some appellants won appeals; but none of those who had done so was victimized; for I think every manager realized that all eyes were on him to see how he would subsequently treat a subordinate who had appealed. (I was very anxious in the early stages on this point, and used to follow the subsequent careers of some of those who had appeared in appeals at my levels; but I never observed or heard of a case which caused me disquiet on this score.) Gradually the system began to operate in a formal and widespread manner.

I have been impressed ever since, in all but a minority of cases, with the sincerity, though not always with the objectivity, of the appellants, and with the fact that nearly all managers have obviously tried to deal impartially with appeal matters. There is, however, a clear case for more understanding on the part of some managers of the principles involved, and of the best procedure to follow. This chapter is a contribution to clearer thinking on the subject.

Executive mechanism or separate social system?

During 1955 a great deal of work was done by the company in re-drafting its social policy. Our thinking at that time led us to the conclusion that our procedure for dealing with grievances was, in fact, a separate social system. This was supported by thinking based on the analogy of the way in which the law was administered in the courts. It was felt that managers, when hearing an appeal, were not in their managerial role but in some sort of 'judicial' role; that the person appealing was not in his executive work role but in the role of an 'appellant'; that a representative who helped a person by arguing for him at an appeal was analogous to a 'counsel' in court. Once we had started this line of thinking it seemed to be clear that we were dealing with a complete group of roles which were not executive in content or in function, and that we had, indeed, analysed out the existence of yet another distinct social system.

In accordance with this thinking, the new edition of the Policy Document, which was adopted in 1956, referred to the appeals mechanism as an appeals *system*, and its terms were appropriate to such an assumption.

Further discussion, however, on an early draft of this chapter has now forced me to the conclusion that we were wrong in 1956. The appeals mechanism is, in fact, an integral part of the executive system. A manager hearing an appeal does so in his managerial role. It is his executive terms of reference which insist that he must: behave impartially, listen carefully to all the evidence, base his decisions on policy rather than his own feelings, and so on. It is not necessary to establish the manager in a separate role as a sort of judicial figure, because the already existing, clear-cut executive policy will ensure the necessary behaviour.

I have, therefore, come to the conclusion that an appeal process is a part of the executive system; and that it can be described quite simply as a mechanism which allows a person to make contacts at every higher level, without by-passing his immediate manager. This changed conception does not, however, seem to call for any amendment of the detailed provisions for handling appeals set out in our Policy Document.

General features of our appeals mechanism

Our appeals mechanism, in general terms, has the following features (I state them briefly at this point, and will go into them in detail later):

(*a*) Every member of the company has the right of appeal against any decision of his manager to the next level of management, and successively to higher levels of management until he reaches the managing director. At most, this can normally involve three levels of appeal only in our company.

(*b*) That, subject to special provisions, he has final right of appeal to an appeal tribunal consisting of a representative, a management member and a tribunal chairman, appointed from outside the company by the chairman of the relevant works council.

(*c*) At each appeal hearing, the person appealing is entitled to the assistance of his chosen representative, and the relevant managers must be present.

(*d*) The task of the manager hearing the appeal is to come to a decision in the light of existing policy, standing orders and precedent. His job is to set aside his personal opinion on the matter, and endeavour to arrive at a decision that is in accordance with our internal policies.

(*e*) Either party to an appeal may refer it to a personnel officer for counselling. The personnel officer may make recommendations to both parties. But these are not binding and, if not accepted, the appeal continues to be heard in the normal way.

Subject-matter of appeals

All appeals are, in the first place, always against the decision of some manager. The subject-matter appears to fall into two categories. One type of appeal is to the effect that the manager is not entitled to make the decision which is the subject of dispute, because his decision is not consistent with standing orders, established policy or precedent. Here are some examples illustrating alleged infringement by managers of their *prescribed* terms of reference under existing policy.

(*a*) A member, having absented himself from work on the day after a holiday, has been refused holiday pay by his manager in accordance with the National Agreement on the subject. The member contends that his manager has not interpreted the National Agreement correctly.

(*b*) A member, being refused an increase of wages, contends that a manager is not entitled to withhold the increase, because his work falls within a category the minimum wage of which is above his existing wage.

(*c*) A member informed by his manager that his performance is not adequate, and that he will not be retained in that command, contends that he has not been given any previous notice of his manager's dissatisfaction; therefore, in accordance with policy, his manager is not entitled to discharge him from his existing role until he has warned him in this way, and given him an opportunity of meeting those criticisms.

The Appeals Procedure

Shortening the procedure

It happens, not infrequently, with this type of appeal that circumstances are new, and the policy which applies is, for example, company rather than factory policy. In such cases, it is often better for a general manager to decide not to hear the appeal, but instead take it to the top of the executive system. If he hears it himself, he may be called upon to give an interpretation in a situation where there is no clear guidance in written policy, and it is likely that his decision will again be the subject of appeal. By deciding to take it to the top without delay, he saves a complete hearing and all the time that it takes. Representatives have recently, in discussion, stressed their own embarrassment about the inefficiency and loss of time taken up by intermediary hearings of an appeal, when they themselves already feel quite certain – because the issue is of a company nature – that it will in the end inevitably have to go to the chief executive for decision.

Cases occur when the decision on the appeal is debated not on the grounds of written policy, but by reference to custom or precedent. In these cases also, there are strong grounds for considering whether they should not go to the top at once, in order to save time.

It has always been possible for a manager to agree that cases should be handled in this manner, but up to now it has happened infrequently. It is clear to me, from the experience of hearing appeals, that there are many instances where time would have been saved by applying such a contraction of the appeal mechanism. Indeed, if it were possible, without actually hearing an appeal, to determine fairly precisely its content, then that content would pre-determine the appropriate level at which it should be heard. Decisions about policy appropriate to a unit should be heard by the unit manager, decisions arising out of factory policy by a general manager, etc. Unfortunately, it is very often necessary to hear an appeal in order to determine its content, and at times an individual appeal can involve several levels of policy.

Appeals about unfair decisions

A second type of appeal seeks to show that a manager, in using his discretion as to which course to pursue, has made a choice that is unfair to a particular individual. In such a case, the argument is not that policy forbids the manager a particular choice, but that his choice is unfair to his subordinate. Here are three examples:

(*a*) A member, while agreeing that his pay is within the agreed bracket for the job, feels that he should be paid higher within that bracket. He claims that his manager is wrong in rating him the same as A and B, and lower than C and D, with whom he considers himself equal in every way.

(*b*) A manager does not give a member certain types of work to do, because he does not rank the member as being sufficiently skilled and careful to keep the risk of 'scrapping' the job within reasonable bounds. The offended member contends that the estimate of his capacity is unfair.

(*c*) A manager, having had many discussions with a member about his shortcomings and having tried to help him by training, decides that the member is not good enough to be retained in his role. The member challenges the soundness of his manager's assessment.

These latter examples are difficult types of appeal cases to deal with. They seem to be the kind of cases which should be referred, if possible, to a personnel officer for counselling. There is a reasonable chance that, as a result of the part played by the personnel officer as an advice-giver, the conflict may be resolved in a manner that is less likely to arise in the atmosphere of the appeal setting, where normally there are only two courses open: either to dismiss the appeal or to uphold it. In most cases it is clearly not realistic for the higher manager to say, in effect, to the lower manager: 'I will uphold this man's appeal for a higher wage, for I think your decision about his worth is wrong, and I (after half an hour's acquaintanceship during this hearing) believe that I can decide his proper wage more accurately than you can.'

My personal practice in hearing appeals, once it has been made quite clear that the appeal is against the way a manager has used his discretionary authority, is to say to the appellant: 'You have a difficult task on your hands. Unless you can show that your manager has come to this decision against you by allowing non-executive matters to influence his judgement, or has in some other way infringed prescribed policy, you cannot hope to win your appeal. My task is to ascertain whether your manager is entitled to make decisions such as the one you feel aggrieved about (and it is clear to me that he is), and to satisfy myself that he had come to his decision, whatever it may be, in an executively realistic manner within prescribed policy'. I cannot say 'You are a good worker' on the basis of personal observation; but I can assess the consistency of the comments of the immediate manager and those of other managers between me and the member appealing. If they are not consistent, then I may feel that personal bias is entering into the manager's decisions and that his decision may need scrutiny and amendment.

It may be asked if there is any real value in hearing these appeals at all in cases where the way in which a manager has used his discretion is the main content. I have no doubt of the value myself – for the following reasons:

(*a*) The appeal has to be heard in order to ascertain what the difference of opinion is about.

(*b*) The member may not be satisfied when, after two or three hearings at different levels, he must face the fact that, in the absence of real evidence of a manager's personal bias, that manager's assessment of him is the accepted basis of the decision and not his own assessment of himself. There is, however, a very large volume of evidence to show that people who contest these 'unfair to me' decisions of their managers, and who fail to get the decision altered, nevertheless do get a much broader perspective as a result of appealing, and are less aggrieved at the end of the procedure than when they started.

(*c*) The higher manager may learn of the difficulty which surrounds the implementation of some of his own policy, and this may cause him to arrange that it be changed.

(*d*) The higher manager learns a good deal about his subordinates on such occasions. This may cause him to feel satisfied or unsatisfied with the manner in which the managerial task is being carried out in that sector of his total command which is concerned with an appeal. If he is not satisfied, he can later take appropriate steps.

Appeals by representatives

The third type of appeal is that made by a group or representative body. The subject-matter may be similar to that of individual appeals; but the appeal made by a group tends to be concerned not so much with the effect of a decision that has been made upon some particular individual, but with the future effect on everybody, if a manager's particular interpretation of our policy is permitted to go unchallenged. I will quote one example of this type of appeal.

A shop committee of representatives appealed against the rate of pay which a man, who had just finished his apprenticeship, was offered to take up a skilled job. The man involved was not present, and the committee explained that the fact they were seeking to get established was that the *grounds* given by the manager for offering a lower rate of pay than was customary in similar circumstances were inappropriate. They sought to prove, for instance, that it was outside company policy for the manager to base his decision to offer a lower rate on the fact that the individual had indicated *lack of enthusiasm* for the job, by saying that he wished, as soon as opportunity arose, to apply for a post in another part of the factory at what he considered to be a higher level. The shop committee were upheld on this, and on two other similar points which they made. They did not, however, win the original appeal, which was for a revision of the individual's rate to the customary level. The individual's rate was marginally adjusted by the judgement and instructions given that, unless within two months it was clear that he was working at a lower level than his colleagues, he was to get the customary rate offered in the department for those joining it at the close of serving an apprenticeship. This was primarily a case of people seeking to prevent what they regarded as a bad precedent being set up by a manager's decision.

We thus have three types of appeal against managerial decisions:

(*a*) Where it is contended that the manager's decision is

wrong, because it is based on an incorrect interpretation of some existing policy, precedent, custom or agreement (Wrong interpretation);

(*b*) Where it is contended that the manner in which a manager has used his discretion is unfair to the individual (Unfair decision);

(*c*) Where the subject-matter is either an alleged wrong interpretation or unfair decision, but the appeal is made by a group rather than an individual (Representatives' appeals).

Analysis of appeals heard

The company does not require that managers should keep records of all the appeals they hear. We do not know, therefore, how many formal appeals actually take place. I, however, do keep records of appeals that come to me as managing director. These figures and brief details about the subject on which the appeals were based give some idea of the scale of operations in the appeals system.

Our formal policy on appeals

What follows is the detail of our company policy on appeals, together with some explanatory comment.

Grounds for Appeal

Every member of the Company shall have the right to appeal against any executive decision or action of an executive superior which affects him and which he considers to be unfair or unjust; inconsistent with either the provisions or the spirit of agreed or normally accepted policy, or not covered by such policy; or contrary to the best interests of the Company (H.1).

A representative shall have the right of appeal on any matter which he considers affects his constituency. The result of such an appeal shall not necessarily affect decisions already made regarding the particular case whose circumstances may have actuated the representative to appeal on behalf of his constituency (H.1.1).

This latter section (H.1.1) was introduced to prevent a situation arising where a manager makes a decision about a member who chooses not to appeal. Thereupon, representatives of

Exploration in Management
ANALYSIS OF APPEALS HEARD BY THE
MANAGING DIRECTOR

	Jan. 53/ Dec. 54	1955	1956	1957	1958
Type of appeal					
Individual	16	9	7	8	7
Group	4	—	1	5	1
	20	9	8	13	8
Grade of membership					
Hourly rated	15	6	6	11	5
Staff	5	3	2	2	3
	20	9	8	13	8
Results					
Disallowed	15	5	5	11	7
Allowed	4	1	3	1	1
Compromise	1	3	—	1	—
Subjects dealt with					
Dismissal	5	2	—	2	1
Sick pay	2	1	1	1	2
Wages payment, expenses, etc.	11	2	2	6	—
Time spent on representative work	1	—	—	—	—
Classification of work available to women	—	—	—	1	—
Reduction of overtime	—	—	—	1	—
Appointments (including operation of S/O)	1	—	4	1	—
Alternative holiday	—	1	—	—	—
Upgrading	—	1	1	—	1
Loan	—	1	—	—	—
Demotion	—	1	—	—	—
Dissatisfaction with job	—	—	—	1	—
Retirement	—	—	—	—	3
Salary level	—	—	—	—	1

other members feel that the decision was an unfair one, and not in accordance with company policy. They fear that it will be regarded by other managers as a precedent. The comment 'shall not necessarily affect decisions already made' is to safeguard against 'retrospective legislation'. It is important that managers should uphold the general principle that a decision made today, in a particular set of circumstances, shall not necessarily be assumed to be grounds for reversal of previous decisions, just because the circumstances look similar. Invalidation of this principle would mean that any decision would have such repercussions on past decisions that change would be rendered very much more difficult.

Establishing an Appeal

The member wishing to appeal shall adopt the following procedure:

> The member shall first appeal to the immediate superior of the supervisor or manager whose action or decision is being appealed against. The appellant and the supervisor or manager whose decision is the subject of appeal both have the right to appeal against the decision of the judging manager and take the appeal to the next higher manager (H.3.1).

It is the responsibility of any manager who feels that his decision is being seriously questioned, either in respect to its conformity with company policy, or on the grounds of the feeling of unfairness which it produces in his subordinates, to say to his subordinate: 'Do you wish to appeal?' and in doing so to convey the following impression: 'I am quite ready to have the correctness of my decision scrutinized by my manager. I feel I am correct, but I could be wrong.' The conveying of such an impression connotes his own confidence in his own judgement. The manager who is worried by his subordinate's desire to appeal is displaying lack of confidence in his own judgement.

I know of more than one case where a subordinate wanted to appeal, not on the grounds that his manager's decision was inconsistent with policy or unfair to him, but because he maintained that any policy which allowed a manager to make such a decision was wrong. Such a situation is not one that can be dealt with by an appeal. Either managers or representatives, if they feel it to be appropriate, can take action to cause policy to be reviewed.

Late appeals

If a manager makes a decision against which a member appeals, implementation of the decision must be delayed until the appeal has been heard. For this reason a member cannot be allowed very long to decide whether or not he wishes to appeal. The Company Policy Document reads as follows on this point:

When, at any stage in an appeal, a member has not given notice of appeal by the beginning of the third working day or night following the working day or night within which the decision was made, then it shall be at the discretion of the responsible manager whether or not the appeal shall be permitted (H.3.5).

The Company Appeal Tribunal

If the appeal reaches the Managing Director and the decision is still not acceptable to both parties, and National Arbitration Procedures do not apply, it can, with the approval of a body set up by the appropriate Works Council, be referred to a Company Appeal Tribunal (H.3.2).

The Company Appeal Tribunal shall consist of:

One member appointed by the Managing Director;
One member appointed by the appropriate Works or Staff Committee:
One independent chairman appointed from outside the Company by the Chairman of the relevant Works Council.

The majority decision of this Tribunal shall be final and binding within the Company (H.3.3).

Although the company's appeal tribunal has formed part of our policy for at least thirteen years, it has never been called upon to deal with an appeal. On two or three occasions, a body set up by the works council has considered whether or not permission should be granted to appeal to the company tribunal. Only once has permission been granted, but on that occasion the appellant left the company before the tribunal could be set up.

The Appeals Procedure

This procedure requires scrutiny and change. It is too onerous a task for the body appointed by the works council to decide whether leave of appeal should be given. This involves a complete hearing of the case all over again. Because it is so cumbersome, the procedure causes much stir and publicity in the company. This is unfortunate and probably inhibits some appeals.

On the other hand, it is clearly impossible to allow any member to take his appeal, however trivial, to the company appeal tribunal without such scrutiny, because the setting up of the latter involves considerable work, expense and time. On the single occasion in 1955 when the chairman of the London factories works council attempted to find a chairman for the tribunal, he experienced great difficulty. Ten days after the appeal, he had still been unsuccessful in finding a suitable person. At that stage, the appellant voluntarily decided to leave the employment of the company.

There seems to be little possibility of obtaining a person reasonably experienced in appeal procedure at short notice; and the setting up of the tribunal is likely to be expensive. Bearing in mind that there is no guarantee that the issue involved will be of real importance either to the individual or the company, it seems that the whole subject of the tribunal should be re-examined. I personally backed its introduction on the basis of the false analogy of procedures at law; but now that this analogy can be seen to be false, re-thinking of this matter is necessary. My current view is that the idea of an independent tribunal is not consistent with the properties of executive systems.

The counselling procedure before a personnel officer

The Policy Document reads as follows on this subject:

Before an appeal reaches the level of Divisional or General Manager, it may be referred by either party to a Personnel Officer. Should his recommendations not be acceptable to both parties, the Personnel Officer may, with the agreement of the intermediate managers concerned, refer the appeal to any level in the Executive System not higher than Divisional or General

Manager. All such intermediate managers shall be entitled to attend the hearing and submit their views (H.3.4).

This procedure is valuable, for an appeal can either be allowed or disallowed; but this enables an appellant, or the manager, time to reconsider the matter and to change his mind without 'loss of face'. It is recognized that personnel officers know company policy more thoroughly than most managers, and that their advice, therefore, tends to foreshadow the final verdict in the matter pretty accurately. The use of this procedure can save much time and, I think, preserves good-will. More use could be made of it with advantage.

A manager defending the correctness of his decision at an appeal

I can remember several occasions over the years when, an appeal being granted, I have been approached later by the managers concerned, because they felt very concerned at my judgement, and urgently wanted to know more of the basis upon which I had made it. These instances have frequently followed the same pattern. The manager has decided to refuse some request, or has decided that one of his subordinates can no longer remain in his immediate command. He has supported his decision by reference to *one or two very specific incidents of failure* on the part of his subordinate in his work. There has been dispute about the facts of the incidents quoted – the failures have *apparently* been isolated ones and not in themselves of a serious nature. The decision has appeared harsh in the circumstances, and the manager has been recommended to discuss the failings with his subordinate, to provide training for him and to supervise him more closely for a period, as a means of helping him to overcome such failures. But his main decision has been overruled.

In the latter discussion, the manager will say: 'But this man has been tried out by me on several different jobs to see if I cannot find him one which he can do competently. I have discussed his failures with him over and over again. He shows no enthusiasm to get down to it, and *the final straw* was the incident on which I took my decision.' I point out to him that it is no good giving the real basis of his decision after the appeal is over. It is my job, as a judging manager, to come to a conclusion on the basis of what is *said* at the appeal. I cannot be clairvoyant and assume what he does not say.

Guidance Note No. 4 in the Policy Document refers to this matter. It reads as follows:

Cases may arise where a manager believes that in order to discharge from his immediate command subordinates who are proving not competent to carry out the work he requires of them, or not able to conform to the generally accepted standards of behaviour, he must produce specific details of some *ad hoc* failure on the part of that subordinate. This may give rise to a situation where a manager who has over a long period formed the conclusion that an immediate subordinate does not conform to these requirements, nevertheless discharges him on a more limited charge. In such a case, if the subordinate appeals he may be able to demonstrate that the facts put forward to support the *ad hoc* charge are not proven. His appeal will then be allowed, and he will remain in his post.

Situations of this kind often arise because a manager has not made clear to his subordinate his dissatisfaction with his performance or behaviour over a period of time. Where managers fail to do this, they can invariably expect to find themselves in difficulty.

Experience shows that cases of this sort frequently resolve themselves because the discussion and working through of relationships which take place during successive hearings in the Appeals System results in the member concerned gaining greater insight into the executive behaviour required of him by his superior. Sometimes the manager concerned gains more knowledge of his subordinate's difficulties and as a result changes his opinion of that subordinate.

If, however, this desirable result does not arise, then the manager concerned, because he has attempted to discharge his subordinate upon incorrect grounds, or because he has failed to inform his subordinate of his dissatisfaction with him, must tolerate what he has experienced as an undesirable situation for a further period of time.

The length of this period will vary according to circumstances, but it must be at least of such duration as will give the subordinate member sufficient time to demonstrate to his manager whether or not he is capable of so changing his behaviour or the manner in which he discharges his executive job as to cause his manager to change his assessment.

Responsibilities of a Manager when hearing an Appeal

To base his judgement on the provisions and intentions of policy, whether or not these are in accord with his own views or those of his superiors or subordinates (H.2.1).

To adopt an encouraging and friendly attitude towards an appellant who might wish to take his case to a higher level (H.2.2).

To deal with appeals with the minimum possible delay (H.2.3).

To encourage the appellant to have present an officially elected representative as his adviser (H.2.4).

I have these provisos to add for the further guidance of managers:

(*a*) Open the appeal by making a statement about anything factual which you know of already, and by asking if, in the opinion of the parties to the appeal, your knowledge is accurate. If this is disputed make it clear that you will let your 'facts' be argued.

(*b*) Discover just what the grievance is by letting the appellant talk first.

(*c*) Sometimes the appellant's statement is not clear. Proceed no further until the position has been clarified. I have sometimes failed to do this, with most unforunate results and a great waste of time. In my experience, every appeal is against the decision of some manager. I am very nearly certain that no other type of appeal is possible. Unless, therefore, the managerial decision against which the appeal is made is clear, the manager hearing the appeal must 'dig' for it. If it cannot be discovered, it will be found that the appeal is not an appeal, but a challenge to some existing policy or a dispute with a colleague, in which case it can be dismissed as an appeal, and steered into some other appropriate channel.

(*d*) Insist that all concerned in the case talk to you, and not to each other. Their job is to convince *you* of their point of view. If you do this, you will prevent the development of wordy arguments that do not help you to come to a decision.

(*e*) The integrity of the whole executive system is at stake in an appeal. Uphold its status and dignity in every possible way:

e.g., avoid, as far as possible, all interruptions to the procedure; if an appellant or a lower manager casts a slur on, or challenges the integrity of the procedure, insist that such remarks are withdrawn before proceeding; if the appellant refuses, terminate the proceedings; if the defendant refuses, take disciplinary action after the proceedings.

(*f*) Two appeals in my recollection have given rise, during the proceedings, to statements by the appellant that, if he did not succeed in his appeal, he proposed to seek the support of others afterwards, to raise the matter with his union or committee, etc. In other words, there was a threat of subsequent action, unless the verdict was in his favour. It is the responsibility of the responsible manager in any such situation to point out that under no circumstances can the appeal be proceeded with under duress, and to insist on an unqualified withdrawal of such remarks in a manner that will satisfy him that it has been made with sincerity. Failing that, he should dismiss the appeal immediately and report the matter to his superior manager.

(*g*) In the law courts, people are allowed to make statements which outside the court would be actionable. It is quite otherwise in a factory.

In the light of this, the responsible manager must refrain from defamatory comment, and must prevent others present making damaging personal remarks about each other or, especially, about persons not present.

I do not wish to leave the impression that people frequently indulge in such comment at appeals. But sometimes in the heat of the moment, somebody may be approaching such comment, and it is important that the responsible manager should be quick to 'nip it in the bud', or immediately insist on a withdrawal if it is in fact uttered.

(*h*) There is a strong tendency at appeals to quote hearsay in support of statements: e.g., one of the parties will say: 'Mr Y, who was this man's manager a year ago, had cause to criticize his work extensively.' The responsible manager must be careful not to accept such statements. They must be supported by the person alleged to have made them, if they are to be made use of.

(*i*) The extent to which evidence from witnesses can be obtained is limited by the fact that it is an executive not a legal procedure. Unsupported statements of what can reasonably be assumed to be the facts should be accepted, if the other party agrees them.

(*j*) Both parties must be given time to state their case in their own way. But it is the duty of the responsible manager to limit expenditure of time by disallowing argument and comment on aspects of the matter which do not assist him to reach a decision.

(*k*) Try and determine if there are any written standing orders or policy bearing on the matter, or policy arising out of established practice and custom, or precedents arising out of management's interpretation of policy, etc. If there is, the application of such policy to the appeal may immediately indicate the proper decision. If it does not, then the task of the responsible manager is to interpret what was the real intention of the policy in such a case. If a manager cannot decide the correct interpretation to place upon such existing policy or standing order, he must send the appeal to his immediate superior.

(*l*) If there is clearly no existing policy on the matter, the manager should exercise the greatest care, remembering that he is making policy by his decision. If the policy he thus has to make covers more than his own extended command, then he must send the case to a higher managerial level.

The Appellant's Adviser

The appellant shall have the right to request any member of the Factory, except managers in his line of command, to advise him (H.4.1).

The appellant, his chosen adviser, if any, and the supervisor or manager whose decision is the subject of appeal, shall all have the right to be present (H.4.2).

Witnesses may be called, but shall be present at the enquiry only long enough to give their testimony and to answer questions arising out of their testimony (H.4.3).

The appeal decision shall be given in the presence of both parties (H.4.4).

Although the policy refers to the appellant's *adviser*, in fact the representatives, who normally act in such a capacity, quite often do all the talking. The reason for this is, I think, that people who appeal are often not very articulate and are anxious about their ability to do credit to their own side of the argument. These 'advisers' become used to the procedure and do a good job on the whole.

Sometimes managers raise the criticism that the adviser will change the whole basis of argument in taking the appeal from one level to a higher level. This can waste time, because had he stated his case at the lower level in the manner subsequently used at the higher level, the decision might have gone in favour of the aggrieved person and saved a hearing. I cannot see how this can be avoided at times. Most of us in any sort of argument tend to shift our ground as we see how the discussion is going.

Advisers sometimes have to help people who have very weak cases, or people who have behaved very stupidly. On the whole, I am very impressed with advisers' conduct. They become skilled in argument and do their best for those they are helping, but not to the point of sacrificing their own integrity. Appeals are time-consuming and arduous, but they also produce a great deal of extremely honest behaviour. In the main they leave behind them a 'good taste'.

An unresolved difficulty

There have been two cases where appeals against loss of jobs at a factory in Scotland have been disallowed by the general manager, and the case has been appealed to the managing director. In each instance, this would have involved either the managing director making a special journey of 400 miles, or, as in fact happened, the retention of the members in a job for which they were not felt to be suitable, until one of his normal visits to the north. This difficult position has not arisen frequently but it is one to which we await a solution.

The effect of appeal decisions on the legislative system

The Policy Document has this to say on the matter:

Decisions by a manager which, in his opinion, involve important interpretations of policy shall be communicated to his extended command through executive channels. In the case of the Managing Director, a file of such interpretations shall be set up and shall be open to all members of the Company (H.5.2).

Important interpretations of policy tend, in effect, to be new policy. Hence, the necessity for committing them to paper, and their inclusion in the standing order books. I have certainly heard many appeals that were based on these published interpretations, and some of the interpretations are constantly referred to by other managers. The form in which these interpretations are issued is rather lengthy, because it is necessary to describe the case leading up to the interpretation.

The work of the appeals procedure has led, over the years, to a considerable amount of amendment both of standing orders and of the Policy Document. On the Sick Pay Standing Order, for example, numerous amendments have been moved at council meetings as a result of complexity and difficulty in its interpretation made evident during an appeal.

The value in an appeal situation of written policy

An appeals procedure seems to be concerned fundamentally with interpretation of our policies, standing orders, conventions, etc. All these are concerned with prescribing the manner in which it is agreed that the company shall operate. Without an explicit appeals procedure, the policy-making work of our factory councils would not, I think, possess the status at present attaching to it. There must be means of ensuring that executive policy is implemented in accordance with its original intention. Conversely, an appeals procedure can gain status and perform a decisive function in settling personal disputes only if there is an appropriate body of *written* policy.

I have always felt reasonably at ease in an appeal, when the job has involved the interpretation of a *written* standing order or *written* policy. When, on the other hand, I have had to listen to what are often contradictory accounts of what is, or is not, convention and practice, or to quote convention myself without the support of written records of its detail, I have invariably felt much less confidence in my competence to make wise decisions. I am sure that this has been the feeling of others who have been involved in such situations.

The Appeals Procedure

Some added values of an appeals procedure

Appeals are most time-consuming. I hear an average of about twelve per year. But I know that general managers have to deal with more than that. They have, by their nature, to be dealt with promptly, and it is often exceedingly difficult at short notice to fit them into a busy programme of duties. The subject-matter can at times seem trivial to a manager. It is too easy to dwell on the difficulties and overlook the benefits which arise from the existence of an explicit appeals procedure. Here are a few samples of the benefits.

One walks through a department and stops to look at some process. An operator seizes the opportunity to begin pouring out the detail of some deep-felt problem or grievance. In the absence of a clearly defined appeals procedure what can one say? But with a clearly established procedure one's course is quite clear. The following type of discussion ensues:

MANAGER: You are very worried about some personal issue, obviously. Have you raised the matter with your own manager?

OPERATOR: Yes; it is his decision that I am cribbing about.

MANAGER: Have you appealed – No? Why not?

OPERATOR (*variously*): What is the use? – I had not thought of that, etc.

MANAGER: Well, I am sorry you are so worried. But you have quite a simple means of redress if it is justified. If your problem is not felt by you to be sufficiently important for you to appeal, then I suggest you forget it. If, on the other hand, you are really troubled, then no doubt you will take the steps necessary to put the matter to the test.

I think it is not unkind to suggest that anybody who grouses but will not appeal is just somebody who enjoys his bit of grousing and can be left to do so. One cannot, however, as a manager, take up this comforting attitude unless an explicit outlet exists for the ventilation of really hard-felt grievances.

Anybody in a senior managerial position in industry is worried at the thought that the policy he has set for his subordinate managers may at times be interpreted harshly or erroneously by them. In the absence of a clearly understood channel of appeal, sub-standard decision can be made by subordinate managers which produce a widespread sense of grievance. This can suddenly burst forth in the form of serious disturbance and conflict. If, however, the channels of appeal are simple and are kept open, it is unlikely that this will happen. An appeals procedure is very like a safety valve of a steam boiler.

The existence of an explicit appeals procedure influences all managers to make decisions with much greater care and precision, and to be more aware of the policies they must observe than would otherwise be the case. In this way, we are prevented from making many mistakes which would cause us far more trouble than that involved in the operation of the appeals procedure itself.

I have already commented at length on the value and necessity of being an adaptable company. I have no doubt that the existence of an explicit appeals procedure assists vitally to get people's cooperation in accepting change. Resistance to change is much concerned with anxiety as to what it holds for the individual: he is helped to overcome his fears if he can feel that, if any result of the change impinges unfairly upon him, it can be ventilated in an appeals procedure if necessary.

Finally, in spite of its difficulties, I have derived great benefit from participating in the operation of the appeals procedure. It is one of the opportunities I get of keeping in touch with how things are going at the base of the executive system. One comes face to face with some unexpected and sometimes unpleasant results of one's own policy, and comes to realize that it was too little considered before being introduced. This is always a salutary experience. Above all, one feels that within this procedure there are some real and worth-while values. It is an essential executive means of attempting to promote natural justice and conscientious dealing within a factory community, and it makes a vital contribution to people's sense of security.

CHAPTER 19

SOME UNEXPLORED PROBLEMS

LOOKING back over the years, it seems to me that growth in size of the company was the most important single factor which helped to generate the need to explore organizational problems. Growth in organizations inevitably means adaptation, and if the necessary insight into social structure is absent, the process of adaptation is slow, painful and full of problems.

There is a wide variety of reasons for assuming that the current tendency for the size of individual industrial units to grow will continue in the future. (These are familiar and I shall not discuss them.) If this is true, then ever-growing pressure for work to be done towards the solution of industrial social problems will be felt. Managers, technicians, craftsmen, clerks and operatives will not be prepared to tolerate for ever the problems, inefficiency and anxieties caused by the present unbalance between the steady growth in the amount of technological research and the situation of near stagnation in the field of social research. The balance must be redressed if we are to avoid increase of trouble in the future.

The period during which this book has been written has, in a sense, been one of considerable frustration for me, and maybe for many others in the company, because I have known what we have to do in the field of personnel and organizational work, and yet economic factors have prevented us from doing it. We need a personnel division, containing the same order of resources of people, brains and facilities as we have deployed in our technical division or in our product research and development organization, in order to implement fully the findings already achieved, and to take the exploration further.

Unfortunately, the company has, during the last few years, been forced in some things to pursue short-term policies, because it has been engaged in a more than usually virulent competitive fight for its markets.

The setting up of a technically based division of adequate

size, concerned with organization and manning, is a project which will yield great benefits in the long term, but is expensive in the short. The gross shortage of people who have both the experience of business, and an educational background suitable for work in this field, means that in order to man such a division we must, to a major extent, train and grow such staff for ourselves. It is this factor which makes the move an expensive one, and will cause our rate of progress in the future to be slower than I should like to see.

This economic difficulty, coupled with the many recognized psychological barriers to work on organizational problems, can build up too easily to the conclusion, 'We have done enough; let us stay further development here'. I want, in this final chapter, to try and inhibit such thinking, for I believe that no field of research offers richer rewards than this one. To this end, I will now try and set out some examples of the known problems which should be tackled, and some of the areas of work where we are apt to blunder along, because we lack explicit knowledge. These examples are not a survey of all the territory to be explored – it is impossible to give such a survey – but a mere indication of some of the known areas where conceptual material is lacking.

Selection of people for roles

I believe that Dr Jaques' research on the 'measurement of responsibility' of work, and on the changing capacity, with age, of people to do work at varying levels of responsibility, is valid and extremely valuable. As yet, however, we have no means of measuring the innate potential capacity of the individual to do varying levels of work. In the absence of this, selection has to be based on intuition, and consequently misfit appointments are numerous. The cost of these mistakes in terms of unhappiness for the individual, and inefficiency for the company, is very serious.

The split at the bottom of the executive system

I have referred to this problem at length in Chapter 14. It manifests itself in a number of ways: e.g., many people occupying roles at the base of the executive system tend to dissociate themselves psychologically from their daily work, and to become identified with goals which are not centred on work; communication from the floor on executive matters tends to be through representatives rather than through executive channels; relations between such people and their managers is of a different order from those that exist elsewhere in the hierarchy; morale tends to be regarded not as a function of creative work well done, but of the extent to which the effect of work on the individual can be ameliorated, and so on. Clearly, the problem has its roots in such areas as the history of the growth of our society, in class divisions of society, in economics, and elsewhere; but I am left with the feeling that lack of insight into organization, manning, selection and equitable methods of deciding the level of pay, play a big part in the general problem. The expenditure of time and effort better to understand exactly what takes place at shop-floor and office-floor level might make a substantial contribution towards solution of one of the major current problems of industry.

Assessment of quantity of work

Potentially, we are now able to measure both the level and amount of work in so-called manual jobs; but we are not able to measure the amount of work done by, say, a manager, a designer, a staff officer, because these men's work is largely mental. It is concerned with making decisions, giving instructions, listening to the ideas of others, reading, coordinating the activity of others, assessing subordinates. Accordingly, we have to rely on intuition to guide us in answering such questions as: 'How many people ought he to have in his extended command to get through the work he has been given?' 'How much space or plant ought he to have?' 'How long ought he and his command to take to complete particular jobs?'

If we have two people satisfactorily carrying out the same level of work, we are not able to say that both should automatically be paid the same salary; for although the performance in each case may be satisfactory, the fact remains that one will be felt to be a faster worker than the other, and there may well be unquantifiable evidence that he gets through more work in the same time. If we were able to quantify the amount of work done by managers, specialists, accountants, salesmen, we should have made a considerable advance.

Production organization structure

We have greatly benefited from the organization of production into units, which are, as far as possible, responsible for a specific finished product, or group of products, rather than for a particular process.

There are often problems in such product delegation to do with the difficulty of duplicating, in each unit, expensive machinery which is required by all the products. Product splits of work sometimes seem to involve the setting up of some units that 'look' too large and others that 'look' too small. There is a case for organizing sections within a unit on a product basis. We do not know the answers to a large range of questions which arise around this subject, and more work might prove very rewarding.

Product research and development organizational structure

Research jobs vary very greatly in content; according to this content, they call for a differential degree of work to be done by persons of widely different knowledge and training. For example, development job A may require to have a senior engineer put in charge of it; but he will require as subordinates a metallurgist and two designers. Job B may have a higher metallurgical content and be best placed in charge of a physicist or a metallurgist, who will require the help of an engineer, a mathematician and some laboratory technicians. Because the tasks entrusted to our total research and development organization are many and varied, both as regards content and the time they will take to achieve, there seems to be a need for continual regrouping of teams around the varying mix of work which has to be undertaken.

There is a tendency for the type of organizational structure that is appropriate for production to get transferred into product development, due to the lack of explicit concepts about product-development organizational structure. Analytic work done in this area might help to increase the efficiency of research and development work.

Some Unexplored Problems

Sales organization

A large amount of analysis has been carried out in this field in recent years, and the considerable changes arising out of it have proved beneficial. During the analysis, it became clear that sales work could be distinguished fairly readily from other types of operational work, by using certain simple criteria which I will not discuss here. Applying these criteria it became evident that there are a considerable number of roles which, though manifestly concerned with production control and other allied functions, are requisitely sales roles. Further research is required to establish just what work these roles contain, and how far it is appropriate to re-position them.

The establishment of more realistic control procedures over expenditure and use of resources

This is a very large area, and it requires exploration and systematic analysis. It is known that many of the figures produced for purposes of control, within standard costing and budgetary control schemes, are poorly adapted to such purposes and, in some cases, useless. Thus a great deal of time is spent in producing data, some of which appears to be little used by managers. Growing up side by side with such conventional financial data are numerous other indices of daily happenings. These have been brought into being by the need of managers for objective information which will give them a better picture of what is happening in their commands.

There appears to be need for a systematic examination of the whole subject, which will explore the realism of using financial data for such purposes, and the exact place of costing data in the whole field of managerial controls.

I hope that this brief list of areas where we have insufficient knowledge will serve as an indication of the much greater field which awaits exploration. Within it will be found the confusions of thinking and the false concepts that lie, I believe, at the root of many problems and troubles which we are now inclined to attribute to psychological causes and the shortcomings of people.

This is not to say that there are no such things as psychological problems in industry; they will abound – in terms of behaviour, relationships, communication, leadership – in any institution where people work together. In the last analysis, the roots of all problems in society lie in the make-up of people; but sociological factors are of great importance, and in my view they have been consistently under-assessed in their effects. This book has focused on such factors, not because I regard them as being of greater significance than psychological factors, but because they are not receiving the attention which is commensurate with their importance.

APPENDIXES

GLOSSARY OF TECHNICAL TERMS[1]

ACCOUNTABILITY: As it is used both in the company, and in this book, this term can be looked on as synonymous with 'responsibility' (see below). It is interesting to note that while the *Oxford Dictionary* defines the term as synonymous with 'responsibility', 'accountability' also suggests the meaning of 'liable to be called to account', which is precisely what a subordinate is liable for in relation to his manager. He is required to give an account of the way in which he has used the resources put at his disposal. In this way the term does, to some extent, illuminate an important aspect of the manager–subordinate relationship.

ADMINISTRATION: The process of interpreting policy and translating it into executive action. (Pol. Doc.)

ADVICE: This term is not defined either in our Policy Document or in this book. It is normally used, however, in its current sense to mean 'opinion given or offered as to action'. Three executive meanings of the term are distinguished in the present book as follows (see also Chapter 3, p. 69):

Instructional advice. This is used to refer to the 'advice' given by a manager to a subordinate. In the strict sense it is really incorrectly used, since the subordinate has no choice but to heed the 'advice' given, whether or not he actually carries out the action recommended.

Responsible advice. This is used to refer to the advice given by a subordinate to a manager; or by someone occupying an executive role to someone else in the organization occupying an executive role, where the former is responsible for giving the advice. In these circumstances, while it remains the responsibility of the advisee to decide whether or not he will heed the advice given, the adviser must retain some responsibility for the quality of the advice he gives, and can be called to account if it proves later to have been ill-founded.

Irresponsible advice. This is used to refer to advice given by one

---

1. The abbreviation, Pol. Doc., appearing after a definition indicates that it is as given in the Company Policy Document.

In some cases the definitions given in this glossary concern concepts which are the subject of extensive description and elaboration in the main part of the book, and in these cases references to the text are given.

member of the organization to another, where the former is not executively responsible for giving such advice. In such a case, both the seeking and the giving of advice is an entirely personal matter, outside formal executive relationships altogether.

ANALYSIS: The dictionary definition of this word is 'the resolution of anything complex into its simple elements; the exact determination of its components'. Four kinds of analysis are referred to in the present book (see also Chapter 1, p. 30):

Analysis of work. The resolution of work into its components. (It should be noted that while this can be achieved in accordance with any categorization found to be convenient, one of the recently developed methods of work analysis in the company, and the meaning normally given to the term in this book, concerns the resolution of work into its prescribed and discretionary components together with the mechanisms used to review the way in which discretion is exercised.)

Executive analysis (of work or of organization). This occurs when an employee member of the company carries out an analysis of work, and the way in which it is distributed between various roles.

Independent analysis (of work or of organization). This takes place when the person carrying out the analysis is not an employee member, and has no executive relationship with anyone in the company. It involves (*a*) complete confidentiality of all communications to the independent analyst unless specific permission is given to make them public; (*b*) the undertaking of analysis of work only at the request of those individuals, managers or groups, responsible for that work.

Organizational analysis. Analysis of work which is allocated to various roles and the way in which the roles are interrelated, whether such roles are established or not.

APPEAL: The process whereby a member causes the decision of another member to be reviewed by the latter's executive superior or the company appeal tribunal. (Pol. Doc.) (See also Chapter 18.)

APPEALS PROCEDURE: The mechanism through which any employed member (or group of members) may question the appropriateness of a manager's decision, as it affects him, in front of a higher manager. (See also Chapter 18.)

APPELLANT: The member or group of members making an appeal. In the course of a case the identity of the appellant may vary at successive stages in the executive system when a judgement is reversed. (Pol. Doc.)

ATTACHMENT: See Role, Specialist.

Glossary of Technical Terms

AUTHORITY: The property attaching to the role which enables its occupant to undertake his activities (utilize resources, etc.). The degree of authority must be consistent with the degree of responsibility. (Pol. Doc.)

Delegate authority. The authority given to an elected representative by his constituents to act on their behalf in accordance with a specific mandate from which he must not depart without reference to them. (Because of the unanimity rule, the concept of delegate has a special connotation. It will be noted that when there is disagreement between delegates, it becomes their responsibility to discover either a new solution or a compromise solution, and to refer the solution arrived at back to their constituent groups for consideration and, if seen fit, ratification.) (Pol. Doc.)

Representative authority. The authority of an elected representative to judge for himself what he considers to be in the best interests of his constituents, and so to vote, without a specific mandate. (Pol. Doc.)

CENTRALIZATION: This is used in the present book to refer to the situation in which a manager sets a policy which applies to levels lower than his immediate subordinates, i.e., a policy which deprives his immediate subordinates of their use of discretion in the matter.

Decentralization. By contrast, this is used to refer to the situation in which a manager sets a policy leaving use of discretion to his immediate subordinates. (See also Chapter 6, p. 103.)

COLLATERAL:

Collateral relationship. The relationship which obtains between colleagues when their work is interdependent.

COMMAND:

The extended command of a manager comprises all the members under his control. (Pol. Doc.)

The immediate command of a manager is that group of members which he makes *immediately* accountable to him. (Pol. Doc.)

COMMITTEE: A body composed of all the elected representatives from a given constituency or electoral unit. (Pol. Doc.)

COMPANY: The legal entity comprising shareholders and the board of directors. (Pol. Doc.)

CONJOINT:

Conjoint relationship. The relationship which obtains between specialists responsible to the same manager.

CONSTITUENCY: A body within an electoral unit whose members have the right to be represented by a common representative or representatives. (Pol. Doc.)

Constituent. Any member of a constituency. (Pol. Doc.)

CONTRACTION: The situation that obtains where the executive chain is contracted, i.e., where a manager makes contact with a member of his extended command who is not his own immediate subordinate. It can occur either in individual instances, as for example when a general manager telephones a shop clerk to get information, or where a manager contracts the whole of his extended command, as when he speaks to all of them together. (See also Chapter 8, p. 131.)

COUNCIL: A body composed of one manager and representatives of all electoral units within his extended command which desire to elect representatives. (Pol. Doc.)

Higher council. One council can be said to be higher than another only where the extended command governed by it contains the extended command governed by the other. (Pol. Doc.)

Part council. A body composed of one manager and representatives of some, but not all, the electoral units within his extended command. (Pol. Doc.)

CROSS-OVER POINT: In relation to any two or more roles, the cross-over point is the most junior manager whose command comprises these roles.

DELEGATION: The process of allocating work to a subordinate role.

DIRECTIVE: Written instructions given by the managing director to his immediate subordinates which will have long-term standing. (See also Chapter 9, p. 144.)

DISCRETION – DISCRETIONARY: The term 'discretion' as used in this book refers to the authority to decide or act according to one's own judgement. It is not used in the sense of the quality of being discreet, i.e. proper, in one's behaviour. (See also Chapter 2, p. 45.)

DIVISION: The non-operational commands of the company, i.e., specialist commands, are referred to as 'divisions'. There are three such commands, personnel, programming, and technical.

ELECTOR: A member of a constituency who has the right to vote. (Pol. Doc.)

Glossary of Technical Terms

ELECTORAL UNIT: A body of members entitled to representation on a legislative body, either directly or through representative committee. (Pol. Doc.)

EXECUTIVE SYSTEM: See System, Executive. (See also Chapter 3, p. 56.)

INSTRUCTION: Any communication from a superior to one or more of his subordinates when they are in their executive roles. This definition includes not only orders, but also requests for information, advice or assistance, the passing of information, etc., which always contain, either explicitly or implicitly, an instruction. (Pol. Doc.) (See also Chapter 15, p. 215.)

Policy instruction. A communication from a manager to any or all of his subordinates, stating the policies which they must observe. It should be noted that policy statements define the boundaries within which a subordinate will be expected to exercise his own judgement and the aims to which he must orient his decisions.

Task and task instructions. A task is a specific job of work, and a task instruction a communication from a manager to a subordinate giving him that specific job of work to do. Task instructions may thus range from 'Post this letter' to 'Place the order for a million pounds' worth of new plant'. Such task instructions are always by definition given within a framework of policy already set.

Staff instructions. A staff instruction is an instruction given by a staff officer within his own manager's policy to any other of that manager's immediate subordinates.

Technical instructions. Instructions given by a staff officer to another staff officer attached by him to one of his manager's subordinates. Such technical instructions are confined to communicating the techniques which the subordinate staff officer is required to use when performing tasks for his own operational manager.

JOB SPECIFICATION: In this book the word 'job' is used as equivalent to the work content of an executive role. A job specification refers to the description of a role, both so far as its work content is concerned (i.e. prescribed limits and objectives, the discretion which must be used in achieving these, and review mechanisms), and also so far as working conditions, social and career considerations, etc., are concerned. (See also Chapter 4, pp. 87-8.)

LEGISLATION: The process of deciding the policy within which executive action will take place. (Pol. Doc.)

LEGISLATIVE SYSTEM: See System, Legislative. (See also Chapter 17, p. 244.)

MANAGER — MANAGERIAL ROLE: A member who has subordinate to him authorized roles into which he can appoint members and determine their work: he is accountable for his subordinates' work in these roles. (Pol. Doc.)

Managerial authority. The term used in this book to refer to the minimal authority attached to a managerial role which has to do with control of work by subordinates, i.e., that a manager must have subordinate roles into which he can appoint members, from which he can remove them, and within which he can set terms of reference and determine differential rewards.

The terms given below are also used in this book to describe specific categories of managerial roles in the company:

Section manager. The lowest level of managerial role such as that directly in charge of operatives on the shop floor.

Unit manager. The manager in charge of a unit of up to about 400 total strength, with section managers subordinate to him.

General manager. A manager responsible to the managing director for the conduct of one of the company's general operational commands, e.g., a manufacturing factory, the research and development organization or the sales organization.

Divisional manager. A manager responsible to the managing director and in charge of one of the company's specialist divisions, i.e., programming, technical or personnel.

Co-manager. Attached specialists are responsible both to a technical manager and to an operational manager, each of whom may be referred to as one of the specialist's co-managers.

MANNING: The process of filling roles in an organization, both in the long and the short term.

MEMBER: Legally, members of the company refers to shareholders. For the purpose of the Policy Document, however, the term 'member' is used to refer to employees, and the term 'shareholders' used whenever shareholders are referred to. (Pol. Doc.)

OPERATING ORGANIZATIONS: Comprise all the business and trading commands of the company. (Pol. Doc.)

OPERATIONAL — OPERATIONAL WORK — OPERATIONAL ACTIVITY: The term 'operational activity' is used to refer to those company activities which it is the concern of the company to carry out. Thus, the Glacier Metal Co. Ltd was established to make, develop and sell bearings and other products at a profit. If it did not make them, did not sell them and (considering the nature of the market) did not develop them, then it would no longer be fulfilling the purpose for which it was established. In this way we can distinguish operational activities from others such as personnel work, production engineering, inspection, etc., which it is not the purpose of the company to carry out, though their effective prosecution may be essential for the operational activities themselves to be conducted. This distinction is important, since it leads to the necessity to make a distinction organizationally between the two kinds of authority appropriate to these two kinds of activity. It should be noted that in more common parlance 'operational activities' are sometimes referred to as 'line' activities, and specialist work as 'functional'.

OPINION SURVEY: Reference of an issue to all those within a constituency so that each member may have the opportunity to state his views individually, but without the results being binding upon the elected representatives. (Pol. Doc.)

ORDER: For the general definition of this word, see Instruction.

Standing orders. This term is used in the company to refer to instructions from the managing director applicable in certain defined circumstances to all members of the company and hence formally sanctioned by council.

ORGANIZATION:

Executive organization. This is used synonymously with the term 'Executive System' (see System, Executive).

Manifest organization. The situation as formally described and displayed.

Assumed organization. The situation as it is assumed to be by the individuals concerned, and there may or may not be consistency between the assumed and the manifest situation.

Extant organization. The situation as revealed by systematic exploration and analysis (it can never be completely known).

Requisite organization. The situation as it would have to be to accord with the real properties of the field in which it exists.

Operating organizations. Comprise all the business and trading commands of the company. (Pol. Doc.)

PERSONAL ASSISTANT: One whose responsibility is to assist his manager in whatever sphere his manager may decide. The personal assistant can convey instructions on his manager's behalf, but does not carry any personal authority to issue instructions. (Pol. Doc.)

POLICY: As the term is used in this book, it refers to the prescribed part of a role or group of roles. On the one hand, it sets what would normally be felt as limitations to discretion, e.g., by prescribing the kind of methods that are to be used, etc., and on the other hand, it sets out the aims, objectives or targets which it is prescribed shall be achieved. In this sense company policy refers to the policy circumscribing the whole company (in the sense of the extended command of the managing director), and definitive policy that which circumscribes the activities of the board of directors. (See also Chapter 6, p. 101.)

POWER: An attribute of an individual or group: the term defines the strength or intensity of influence that a given body or individual is potentially capable of exerting at any given time, regardless either of the role assumed or authority carried.

PRESCRIPTION: The means of achieving a desired result as specified by a member who is executively responsible for giving such specifications to other members not in the same line of command. (Pol. Doc.)[1]

REFERENDUM: Reference of an issue to the electoral unit by ballot. The result of the ballot is binding upon those who have decided to conduct the referendum. (Pol. Doc.)

REPRESENTATIVE: See Role, Representative.

Representative system. See System, Representative.
Representative authority. See Authority, Representative.
Representative committee. See Committee, Representative.

RESPONSIBILITY: This is the obligation a person takes on to do the work allocated to him. (Pol. Doc.)

ROLE: A position in a system which is filled by specified means (e.g. election, appointment): every role carries specified responsibility and authority which are taken on by the member assuming the role. (Pol. Doc.)

Executive role. A position in the executive system which a member takes up by entering into an employment contract; in his executive role he has to discharge specified responsibilities and carry specified authority. (Pol. Doc.)
Role relationships. The relationships defining the behaviour required between the occupants of any roles in any of the systems of the operating organizations. (Pol. Doc.)

1. It should be noted that this term was originally developed and appears in our Policy Document as a means of defining a certain kind of relationship between a specialist and another member not in the same line of command. It is still used as such in the company but, used in this sense, its meaning should be kept distinct from the term 'prescribed', where reference is made to that part of the work-content of a role about which the occupant has no authorized choice.

Executive role relationships. The relationships obtaining between positions in the executive system. (These include such relationships as superior-subordinate, collateral, staff, etc.) (Pol. Doc.)

Representative role. Any role in the representative system, which a member takes up by election and in which he acts on behalf of the constituency or electoral unit which elected him. (Pol. Doc.)

Specialist role. A role in which the occupant is accountable for assisting a manager through the discharge of one or more responsibilities. (As detailed in the Policy Document.) (See also Chapter 13, p. 177.)

Supervisory role. See Supervisor.

Managerial role. See Manager.

SERVICE: Is an activity carried out by one member at the request of another, not in the same line of command, which it is his executive responsibility to perform for others. (Pol. Doc.)

SPECIALIST: See Role, Specialist.

STAFF WORK: The work carried out by a specialist with staff responsibility.

STRUCTURE – SOCIAL STRUCTURE: The social structure of a company is the more or less recognizable organizational pattern made up of what is variously referred to as 'the authority chart', 'the hierarchy of positions' or 'the managerial tree'. It includes also the consultative or representative system, various grouping systems and other types of stratification; structure in this sense is made up of a network of positions which can be occupied by individuals, i.e., roles.

SUPERVISOR: A member who assists his manager by assigning appropriate work to those members of his manager's immediate command allocated to him, and seeing that this work gets done. (Pol. Doc.) (See also Chapter 14, p. 202.)

SYSTEM:

Executive system. Comprises the network of positions to which the company's work is assigned. It is made up of positions which shall be called 'Executive Roles'. The executive system includes all members of the operating organizations, a member being in his executive role while he is carrying out his job responsibility. (Pol. Doc.) (See also Chapter 3, p. 56.)

Representative system. Comprises constituents, elected representatives and elected committees, electoral units and constituencies. (Pol. Doc.) (See also Chapter 16, p. 222.)

Legislative system. Comprises councils and part councils, in which the executive and representative systems meet, and by means of which every member can participate in formulating policy, and in assessing the results of the implementation of that policy. (Pol. Doc.) (See also Chapter 17, p. 244.)

TECHNIQUE: This term is used in the company to denote the method or methods by which any particular task is carried out.

TIME-SPAN OF DISCRETION: The maximum period of time that a subordinate may continuously use sub-standard discretion in carrying out his work before this fact becomes apparent to his manager.

WORK: The totality of discretion which a member is expected to exercise, and the prescribed acts he must discharge, in carrying out the responsibilities of the role which he occupies.

Discretionary act. An act or course of action adopted by a member in doing his work, where the policy set for him left alternative courses of action from among which he had to choose.

Prescribed act. An act or course performed by a member in doing his work, where the policy set for him allowed him no choice. (Pol. Doc.) (See also Chapter 3, p. 65.)

APPENDIX 2

COMPANY POLICY DOCUMENT

(Policy controlling the Operating Organizations of
the Glacier Metal Co. Ltd and its Subsidiary Companies drawn
up March 1956)

A.[1] PREAMBLE
C. ACHIEVEMENT OF THE PURPOSE OF THE COMPANY
D. STRUCTURE OF THE OPERATING ORGANIZATIONS
E. THE EXECUTIVE SYSTEM
F. THE REPRESENTATIVE SYSTEM
G. THE LEGISLATIVE SYSTEM
H. THE APPEALS SYSTEM

A PREAMBLE

A.1 The broad purposes and legal constitution of the Company are laid down in the Memorandum and Articles of Association which govern the activities of the Shareholders and the Board of Directors.

A.2 This document sets out the policy within which the Board of Directors, in consonance with Works Councils, directs that the Operating Organizations of the Company shall be governed.

A.3 This policy assumes that shareholders and members[2] individually and collectively want to go to the very limit in trying to work out policies which are in the best interests of the Company and its members as a whole, and that they are willing to tolerate some shortcomings in policy in order to achieve this end. These assumptions are embodied in the principle that Councils shall pursue their deliberations until they reach unanimous agreement.

A.4 It is realized that when, after a serious attempt to reach unanimous agreement has been made, differences of viewpoint prove irreconcilable, action may be forced by the section which

1. Section B of the Policy Document in its current form is a list of definitions; all of these, plus many more established in this book, appear in the Glossary.
2. See Glossary, 'Member'.

has the most power. The use of power in this way shall be regarded not as a normal alternative to the methods of legislation laid down in this document, but as the inevitable consequence of a breakdown in these methods.

A.5 The desired interaction between the Executive and Representative Systems does not impair the scope either of managers or of representatives. Indeed, great responsibility and authority will have to be accepted by managers for the leadership of their subordinates: and elected representatives will have to occupy fully their elected roles in the sense of knowing policy, of being able to speak responsibly on behalf of their constituents, and of being able to integrate their views with those of representatives of other groups.

A.6 It is the responsibility of members to keep themselves informed about those aspects of policy which are likely to affect them. They are expected to interpret the provisions of this policy reasonably and intelligently, with due regard to the interests of the Company, bearing in mind that it is not possible to provide for every eventuality.

A.7 In carrying out their work members shall conform to the policy as set out in this document.

C. ACHIEVEMENT OF THE PURPOSE OF THE COMPANY

C.1 The purpose of the members employed by the Company is the continuity of a working community, the conditions of which will promote the physical and mental well-being of members and, taking into account all circumstances, will provide them with the highest possible return for work done. The purpose of the members in this respect is consistent with the legal purpose of the Company as set out in the Memorandum of Association dated 6 December 1935 in that both will best be achieved by:

C.1.1 Ensuring that the Company is able to maintain a high position in the competitive market by reason of its standards of price, quality and service to customers. This involves research, development and achievement of high technical and organizational efficiency.

C.1.2 Providing such dividends for its shareholders as will represent a reasonable and fair return for their capital investment.

C.1.3 Ensuring that every member is paid at a level consistent with the role into which he contracted, and that he gets a level of work consistent with his capacity, if such work is available.

C.1.4 Providing reserves sufficient to safeguard the Company and all who work within it.

C.1.5 Providing the maximum practicable facilities for the health, safety and well-being of all members employed by the Company.

D. STRUCTURE OF THE OPERATING ORGANIZATIONS

D.1 The Operating Organizations contain the Executive System, the Representative System, the Legislative System and the Appeals System.

The purpose of defining these systems is:

(*a*) To ensure that clear responsibility and equivalent authority are carried by individuals, committees and Councils,

(*b*) To provide a means whereby a manager can achieve such understanding with both his own manager and his subordinates as to make him free to act with decision,

(*c*) To assure to members the right to take part in formulating the policies within which authority over them will be carried by their managers; and, conversely, to place the responsibility for policy-making on all members, whether or not this right is exercised,

(*d*) To ensure that no changes in legislated policy are made without a unanimous vote in favour of them by the appropriate Council Meeting,

(*e*) To provide means whereby the implementation of policy may be subjected to scrutiny, and, where necessary, policy modified.

(*f*) To provide a sanctioned system of arbitration to which disputes between individuals on the interpretation of policy may be referred.

D.2 *Executive System:* There shall be an Executive System through which the day-to-day business of the Company shall be carried out. Within this System, each role will carry responsibilities for which the member occupying the role shall be personally accountable to his manager. Each role shall be vested with that authority necessary for the member to carry out his work.

D.3 *Representative System:* There shall be a Representative System by means of which members may express their views through their elected representatives.

D.4 *Legislative System:* There shall be a Legislative System to determine by unanimous agreement at Council Meetings legislative policies which best meet the requirements of the Company and of the members of the Operating Organizations. A Council shall only be formed where the members of a given command feel the need for their own policy-making body.

D.5 *Appeals System:* There shall be an Appeals System to allow a member or members to cause to be reviewed by a higher authority any acts of their executive superior which they feel to be inconsistent with or outside the spirit of agreed policy.

E. THE EXECUTIVE SYSTEM

General Responsibilities

E.1.1 Notwithstanding any responsibilities laid down in this policy, every member of the Operating Organizations shall:

(a) refuse to carry out instructions or to provide services which appear to be unlawful,

(b) take action in an emergency to ensure people's safety and protect the Company's interests and property, and notify the appropriate manager of his action,

(c) refuse services or otherwise attempt to prevent another member performing or continuing to perform an act which he considers to be seriously damaging, dangerous or unlawful.

General Executive Accountability

E.2.1 A member shall be accountable for the results of all his executive activities to his own immediate manager.

E.2.2 A member shall question any instructions which he does not feel able to carry out within the policy set and with the facilities available to him. In the absence of any such query, his manager may take it that the member has accepted the instruction as being reasonable.

E.2.3 A member shall decide whether to raise with his manager points not clear in or not governed by policy or Standing Orders.

E.2.4 When a member raises a question with his manager, his manager shall try to give him an immediate decision. If he cannot give an immediate decision, he must commit himself to give a decision by a specified time.

Company Policy Document

Assignment and Assessment of Work

E.3 A manager shall be accountable for the work assigned to him, including the work which he assigns to members under his command. In assigning work, a manager shall determine the extent to which he requires his subordinates to make reference to him before making their own decisions.

E.4 A manager shall appoint, train and maintain as his immediate command a team of subordinates who are competent to carry out the work he requires of them, and who conform to the generally accepted standards of conduct. He shall assign and display an order of seniority among a sufficient number of his subordinates to ensure that his work is done in his absence.

E.4.1. He shall set standards of executive performance and attainment for his immediate subordinates, and shall make these standards clear to them.

E.4.2 He shall assign work to each of his immediate subordinates at a level consistent with the standards he has set.

E.4.3 He shall judge the executive performance of each of his subordinates in relation to the standards he has set, and their conduct in relation to the standards accepted in the Company.

(a) He shall ensure that each subordinate is rewarded at a level appropriate to the work of his executive role.

(b) In the event of a subordinate performing below the standards he has set or contrary to the generally accepted standards of conduct, he shall acquaint him of this fact, and in the event of continued inadequacy, he shall decide whether to retain him in his command.

E.4.4 A manager shall limit his immediate command to the number of people he can effectively control, and amongst whom he can maintain cooperation.

E.4.5 The above clauses shall not necessarily apply to a manager on probation or in training, the extent of whose responsibilities his immediate manager shall decide.

(Assistance in the interpretation of Assignment and Assessment of Work as set out in sections E.3 and E.4 may be obtained by reference to the Guidance Notes (on p. 329).)

Supervision of Work

E.5.1 A supervisor shall apportion and assign work to those of his manager's subordinates allocated to him.

E.5.2 A supervisor shall judge whether his manager's sub-ordinates are performing executively at a satisfactory level and conforming to general conduct requirements. When in his estimation they are not doing so, he shall inform them of this fact, and shall give them the necessary instructions to ensure that the required results are achieved.

E.5.3 A supervisor shall report to his manager his assessment of the quality of the work and conduct of his manager's sub-ordinates, recommending advancement or discipline when-ever he considers this to be appropriate.

Contraction of Executive Lines

E.6 A manager shall, when he feels such action to be necessary, contract the executive lines in his command; i.e., make executive contact with any member or members of his extended command, either directly, or indirectly through the intermediate subordinates.

E.6.1 When he makes such contact in the absence of the intermediate members, he must recognize that he has removed responsibilities from his subordinates down to and including the manager of the member with whom he is making contact. He must, therefore (except where he judges that his instruction does not interfere with the existing executive relationship between a member and his immediate superior): (*a*) cause the intermediate subordinates to be informed of his action with the least possible delay, (*b*) arrange for the member to return to the command of his manager when he has completed the designated task, or by other means restore in due course the responsibilities he has removed from the intermediate subordinates.

E.6.2 When the contraction includes the intermediate mem-bers, no such special subsequent action is necessary.

Seeking Prescriptions and Services

E.7 A manager shall inform the members of his immediate com-mand to what extent they are authorized to seek services and prescriptions from others.

E.8 A member shall seek from an appropriate member those prescriptions and services which he is authorized to obtain, and which are required to carry out his work.

E.8.1 A member shall be accountable for deciding whether to implement or reject any prescription received.

E.8.2 A member who considers that his manager has failed

to provide adequat: facilities for him to obtain prescriptions or services, shall decide whether this endangers the discharge of his responsibilities and whether to approach his manager. If he does make such an approach, he will state the nature of the service required, in order that his manager, if he agrees the service to be inadequate, may either:

(*a*) refer the matter to higher executive level,

(*b*) alter the responsibilities, or

(*c*) arrange to provide the required service.

E.8.3 A member who is authorized to request another member for a prescription or service, is entitled to comment directly to that member on the quality of the prescription or service provided. This applies even when the work involved in providing the service is executed by a subordinate of the service-providing member.

E.8.4 A member receiving a prescription or service shall be accountable for providing all reasonable information on the results of the prescription or service, if requested to do so by the prescribing member.

Providing Prescriptions and Services

E.9 A manager shall set terms of reference to each member of his immediate command in regard to responsibilities the member carries for providing prescriptions and services.

E.10 A servicing or prescribing member shall:

E.10.1 Give prescriptions or services within his terms of reference at the request of an authorized member.

E.10.2 Offer to provide prescriptions or services when he feels these would be of benefit.

E.10.3 Be accountable for the quality of any prescription or service rendered.

E.10.4 Use his best endeavours to get his prescriptions or services accepted, but shall recognize that the member requesting the service is accountable to his own manager for the results of either accepting or rejecting a prescription, and therefore must make his own decision on the matter.

E.10.5 Use his best endeavours to dissuade a member from seeking a service which he feels is inappropriate, but shall recognize that a member who requests a service is entitled, if he insists, to receive any service which the servicing or prescribing member is authorized to give.

E.10.6 Be accountable for obtaining any available information which he feels to be necessary on the results of his services and prescriptions.

Communications and Fact-finding

E.11 In communicating with his immediate superior, a manager shall give his own assessment, and any reservations he may have, taking into account the views of his subordinates. In communicating with his immediate subordinates, a manager shall give his own instructions, taking into account in so doing the requirements of his immediate superior.

E.11.1 A manager shall give his immediate command all necessary information and explanation, indicating that which is confidential.

E.11.2 A manager shall ensure that his immediate subordinates have such access to him as is reasonably necessary to enable them to carry out their work.

E.11.3 A manager may contract the whole or part of his extended command whenever he is dealing with a matter which applies equally to the whole or part of his extended command.

E.11.4 A manager shall decide when, for the purpose of making decisions or assisting his own manager to do so, he shall ascertain facts and feelings from his subordinates, specialist services or outside sources of information he is authorized to use.

E.11.5 A manager shall from time to time inspect the work of his subordinates and, in the light of this inspection, review his instructions to ensure that they are achieving the desired results.

Reporting on the Executive Activities of Members

E.12.1 A manager shall report to his own immediate subordinates his assessment of their activities.

E.12.2 A member may discuss any of his subordinates without their knowledge with any other member superior to that subordinate and in the same line of command.

E.12.3 A manager shall not ask a subordinate to report on any members except those within that subordinate's extended command.

Procedure for Dealing with Disagreements
General Responsibilities of Managers with Respect to Disagreements

E.13.1 A manager is accountable, where there is a conflict which affects the efficiency between one of his subordinates and another member, for ensuring that his subordinate takes the matter up with the other member with a view to resolving the conflict.

E.13.2 A manager shall discuss with the individuals concerned personal conflicts between members of his immediate command, which in his opinion they have failed to resolve and which reduce his command efficiency.

E.14 A manager is accountable for encouraging his own immediate subordinates to state to him their opinions, whether or not they are in accord with his own. A subordinate should, whenever he feels strongly about the matter, state his differences of opinion with his manager to that manager.

E.14.1 In the case of a difference of opinion between himself and a member or members of his immediate command, a manager shall manifest his readiness to submit such a difference to his own manager, should the subordinate so desire.

E.14.2 A manager shall draw the attention of members to their right to use the appeals procedure.

Disagreements on Interpretation of Policy

E.15 Where there is a disagreement between two members with respect to the interpretation of policy, the following procedure shall be adopted.

E.15.1 In the case of two members in the same line of command, they shall take the matter up with the next higher manager.

E.15.2 In the case of two colleagues, they shall take the matter up with their manager.

E.15.3 In the case of any other two members, they shall take the matter up with either of their managers.

E.16 In all three cases above, the manager approached shall first of all determine whether the policy in question is his.

E.16.1 Where the policy is his, he shall give an interpretation.

E.16.2 Where the policy is not his, he shall give an interpretation where he feels in a position to do so, or where he knows that a previously authorized interpretation exists.

E.16.3 Where he does not consider himself to be authorized to give an interpretation of policy, the matter shall be referred higher up the executive line to the point where an interpretation can be given; this interpretation shall then be communicated to the members concerned.

E.17.1 Where any of the members concerned consider the interpretation of policy which they receive to be inconsistent with legislated policy, the manager giving the interpretation shall then (if he has not already done so) cause an interpretation to be obtained executively from the management member of the legislating Council, and will communicate it to the members concerned. If these members are still dissatisfied, they should seek to have the matter raised with the legislating Council.

E.17.2 Where either party or the manager who has heard an appeal feels that his decision is a correct interpretation of existing policy, but that the existing policy is unsatisfactory, then he must petition either his manager or the body through which he is represented to table an amendment before the appropriate Council. If the amendment is adopted, it shall not affect previous judgements given, unless the amending Council so decides.

E.17.3 Decisions given by a manager on matters relating to the interpretation of policy shall, unless challenged, have the standing of interpretations of policy governing his extended command. They shall be communicated to his manager, after which they shall be communicated to his extended command through executive channels. In the case of the Managing Director, a file of such interpretations shall be maintained and shall be open to all members of the Company.

Manning of the Operating Organizations

E.18.1 The Managing Director shall be the only person having executive authority in all the Operating Organizations of the Company. Members of the Board shall have no direct executive authority unless employed as managers, when they shall have the authority appropriate to their executive roles.

E.18.2 The appointment of General and Divisional Managers shall be made by the Managing Director, assisted by a Selection Board comprising the Personnel Division Manager and such other members as are felt by the Managing Director to be necessary.

E.18.3 All appointments shall be in accordance with the appropriate policy, taking into account the following broad principles:

(a) Selection procedures shall be designed to find people whose mental and physical calibre is properly suited to the work involved and to the Company's potential requirements. Due regard shall be had for the colleagues and subordinates (if any) of the role to be filled, and the selection methods used shall include any appropriate scientific procedures.

(*b*) Provided suitable candidates are available, vacancies within the Operating Organizations shall be filled by existing members according to agreed procedure.

(*c*) The excellence of a member's performance in his existing job, or the absence of a suitable replacement for him, shall not be a valid reason for refusing him transfer to the post for which he has been selected, or for delaying his transfer unduly.

E.18.4 A manager shall have the right to dismiss a subordinate from his own immediate command. When taking such action he shall – in the following order –

(*a*) inform his own manager,

(*b*) inform the member so that he may seek alternative employment in the Operating Organizations,

(*c*) inform Personnel Department.

The dismissal is subject to appeal. If the appeal is not upheld, or if the subordinate is unable to find alternative employment in the Operating Organizations within the period of notice, the manager's notice of dismissal shall be taken as dismissal from the Company.

E.18.5 A manager may, in the case of gross misconduct, dismiss a subordinate from the Company, subject to appeal, without delay or prior reference to the Personnel Department.

Conditions of Service

E.19 The Conditions of Service of all members employed by the Company shall conform to the following general principles:

E.19.1 The minimum standards of service shall not be lower than such minimum standards as are the subject of Agreements between Trades Unions and Management, or National Agreements between Trades Unions and Association of Employers.

E.19.2 The Conditions of Service of all members of the Operating Organizations shall be reviewed from time to time, to ensure that a reasonable balance is maintained between individuals and between groups.

E.19.3 Any member or groups of members shall have the right to bring to the notice of Management, through the

Executive or Representative System, cases where adjustment of Conditions of Service appears necessary.

Special Arrangements outside Conditions of Service

E.20 Where a manager decides to arrange for a subordinate to receive special treatment outside Conditions of Service (which include wages and salary), he shall take into account all or any of the following factors:

(a) the value or potential value to the Company of qualifications, experience and skill,

(b) service rendered to members through any of the Company's institutions,

(c) past service or length of service of notable value to the Company,

(d) special qualifications or attributes which enable the individual to command a high valuation of his services in the Glacier community,

(e) degree of danger, inconvenience or special hardship entailed in the job by irregular hours, uncomfortable working conditions, absence from home, or other reasons.

Legislative Responsibilities

E.21.1 A manager's executive action shall be within the terms of the agreed policy, or, where there is no agreed policy, in line with precedent or custom in his extended command. (See footnote.) Where he finds it necessary to make a decision which he feels is not covered by existing policy or precedent, he shall decide whether or not it is sufficiently important to report to his manager or to bring before the appropriate Council.

E.21.2 A manager, when getting a workable policy agreed by means of the Legislative System, shall take into account:

(a) the effect on his executive subordinates,

(b) the policy of his manager,

(c) whether there is any likelihood of a given decision having effects outside his extended command.

E.21.3 A manager shall review his executive decisions where

Note: It must be clear that there is a difference between policy and actions implementing policy. Managers carry responsibility for making decisions in the implementation of policy, and must make such decisions as seem appropriate to them, whether or not they have the full support of their subordinates.

these are questioned by representatives, and shall ensure that they are in line with policy or precedent.

E.21.4 A manager shall report newly agreed local policies to his manager.

E.21.5 A manager shall report to his Extended Command Council all important matters of policy on which decisions have been made by Councils within his extended command.

E.21.6 A manager shall, when requested to meet with representative committees or representatives, do so as soon as reasonably possible.

E.21.7 A manager shall, if necessary, clarify his terms of reference with his manager in advance of meeting with representatives, so as to determine the limits of the discretion he has on the subject under discussion.

E.21.8 A manager shall recognize that the views put forward by a representative are views he is expressing for his constituents, and may or may not be the same as those that the representative would express in his executive role. A manager shall not use his executive authòrity to influence other members with regard to their representative activities.

E.21.9 When a manager makes contact with a member whom he knows to occupy a representative role, he shall inform him whether he is being contacted in his representative role or in his executive role.

E.21.10 A manager shall provide such means and safeguards as will enable representatives and representative committees to carry their representative responsibilities.

E.21.11 The management member of a Council shall arrange for the provision of the services (minutes, information, etc.) necessary to the Council to get its work done.

F. THE REPRESENTATIVE SYSTEM

Conditions governing the Election of Representatives

F.1 Each member who is eligible to vote shall vote only for those members standing for election in his own constituency or electoral unit.

F.1.1 Each factory shall be divided into electoral units, and each electoral unit shall have a representative committee. The boundaries of the electoral units of a factory shall be defined or approved by the Works Council of that factory.

F.1.2 Each electoral unit may be divided into constituencies according to administrative convenience, for the purpose of electing representatives to the representative committee. The boundaries of any constituency shall be defined by the representative committee of the electoral unit within which the constituency is created.

F.1.3 Where constituencies are sufficiently large, they may be divided into sub-constituencies, each of which will elect representatives to a constituency representative committee.

F.1.4 Any sector of the Operating Organizations not below unit status may have its own legislative body. The definition of electoral units and constituencies shall be a matter for decision by the members of the sector.

F.2 The members of each electoral unit shall have the right to determine the conditions of franchise in the constituencies comprising the electoral unit, subject to the following conditions:

F.2.1 Conditions governing the franchise shall be determined by a referendum of all those within the electoral unit who are eligible to vote, provided that not less than two-thirds of the valid votes are in favour of the conditions.

F.2.2 No member shall be disfranchised unless he has a reasonable opportunity to enfranchise himself should he wish to do so.

F.2.3 Where a constituency contains disfranchised members, the elected representatives of that unit shall, in acting for the constituency, act also on behalf of the disfranchised members.

F.2.4 Because the structure of representative committees is of vital importance to the efficient running of the Operating Organizations, any proposal for the amendment of conditions of election or constitution of a representative body should, wherever possible, be the subject of discussion between the responsible manager and the representative body.

Rights and Responsibilities of Constituents

F.3 Each in his role as constituent:

F.3.1 Has rights to participate in the election of his representatives in accordance with the regulations laid down in each electoral unit.

F.3.2 Should cooperate with his representative and the other members of his constituency in deciding the general lines to be followed by his representative when discussing policy.

F.3.3. Should, as far as possible, vest representative authority in his elected representative.

F.3.4 Must accept the consequences of not keeping himself informed about those aspects of policy which are likely to affect him.

F.3.5 Must accept the executive actions arising out of and consistent with the policies which his representative agrees on his behalf.

F.3.6 Should pass to his representative any information which will enable his representative to be aware of the main interests of his constituents, including special interests such as Trade Union interests where these exist.

F.3.7 May seek advice on an executive matter from his representative at any time, but may only seek action through his representative if he has first taken the matter up with the member concerned and has been unable, after a reasonable time, to obtain satisfaction.

Responsibilities of Elected Representatives

F.4 A representative is accountable to that constituent group or electoral unit which elects him; and it is his responsibility:

F.4.1 To make himself aware of the main interests of all in his constituency.

F.4.2 To represent the point of view of his constituents in committees and Councils, even where this may mean presenting a point of view contrary to his own personal opinion or his view in his executive role.

F.4.3 To allow Councils or committees to work with the greatest possible realism by judging when to state any views held by minorities within his constituency or committee.

F.4.4 To judge when reference to constituents is necessary, and when to accept responsibility for acting without such reference.

F.4.5 To initiate proposals for change which would be in the best interests of his constituents.

F.4.6 To take appropriate steps when in his judgement executive actions or the actions of his constituents are inconsistent with policy.

F.4.7 To assist his constituents to understand the executive implications of the agreements he has accepted on their behalf.

F.4.8 To familiarize himself with the Constitution and

Standing Orders of those bodies of which he is a member and with established rules of procedure.

F.4.9 To know policy, and in particular to understand those aspects of policy which are of most immediate concern to his constituents.

F.4.10 To ensure, before taking up an appeal with and on behalf of a constituent, that the constituent has in the first instance taken the matter up with the manager concerned.

F.4.11 To act as adviser to any of his constituents in cases of appeal when requested to do so.

Responsibilities of Committees

F.5.1 To serve the best interests of their constituents by arriving at conclusions which take account of the facts of the case and possible implications for the future.

F.5.2 To decide when reference to their constituents is necessary, and the means by which this reference should be made.

F.5.3 To meet as soon as reasonably possible at the request of their constituents or of the manager accountable for their constituents.

F.5.4 To determine, when questioning Management's implementation of policy or when taking up some difference of viewpoint, whether they are questioning the manner in which the policy is being interpreted or the policy itself.

F.5.5 To frame constitutions for regulating their conduct.

G. THE LEGISLATIVE SYSTEM

General

G.1.1 Legislated Policy governing all the Operating Organizations shall be decided by agreement between the Chief Executive of the Company and the representative members of the appropriate Factory Councils, and shall be built up from:

(a) the decisions of the Legislative System,

(b) policy arising out of established practice and custom, until amended by the Legislative System,

(c) precedents arising out of Management's interpretation of policy (unless challenged) until amended by the Legislative System.

G.1.2 Legislated Policy governing any sector of the Operating Organizations (e.g., Factory Policy, Unit Policy, Section

Policy) shall be built up as above, but shall be decided between the chief executive of that sector and the representatives of the members of his command.

G.1.3 Any member employed by the Company shall have the right to propose amendments to existing policy, through either the Executive or Representative System.

G.1.4 Part Councils shall be for exploratory discussion only, and shall submit any proposals on policy to the Extended Command Council for decision.

Responsibilities of Councils

G.2.1 To find policies which, by unanimous agreement, best meet the requirements of the Company and of the members of the Operating Organizations.

G.2.2 To accept, pending a unanimous decision, either

   (*a*) the continuation of existing policy, or

   (*b*) such immediate decisions as the manager concerned thinks fit, where the matter under consideration is not covered by existing policy, and where the interests of the Company demand that action be taken. Such acceptance shall be without prejudice to the final decision of the appropriate Council or Councils,

and to make every effort to reach a unanimous decision without delay.

G.2.3 To attempt to discover either new or compromise solutions when difficulties arise in getting unanimous adoption of a proposal on which there is no existing policy.

G.2.4 To review such policy decisions as are called into doubt.

G.2.5 To ensure that it has adequate knowledge of the views within the extended command for which it legislates, using such methods as opinion surveys or referenda when it unanimously agrees them to be necessary.

G.2.6 To refuse to accept the result of a ballot in any of the electoral units which it governs, should there be adequate evidence that improper practices have been used.

G.2.7 To take the necessary action in the event of failure to agree a proposal of policy, should any member or members of the Council exercise their right to require that the matter be referred to the next higher Council through either the Executive or the Representative System.

G.2.8 To determine whether policies arrived at could cover a wider sphere of influence, and where this is the case to pass the matter higher up the Executive or Representative System for consideration by a higher Council.

G.2.9 To arrange where possible sufficient advance notice of agendas to allow managers and representatives to establish their terms of reference.

G.2.10 To ensure that the business of each Council meeting is conducted within the terms of policy.

G.2.11 To ensure that Minutes are kept of all decisions taken.

G.2.12 To convene extraordinary meetings at any time at the request of the responsible manager or any of the constituent bodies.

G.2.13 If the highest Council in any one of the Company's factories is unable to reach agreement on a major principle after a serious attempt to work through the difficulties, then the matter shall be referred to a joint meeting of delegates from all the Factory Councils and the Managing Director.

H. THE APPEALS SYSTEM

Grounds for Appeal

H.1 Every member of the Company shall have the right to appeal against any executive decision or action of an executive superior which affects him and which he considers to be unfair or unjust; inconsistent with either the provisions or the spirit of agreed or normally accepted policy, or not covered by such policy; or contrary to the best interests of the Company.

H.1.1. A representative shall have the right of appeal on any matter which he considers affects his constituency. The result of such an appeal shall not necessarily affect decisions already made regarding the particular case whose circumstances may have actuated the representative to appeal on behalf of his constituency.

Responsibilities of a Manager when hearing Appeals

H.2.1 To base his judgement on the provisions and intentions of policy, whether or not these are in accord with his own views or those of his superiors or subordinates.

H.2.2 To adopt an encouraging and friendly attitude towards an appellant who might wish to take his case to a higher level.

H.2.3 To deal with appeals with the minimum possible delay.

H.2.4 To encourage the appellant to have present an officially elected representative as his adviser.

General Procedure

H.3 The member wishing to appeal shall adopt the following procedure:

H.3.1 The member shall first appeal to the immediate superior of the supervisor or manager whose action or decision is being appealed against. The appellant and the supervisor or manager whose decision is the subject of appeal both have the right to appeal against the decision of the judging manager and take the appeal to the next higher manager.

H.3.2 If the appeal reaches the Managing Director and the decision is still not acceptable to both parties, and National Arbitration Procedures do not apply, it can, with the approval of a body set up by the appropriate Works Council, be referred to a Company Appeal Tribunal.

H.3.3 The Company Appeal Tribunal shall consist of:

One member appointed by the Managing Director;

One member appointed by the appropriate Works or Staff Committee;

One independent chairman appointed from outside the Company by the Chairman of the relevant Works Council.

The majority decision of this Tribunal shall be final and binding within the Company.

H.3.4 Before an appeal reaches the level of Divisional or General Manager, it may be referred by either party to a Personnel Officer. Should his recommendations not be acceptable to both parties, the Personnel Officer may, with the agreement of the intermediate managers concerned, refer the appeal to any level in the Executive System not higher than Divisional or General Manager. All such intermediate managers shall be entitled to attend the hearing and submit their views.

H.3.5 When, at any stage in an appeal, a member has not given notice of appeal by the beginning of the third working day or night following the working day or night within which the decision was made, then it shall be at the discretion of the responsible manager whether or not an appeal shall be permitted.

Procedure at Hearings

H.4 At all hearings of any appeal:

H.4.1 The appellant shall have the right to request any member of the factory, except managers in his line of command, to advise him.

H.4.2 The appellant, his chosen adviser, if any, and the supervisor or manager whose decision is the subject of appeal, shall all have the right to be present.

H.4.3 Witnesses may be called, but shall be present at the enquiry only long enough to give their testimony and to answer questions arising out of their testimony.

H.4.4 The appeal decision shall be given in the presence of both parties.

H.4.5 When it is in the interests of the Company that an appeal be heard, and the appellant fails to attend or appoint an adviser to act for him, the manager hearing the appeal may request the officers of the appellant's elected committee to appoint a person to act for the appellant, and the appeal shall proceed.

H.4.6 The original appellant and his adviser shall have the right to be present at all hearings.

Definition of Policy resulting from Appeals

H.5.1 Appeal decisions given by a manager on matters relating to the interpretation of policy shall, unless challenged, have the standing of interpretations of policy governing his extended command.

H.5.2 Decisions by a manager which, in his opinion, involve important interpretations of policy shall be communicated to his extended command through executive channels. In the case of the Managing Director, a file of such interpretations shall be set up and shall be open to all members of the Company.

H.5.3 Decisions given by managers which are not challenged, and which appear to them to be important interpretations of policy, shall be communicated to the management group of which they form part.

H.5.4 Where either party feels that the decision in an appeal is a correct interpretation of existing policy but that the existing policy is unsatisfactory, then he must petition either his manager or the body through which he is represented to table an amendment before the appropriate Council. Such amendments, if agreed by the appropriate bodies, shall not affect previous judgements given.

Company Policy Document

Guidance Notes on Assignment and Assessment of Work –
Sections E.3 and E.4.

(1) The requirements of this section shall not be construed as disallowing Scottish Precision Castings Limited from continuance of its existing practices in regard to the award of merit rates.

(2) No manager is given unlimited discretion, because delegation is always within the terms of some policy. A manager shall set such policies for his subordinates as he deems appropriate, within the policies to which he himself is subject. For instance, decisions about pay and salary increases are always made by managers within Company and Factory Policy, and conditioned by such further guidance in principle as may be given by a manager to his subordinate managers. The policy states that, given that framework, the manager immediately in command of a group of members shall make the decisions as to whether a member shall be given a pay increase, and how much.

(3) This policy means that a manager is responsible for ensuring that all decisions about penalties and rewards made by others within his extended command are within the policy set. This being so, then a manager who is unable to set his subordinate managers a policy which he feels gives sufficiently clear guidance, would be entitled to instruct his subordinate managers to discuss their ideas with him before making decisions. Such an instruction might be necessary, for instance, in order to ensure that individual managers were made aware of the possible effect of their decisions about awards or penalties outside their own commands before making them (see also E.3).

(4) It may be difficult for managers to grasp the implications of the policy contained in E.4. Guidance is therefore given as follows:

Cases may arise where a manager believes that in order to discharge from his immediate command subordinates who are proving not competent to carry out the work he requires of them, or not able to conform to the generally accepted standards of behaviour, he must produce specific details of some *ad hoc* failure on the part of that subordinate. This may give rise to a situation where a manager who has over a long period formed the conclusion that an immediate subordinate does not conform to these requirements, nevertheless discharges him on a more limited charge.

In such a case, if the subordinate appeals he may be able to demonstrate that the facts put forward to support the *ad hoc* charge are not proven. His appeal will then be allowed, and he will remain in his post.

Situations of this kind often arise because a manager has not made clear to his subordinate his dissatisfaction with his performance or behaviour over a period of time. Where managers fail to do this, they can invariably expect to find themselves in difficulty.

Experience shows that cases of this sort frequently resolve themselves because the discussion and working through of relationships which take place during successive hearings in the Appeals System result in the member concerned gaining greater insight into the executive behaviour required of him by his superior. Sometimes the manager concerned gains more knowledge of his subordinate's difficulties and as a result changes his opinion of that subordinate.

If, however, this desirable result does not arise, then the manager concerned, because he has attempted to discharge his subordinate upon incorrect grounds, or because he has failed to inform his subordinate of his dissatisfaction with him, must tolerate what he has experienced as an undesirable situation for a further period of time.

The length of this period will vary according to circumstances, but it must be at least of such duration as will give the subordinate member sufficient time to demonstrate to his manager whether or not he is capable of so changing his behaviour or the manner in which he discharges his executive job as to cause his manager to change his assessment.

Managerial Policy Governing Implementation of Organizational Concepts

AA. DEFINITIONS

AA.1 *Specialist Role:* A role in which the occupant is accountable for assisting a Manager through the discharge of one or more of the following responsibilities:

(*a*) *Advisory responsibility* – for giving technical advice and assistance to his Manager (or Operational Co-Manager).

(*b*) *Service-providing responsibility* – that of providing services or prescriptions.

(*c*) *Staff responsibility* – that of assisting a Manager in the coordination of the work of that Manager's immediate subordinates in a particular field by exercising authority and issuing instructions on his behalf.

(*d*) *Technical coordination responsibility* – that of operating one or more of the following mechanisms (as instructed) for the coordination of the technical aspects of specialist work:

(i) *Technical Guidance:* Where a specialist is accountable for giving advice and guidance to other specified members.

(ii) *Inspection:* Where a member is instructed to review, assess and report upon the effectiveness of work which is in his specialist field but which is not directly under his executive control.

(iii) *Attachment or Secondment: Attachment* – the process of deploying a specialist from a Specialist Division to an established position under a Manager. *Secondment* – the temporary deployment of a specialist to a position under a Manager.

AA.2 *Specialist Division:* Part of the structure of the Company into which specialist roles are grouped and from which they may be attached or seconded to an Operational Co-Manager.

AA.3 *Specialist Manager:* A Manager carrying responsibilities which facilitate the achievement of the Company's operational activities.

AA.4 *Specialist Co-Manager:* The part-managerial role which a Specialist Manager takes up in relation to a specialist whom he has attached to an Operational Manager.

AA.5 *Specialist Subordinate:* The part-subordinate role which an attached or seconded specialist takes up in relation to his Specialist Co-Manager.

AA.6 *Operational Manager:* A Manager in charge of the whole or part of the Company's product developing, manufacturing or selling activities.

AA.7 *Operational Co-Manager:* The part-managerial role which an Operational Manager takes up in relation to a specialist attached to him.

AA.8 *Attached (or Seconded Subordinate):* The part-subordinate role which an attached specialist takes up in relation to his Operational Co-Manager.[1]

AA.9 *Manager:* A member who has authorized roles subordinate to him, into which he can appoint members and determine their work; he is accountable for his subordinates' work in those roles.

BB. POLICY GOVERNING ADVISORY RESPONSIBILITY

BB.1.1 A specialist is accountable for making such recommendations in his own field to his Manager (or Operational Co-Manager) as he considers will facilitate the discharge of that Manager's responsibilities.

BB.1.2 Where a Manager accepts the recommendations of one of his specialists, then the recommendation itself and any implementation become his responsibility, and he is personally accountable for the results.

CC. POLICY GOVERNING STAFF RESPONSIBILITY AND AUTHORITY

Responsibilities of a Manager assigning Staff Responsibility

CC.1 A Manager assigning staff responsibility and authority to a specialist shall ensure that he has set and made known to his other subordinates the terms of reference within which he is instructing his specialist to act.

CC.1.1 Where he has more than one specialist to whom he has given staff responsibility and authority, a Manager shall be accountable for ensuring that the policies he sets are sufficiently consistent to obviate a situation where his subordinates are asked to work inconsistent policies in different specialist fields.

Responsibilities of a Specialist exercising Staff Authority

CC.2 A specialist with staff responsibility shall have the

1. *Note:* An attached or seconded specialist is accountable to two members, each of whom performs a part of the functions of his manager. Thus, an operational co-manager and a specialist co-manager between them exercise in relation to that specialist the full rounded authority of his manager. It is impossible to consider giving a specialist two managers unless there is a clear delineation stating which part of the function of manager, with respect to him, each exercises. This delineation is set out in part 'D' of this directive.

authority to make decisions and issue instructions on behalf of his Operational Manager to his Manager's immediate subordinates within the field for which he is accountable, and within the terms of reference set by that Manager. A Specialist Manager may, in agreement with his operational colleagues, formulate terms of reference within which (*a*) his subordinates may issue instructions on his behalf, (*b*) he may issue instructions for his operational colleagues to their specialist subordinates.

CC.2.1 Specialists with staff authority shall carry responsibility for integrating their work one with the other in order to avoid inconsistent detailed instructions being given to their Manager's immediate subordinates.

CC.2.2 Where, in the judgement of a specialist with staff responsibility, legislated policies or his Manager's instructions are not being effectively implemented, he cannot be considered to have discharged his responsibility until he has so informed the subordinate concerned, and, failing a change, reported back to his Manager.

CC.2.3 In judging whether his Manager's instructions are being effectively implemented, a specialist with staff authority who is also a Specialist Manager attaching specialists to his Manager's subordinates, must judge whether the attached personnel are giving the necessary technical assistance. Where, in the judgement of the Specialist Manager, adequate technical assistance is not being given, he shall take such steps as are necessary to train the attached subordinate, or jointly to decide with the Operational Manager to make a replacement.

Responsibilities of Members subject to Staff Authority

CC.3.1 Where a member requires direction in a field for which his Manager has assigned responsibility to a specialist, he shall consult with that specialist.

CC.3.2 Where a member receives from one of his Manager's specialists carrying staff authority an instruction which he does not find acceptable, he will normally consult with that specialist, but may take the matter direct to his Manager.

CC.3.3 In the event of a member receiving inconsistent instructions from two members with staff authority, he shall inform them of the fact to enable them to integrate, and, failing integration, shall inform his Manager so that he may coordinate; the member shall take such action as is necessary during the interim according to his discretion.

Technical Guidance

DD.1.1 A Manager assigning technical guidance responsibility to a specialist shall ensure that all of his subordinates concerned are informed of his instruction.

DD.1.2 Where a specialist is assigned technical guidance responsibility, he shall make contact with the members concerned in order to discover whether there is any assistance that he can give and to present any technical information which he considers might be of value in their work.

Inspection

DD.2.1 Where a Manager wishes one of his specialists to carry out an inspection, he shall instruct him to do so, and shall inform those of his subordinates concerned of this instruction.

DD.2.2 Before reporting back to the Manager concerned, the inspecting member shall discuss his report with the appropriate Manager in the same immediate command as himself.

Attachment

DD.3 Managerial authority and accountability with regard to attached specialists shall be shared between the Operational Co-Manager and the Specialist Co-Manager in the following manner:

DD.3.1 The two Co-Managers shall be jointly accountable for the selection of the attached specialist and for his merit assessment.

DD.3.2 Only the Operational Co-Manager shall assign operational responsibilities to attached specialists, and he shall be accountable for –

(a) informing the Specialist Co-Manager of any major changes he introduces in the operational use of the attached specialist;

(b) the type of responsibility he assigns; and

(c) the discipline of the attached specialist in the discharge of these responsibilities.

DD.3.3 The Specialist Co-Manager shall set the terms of reference governing the techniques which an attached specialist uses in the discharge of his responsibilities, and he shall be accountable for –

   (*a*) informing the Operational Co-Manager of any major changes which he makes in the technical terms of reference which he sets;

   (*b*) ensuring his specialist subordinates are technically equipped to carry out the requirements of the roles which they occupy; and

   (*c*) the technical discipline of specialist subordinates.

DD.4 In the case of appeals being taken up a line of command which includes co-management, the following procedure shall obtain when an appeal reaches the level of Co-Managers:

   (*a*) if the appeal is on a purely operational matter, it shall be taken through the operational line of command;

   (*b*) if it is on a purely technical matter, it shall be taken through the specialist line of command;

   (*c*) if the appeal is against a decision on a matter involving the total sphere of a member's work, he shall appeal to his Co-Managers at the next level and upwards to the Managing Director.

BIBLIOGRAPHY
ON THE GLACIER PROJECT

BROWN, WILFRED, 'Principles of Organisation', *Monographs on Higher Management*, no. 5, Manchester Municipal College of Technology, December 1946

'Some Problems of a Factory', *Occasional Paper No. 2*, Institute of Personnel Management, London, 1952

Exploration in Management, William Heinemann, London, 1960

'Selection and Appraisal of Management Personnel,' *The Manager*, vol. XXVIII, no. 6, 1960

Piecework Abandoned, Heinemann, London, 1962

'What is Work?', *Harvard Business Review*, September 1962; *Scientific Business*, August 1963

'A Critique of some Current Ideas about Organisation', *California Management Review*, September 1963

'Judging the Performance of Subordinates', *Management International*, 1964, vol. 4, no. 2

BROWN, WILFRED, and JAQUES, ELLIOTT, *Product Analysis Pricing*, Heinemann, London 1964

'The Business School Syllabus – A Systematic Approach', *The Manager*, April 1964

Glacier Project Papers, Heinemann, London 1965

BROWN, WILFRED, and RAPHAEL, WINIFRED, *Managers, Men and Morale*, MacDonald and Evans, London, 1948

HILL, J. M. M., 'A Consideration of Labour Turnover as the Resultant of a Quasi-Stationary Process', *Human Relations*, vol. IV, no. 3, 1951

'The Time-Span of Discretion in Job Analysis', *Tavistock Pamphlets No. 1*, Tavistock Publications, London, 1957

'A Note on Time-Span and Economic Theory', *Human Relations*, vol. XI, no. 4, 1958

JAQUES, ELLIOTT, 'Studies in the Social Development of an Industrial Community', *Human Relations*, vol. III, no. 3, 1950

The Changing Culture of a Factory, Tavistock Publications, London; Dryden Press, New York, 1951

'On the Dynamics of Social Structure', *Human Relations*, vol. VI, no. 1, 1953

Measurement of Responsibility, Tavistock Publications, London; Harvard University Press, Cambridge, Mass., 1956

'Fatigue and Lowered Morale Caused by Inadequate Executive Planning', *Royal Society of Health Journal*, vol. 78, no. 5, 1958

'An Objective Approach to Pay Differentials', *The New Scientist*, vol. 4, no. 85, 1958

'Standard Earning Progression Curves: A Technique for Examining Individual Progress in Work', *Human Relations*, vol. XI, no. 2, 1958

'Disturbances in the Capacity to Work', *International Journal of Psycho-Analysis*, vol. XLI, 1960

Equitable Payment, Heinemann, London, 1961

'Objective Measures for Pay Differentials', *Harvard Business Review*, January–February 1962

'A System for Income Equity', *New Society*, 12 December 1963

'Economic Justice – by Law?' *Twentieth Century*, Spring 1964

National Incomes Policy: A Democratic Plan, Pamphlet published by K.-H. Services Ltd, May 1964

Time-Span Handbook, Heinemann, London, 1964

'Level-of-Work Measurement and Fair Payment: A Reply to Professor Beal's Comparison of Time-Span of Discretion and Job Evaluation', *California Management Review*, Summer 1964

'Two Contributions to a General Theory of Organisation and Management', *Scientific Business*, August 1964

'Social-Analysis and the Glacier Project', *Human Relations*, vol. XVII, no. 4, November 1964

JAQUES, ELLIOTT, RICE, A. K., and HILL, J. M. M., 'The Social and Psychological Impact of a Change in Method of Wage Payment', *Human Relations*, vol. IV, no. 4, 1951

RICE, A. K., 'The Use of Unrecognised Cultural Mechanisms in an Expanding Machine-Shop', *Human Relations*, vol. III, no. 2, 1951

'An Examination of the Boundaries of Part-Institutions', *Human Relations*, vol. IV, no. 4, 1951

'The Relative Independence of Sub-Institutions as Illustrated by Departmental Labour Turnover', *Human Relations*, vol. V, no. 1, 1952

RICE, A. K., HILL, J. M. M., and TRIST, E. L., 'The Representation of Labour Turnover as a Social Process', *Human Relations*, vol. III, no. 4, 1950

RICE, A. K., and TRIST, E. L., 'Institutional and Sub-Institutional Determinants of Change in Labour Turnover', *Human Relations*, vol. V, no. 4, 1952

INDEX[1]

1. This Index refers readers to the text of the book itself, but it does not cover the Glossary of Terms (p. 299) which in itself is arranged in alphabetical order, nor does it index the Company Policy Document which is set out in a form which allows easy reference by the reader.

MORE ABOUT PENGUINS
AND PELICANS

Penguinews, an attractively illustrated maga-
zine which appears every month, contains
details of all the new books issued by Penguins as they are published. Every four
months it is supplemented by *Penguins in
Print*, which is a complete list of all books
published by Penguins which are still available.
(There are well over three thousand of these.)

A specimen copy of *Penguinews* can be
sent to you free on request, and you can
become a regular subscriber at 4s. for one
year (with the complete lists). Just write to
Dept EP, Penguin Books Ltd, Harmondsworth, Middlesex, enclosing a cheque or
postal order, and your name will be added to
the mailing list.

Some other books published by Penguins
are described on the following pages.

Note: *Penguinews* and *Penguins in
Print* are not available in the U.S.A. or
Canada

THE BUSINESS OF MANAGEMENT

Roger Falk

What makes a manager? Is management today a science or is it an art? Roger Falk, a leading business consultant, explains the qualities that make a manager and the problems that business management has to face if it is to meet the challenges of the next ten years or so. He discusses business methods, selection, human relations, training, etc., and illustrates his points about management with a number of fascinating case-histories, both successes and failures.

'If you are a manager of any kind (whether shoe-shop, railway station, or oil refinery), buy it and read it . . . If you are not a manager, there is still a lot to be learnt for little time and money' – *Spectator*

'Practical and progressive' – *Financial Times*

EQUITABLE PAYMENT

A General Theory of Work, Differential Payment and Industrial Progress

Elliott Jaques

One of the cruxes of Britain's current industrial situation is the controversial system of wage bargaining which has led to a severe and chronic social malaise. Professor Jaques believes that the methods of wage negotiation at present in use are inherently socially disruptive.

This book presents a radical alternative, a theory founded on the solid experience of more than twelve years of practical research and experiment at the Glacier Metal Company's factory. It describes a method by which fair payment may be discovered for any level of work, from the shop floor to the board of directors.

'A landmark in the history of industrial relations' – *Financial Times*

'Professor Jaques' theory offers a way out of many of the country's difficulties' – *Accountant*

NOT FOR SALE IN THE U.S.A. OR CANADA

ECONOMIC PLANNING AND
DEMOCRACY

Firmin Oulès

The currents of economic planning and democratic freedom run counter. Hence one of our acutest dilemmas.

Professor Oulès, leader of 'The New Lausanne School' of economists, faces this difficulty squarely in a new Pelican in which he effectively 'de-mystifies' the economic complex of Western Europe, laying bare the forces which determine the array of facts and figures we call economics. His examination is both honest and intelligent, and he comments forcefully on the anti-democratic trend of 'indicative planning', as practised notably in France.

As an alternative Professor Oulès makes his own recommendation. It is for 'planning by enlightenment' – a concept which combines budgetary coordination, at the national level, with the systematic provision of enough data for industry, finance, commerce, and labour to act rationally yet freely.

Economic Planning and Democracy is at once a brilliantly clear exposition of the material realities of trade and industry and a constructive solution of a problem which is today admitted by most politicians and economists.

MATHEMATICS IN MANAGEMENT

Albert Battersby

Sophisticated methods of planning, control, and decision-making, together with the advent of the electronic computer, have already brought mathematics well to the fore in modern industry and commerce. At the present rate of advance, mathematics will soon be an indispensable tool of the intelligent manager.

Mathematics in Management has been specially written, for managers and others, to provide a sound basis of knowledge about the methods of operational research now being applied in public industries and services, to save resources and prune expenditure. Some such account is urgently needed, since general education has not kept pace with advances in this field, and mathematicians have difficulty in 'talking' to managers.

Among the particular topics covered by Albert Battersby in this Pelican are network analysis, simple functions, linear programming, simulation, and electronic computers. The author employs a minimum of mathematical notation in his text and, wherever possible, makes his points with the help of drawings. He has also included a set of exercises with full solutions.